A VIEW FROM
THE HIGHLANDS

The ISEAS – Yusof Ishak Institute (formerly Institute of Southeast Asian Studies) is an autonomous organization established in 1968. It is a regional centre dedicated to the study of socio-political, security, and economic trends and developments in Southeast Asia and its wider geostrategic and economic environment. The Institute's research programmes are grouped under Regional Economic Studies (RES), Regional Strategic and Political Studies (RSPS), and Regional Social and Cultural Studies (RSCS). The Institute is also home to the ASEAN Studies Centre (ASC), the Temasek History Research Centre (THRC), and the Singapore APEC Study Centre.

ISEAS Publishing, an established academic press, has issued more than 2,000 books and journals. It is the largest scholarly publisher of research about Southeast Asia from within the region. ISEAS Publishing works with many other academic and trade publishers and distributors to disseminate important research and analyses from about Southeast Asia to the rest of the world.

A VIEW FROM THE HIGHLANDS

Archaeology and settlement history of
West Sumatra, Indonesia

EDITED BY
MAI LIN TJOA-BONATZ

YUSOF ISHAK
INSTITUTE

First published in Singapore in 2020 by
ISEAS Publishing
30 Heng Mui Keng Terrace
Singapore 119614

E-mail: publish@iseas.edu.sg
Website: http://bookshop.iseas.edu.sg

All rights reserved. No part of this publication may be reproduced, stored in a retrieval system, or transmitted in any form, or by any means, electronic, mechanical, photocopying, recording or otherwise, without the prior permission of the ISEAS – Yusof Ishak Institute.

© 2020 ISEAS – Yusof Ishak Institute

The responsibility for facts and opinions in this publication rests exclusively with the authors and their interpretations do not necessarily reflect the views or the policy of the publisher or its supporters.

ISEAS Library Cataloguing-in-Publication Data

Name: Tjoa-Bonatz, Mai Lin, editor.
Title: A view from the highlands : archaeology and settlement history of West
 Sumatra, Indonesia / edited by Mai Lin Tjoa-Bonatz.
Description: Singapore : ISEAS – Yusof Ishak Institute, 2020. | Includes
 bibliographical references and index.
Identifiers: ISBN 978-981-4843-01-0 (paperback) | ISBN 978-981-4843-02-7 (pdf)
Subjects: LCSH: Excavations (Archaeology)—Sumatra—Indonesia. | Minangkabau
 (Indonesian people)—Material culture. | Minangkabau (Indonesian
 people)—History. | Indonesia.
Classification: LCC DS641 V67

Typeset by International Typesetters Pte Ltd

CONTENTS

List of Tables	vii
List of Maps	viii
List of Figures	ix
List of Colour Plates	xiv
Abbreviations and Acronyms	xv
Preface and Acknowledgements	xvi
About the Contributors	xxv

1. Research History, Methods, and Objectives   1
   - 1.1 Research History   1
     Mai Lin Tjoa-Bonatz
   - 1.2 Megalithic Complexes in the Highlands of Sumatra   5
     Mai Lin Tjoa-Bonatz
   - 1.3 Settlement Archaeology and State Formation   7
     Mai Lin Tjoa-Bonatz
   - 1.4 A Highland Perspective   11
     Mai Lin Tjoa-Bonatz
   - 1.5 The "Age of Commerce" and the Fourteenth Century   14
     Mai Lin Tjoa-Bonatz
   - 1.6 Documentation Techniques   15
     Mai Lin Tjoa-Bonatz
     - 1.6.1 Surveys and Aerial Images   15
       Mai Lin Tjoa-Bonatz
     - 1.6.2 Geophysical Surveys   17
       Benjamin Vining
     - 1.6.3 Excavating in a Minangkabau Community   20
       Johannes Greger

2. Early Histories: Historiography and Archaeological Surveys 30
    Mai Lin Tjoa-Bonatz
    2.1 The Minangkabau and Adityavarman 30
    2.2 The Archaeological Context of Adityavarman's Inscriptions 42
    2.3 Gold Processing 72
    2.4 The Royal Court of Pagaruyung Seized Power in the Seventeeth Century 74
    2.5 Memories in Stone: Council Meeting Places and Burial Sites 79

3. Excavations 91
    3.1 The Prehistoric Settlement Site of Tanah Lua 91
        Dominik Bonatz
    3.2 Adityavarman's Royal Centre? The Settlement Site on Bukit Gombak 96
        Dominik Bonatz
    3.3 The Burial Site on Bukit Kincir 120
        Johannes Greger
    3.4 The Settlement Site on Bukit Kincir 127
        Annika Hotzan-Tchabashvili

4. Material Culture Studies 134
    Mai Lin Tjoa-Bonatz
    4.1 Ceramics 134
        4.1.1 Earthenware 135
        4.1.2 Imported Ceramics 159
    4.2 Stone Artefacts 172
        4.2.1 Flaked Lithic 173
        4.2.2 Ground Stone Tools 179
    4.3 Glass Vessels and Glass Beads 186
    4.4 Metal Objects 189
    4.5 Finds at the Burial Site 196

5. Conclusion 203
    Mai Lin Tjoa-Bonatz

Bibliography 212

Index 231

LIST OF TABLES

1.1	Distribution and Density of Sherds Retrieved at the Excavated Sites of Bukit Gombak, Bukit Kincir, and Tanah Lua	22
3.1	^{14}C-dating and TL-dating for Bukit Gombak (Trenches A–D, M), the Settlement Site (Trenches O, P, R), and Burial Site (Trenches G, L) on Bukit Kincir, and Tanah Lua	94
4.1	Chemical Analyses of Earthenware Sherds from Bukit Gombak and Bukit Kincir	136
4.2	Distribution of Earthenware Shard Types in the Excavated Areas of Bukit Gombak, Bukit Kincir, and Tanah Lua	142
4.3	Detailed Distribution of Earthenware Shard Types in the Excavated Areas of Bukit Gombak, Bukit Kincir, and Tanah Lua	150
4.4	Distribution of Imported Ware Types in the Excavated Areas of Bukit Gombak and Bukit Kincir	160
4.5	Stone Artefacts from Bukit Gombak, Bukit Kincir, and Tanah Lua	174
4.6	Other Small Finds in the Excavated Areas of Bukit Gombak and Bukit Kincir	176

LIST OF MAPS

If not stated differently, all maps, figures and colour plates are of the "Tanah Datar Project".

1	The Tanah Datar district in the province of West Sumatra, Indonesia	xviii
2.1	Archaeological sites and monuments in the district of Tanah Datar: (A) Burial sites (B) Settlements (C) Inscriptions (D) Meeting places and other stone remains	44
2.2	West Sumatra in 1724	77
2.3	Tanah Datar in 1887–92	78
3.1	Topographical plan of Bukit Gombak, Bukit Kincir, and Tanah Lua showing the excavated areas in 2011 and 2012	97
4.1	Distribution of earthenware sherd types in the excavated areas of Bukit Gombak and Bukit Kincir	137
4.2	Distribution of imported ceramics in the excavated areas of Bukit Gombak and Bukit Kincir	162

LIST OF FIGURES

1.1	Erected stone with mirrored spirals from Bawah Parit, Lima Puluh Kota regency	2
1.2	Erected stone with mirrored spirals, foliage and triangles originating from the Mahat valley, Lima Puluh Kota regency, now in the Museum Nasional Indonesia, Jakarta (no inv. no.)	3
1.3	The "dendritic model" of Bennet Bronson from 1977	13
1.4	Magnetic anomalies (annotated) that correspond to modern features visible on the surface	18
1.5	Magnetic anomalies without correspondence with modern surface features and which possibly are archaeological in origin	19
1.6	Fireplace was set up on the excavation site	27
2.1	Head Sikatimuno, heirloom of the king of Pagaruyung	33
2.2	Dagger Si Mandang Giri depicting a male and female Buddhist deity, fourteenth century, heirloom of the king of Pagaruyung	34
2.3	The statue of amoghapasa was brought to Dharmasraya in 1286 and re-consecrated by Adityavarman in 1347, now in the Museum Nasional Indonesia, Jakarta (inv. no. 6469)	38
2.4	The Bhairawa statue associated to Adityavarman from Sungai Langsat, Padang Roco, now in the Museum Nasional Indonesia, Jakarta (inv. no. 6470)	40

2.5	Inscriptions of Adityavarman: the one dated to 1356 from Bukit Gombak (called Bukit Gombak I) is the largest erected stone seen on the photo of *c.* 1910	48
2.6	Detail of the inscription Bukit Gombak I: Adityavarman's symbol	49
2.7–2.8	Two fragments of the legs and upper body, orginating from Bukit Gombak, now at the BPCP in Batusangkar (inv. nos. 033/BCB/B/A/12/V/2008, 034/BCB/B/A/12/V/2008)	49
2.9	Three fragments of a Bodhisattva statue with long hair, Central Javanese Period (700–900): Lotus base, badly restored, originating from Bukit Gombak, now at Bundo Kanduan in Batusangkar	49
2.10–2.11	Female water spout and its backview, originating from Bukit Gombak, now at Bundo Kanduan in Batusangkar	50
2.12	The inscriptions above a water channel at Batu Papahat of 135(?) are lost	51
2.13	Irrigation channel built by Adityavarman	52
2.14	The in-situ inscription Saruaso I of 1374	55
2.15	Burial ground of the kings of Saruaso	56
2.16	The in-situ inscription of Ponggongan covered by a roof, today found in the middle of rice fields	58
2.17–2.19	Excavation at a gold workshop at Ponggongan, sixteenth to seventeenth centuries: remains of a stone wall	59
2.20	An inscribed stone mortar of 1375, originating from Ponggongan, now at Pagaruyung	60
2.21	A three-tiered stepped stone of unknown purpose from Gudam, now at Pagaruyung	61
2.22	The in-situ inscription Kubarajo I mentions Adityavarman	62
2.23	Stone slabs are used as seats at Kubarajo, the central stone is the inscription Kubarajo II	63

List of Figures   xi

2.24	Paper estampage of the in-situ inscription Kubarajo II	63
2.25	Paper estampage of the ornamented stone slab at Kubarajo	63
2.26–2.27	The in-situ inscription at Rambatan and its paper estampage	67
2.28–2.29	The in-situ inscription on a rock at Pariangan and its paper estampage	68
2.30–2.31	The in-situ inscription at Ombilin facing the Singkarak Lake, *c.* 1910	69
2.32	The pierced stone at Batu Batikam near Pagaruyung that has allegedly been pierced with a mythical kris	80
2.33	Stone seats for council meetings at Batu Batikam near Pagaruyung	81
2.34	Simawang, the largest burial ground in Tanah Datar, contains 237 stones of various sizes and shapes	83
3.1	The prehistoric site of Tanah Lua	92
3.2	Aerial view of the prehistoric excavation site of Tanah Lua	92
3.3	Digital elevation model of Bukit Gombak	98
3.4	Aerial view (from north to south) over the central plateau of Bukit Gombak and the southern slope of Bukit Kincir: in the foreground are the excavation trenches	98
3.5	Bukit Gombak: excavation of Trench C, in the background is Mount Merapi	99
3.6	Bukit Gombak: excavation plan of Trench C	101
3.7	Bukit Gombak: excavation plan of the west-section of Trench C	103
3.8	Bukit Gombak: excavation plan of Trench D	105
3.9	Bukit Gombak: excavation plan of Trench A	107
3.10	Bukit Gombak: excavation of Trench N at a paved street	109
3.11	Bukit Gombak: excavation plan of Trench N at a paved street	110

3.12	Bukit Gombak: the water spring, Trench S	112
3.13	Bukit Gombak: excavation plan of the water spring, Trench S	112
3.14	Bukit Gombak: excavation of the west-section of the water spring, Trench S	113
3.15	Bukit Gombak: excavation of Trench F in 2011, groundplan of a house on stilts	115
3.16	Bukit Gombak: excavation of outdoor-hearths in Trench M	115
3.17	Bukit Gombak: excavation plan of Trenches F, M, and T in 2012, around the house on stilts	116
3.18	Burial place on Bukit Kincir: erected stones (Structure 1)	120
3.19	Burial place on Bukit Kincir: grave pits in Trench L	121
3.20	Burial place on Bukit Kincir: aligned stones in Trench G (Structure 2)	121
3.21	Burial place on Bukit Kincir: aligned stones in Trench L3 (Structure 2)	122
3.22	Burial place on Bukit Kincir: aligned stones in Trench L3 (Structure 2)	122
3.23	Burial place on Bukit Kincir: excavation plan of Trenches G, H, L1–L3, and Q	123
3.24	Bukit Kincir: excavation plan of Trenches O, P, and R at the settlement site	129
3.25	Settlement site of Bukit Kincir: excavation of Trench P with remains of burnt clay of a metal working site	131
4.1	Earthenware of Tanah Lua	141
4.2	Restricted vessel of Bukit Gombak	145
4.3	Restricted vessel of Bukit Gombak	146
4.4	Unrestricted vessel of Bukit Gombak	148
4.5	Other earthenware finds of Bukit Gombak	149
4.6	At the pottery workshop in Galo Gandang, bamboo loops ensure an even diameter and normative size; paddle and anvil are used to form the vessel	152

4.7	Ceramic tools of Ponggongan (A), Bukit Gombak (B–C), and Bukit Kincir (D–F)	155
4.8	Earthenware of Bukit Kincir	156
4.9	Vessel of the burial site	157
4.10	Decoration of Tanah Lua (A–C), Bukit Gombak (D–K), and Bukit Kincir (L–N)	158
4.11	Chinese ceramics of Bukit Gombak	167
4.12	Chinese ceramics of Bukit Kincir (A) and Bukit Gombak (B–I)	168
4.13	Chinese ceramics of Bukit Gombak	169
4.14	Flaked lithics of Bukit Gombak and Tanah Lua	178
4.15	Adzes of Tanah Lua, Bukit Gombak, and Bukit Kincir	181
4.16	Ground stone tools of Bukit Gombak	182
4.17	Ground stone tools of Bukit Gombak	184
4.18	Flaked lithics of Bukit Kincir	185
4.19	Ground stone tools of Bukit Kincir	187
4.20	Metal objects of Bukit Gombak	191

LIST OF COLOUR PLATES

1. Imported monochrome ceramics of Bukit Gombak (A–E, H–N) and Ladang Rojo (F–G)
2. Imported blue-and-white dishes of Bukit Gombak
3. Metal fragments of Bukit Gombak (A, C–D) and of Bukit Kincir (B)
4. Archaeometric analyses of seven pottery samples from Bukit Gombak and Bukit Kincir: clay raw material, thermal behaviour after refiring

ABBREVIATIONS AND ACRONYMS

BPCP	Balai Purbakala dan Cagar Budaya (Centre of Antiquities and Cultural Property)
DFG	Deutsche Forschungsgemeinschaft (German Research Foundation)
EFEO	École française d'Extrême-Orient (French School of Asian Studies)
FU Berlin	Freie Universität Berlin
KAAK	Kommission für Archäologie Außereuropäischer Kulturen (Commission for Archaeology of Non-European Cultures)
MAMS	Curt-Engelhorn-Zentrum Archäometrie
MF	Magnetic feature
OSL	Optically stimulated luminescence
BPPP	Balai Pelestarian Peninggalan Purbakala (Centre of Antiquities and Cultural Property)
PUSLIT ARKENAS	Pusat Penelitian dan Pengembangan Arkeologi Nasional (National Research Centre for Archaeology)
RISTEK	Kementerian Riset dan Teknologi Republik Indonesia (Ministry of Research and Technology of Indonesia)
VOC	Verenigde Oostindische Compagnie (Dutch East Indies Company)
WD-XRF	Wavelength-dispersive x-ray fluorescence

PREFACE AND ACKNOWLEDGEMENTS

This volume concerns the historical archaeology of Sumatra, whose past has been neglected by researchers in comparison with other islands of the Indonesian archipelago such as Java, Bali, and Sulawesi. In particular, historians have assumed that highland Sumatra played a marginal role in the formation of the riverine trading kingdoms such as Melayu and Srivijaya in the seventh to the fourteenth centuries, places that were well-known to foreign traders and are better documented. However, little is known about the origins of the settlement processes that created the unique ethnic and cultural diversity of Indonesia's highland regions, or the demographic, political, and cultural developments that followed. This book analyses the rise of the settlement system in the heartland of the Minangkabau region in the highlands of West Sumatra. Historians have studied European sources and indigenous writings (Dobbin 1975; 1983; Drakard 1990; 1999; 2008–9), but the pre-colonial settlement history is poorly understood. An examination of the settlement and material culture from the fourteenth to the seventeenth centuries reveals growing social complexity in the region.

At the centre of this research lies a mountain called Bukit Gombak. Excavations suggest its identification with the royal centre of Adityavarman, the last Buddhist king of Sumatra, in Tanah Datar, a fertile plain in the highlands of West Sumatra. Buddhist artefacts and stone inscriptions document his reign (c. 1347–75),[1] which also produced more epigraphic material than any other ancient Indonesian polity. Drawing upon recent archaeological investigations, this volume explores the regional settlement pattern arising from Adityavarman's highland interregnum, and provides the first attempt to place the archaeological remains and the landscape of Tanah Datar in a cultural-historic synthesis.

The book explores the role of upland zones in the development of complex settlement systems in Southeast Asia, based on archaeological evidence and a close examination of the material culture of pre-state and early state systems in the highlands of Sumatra during the fourteenth century. This process occurred later than in the lowlands but was contemporaneous with developments in other highland regions in Southeast Asia. The research is important for understanding a core cultural region of West Sumatra, today the homeland of the Minangkabau, but it also facilitates evaluation of the settlement pattern, technology, cultural affiliation, and external links of Sumatra's highland in the development of precolonial Indonesia.

The research involved geophysical surveys, magnetometry, drone-based aerial surveys and detailed studies of metal, ceramics and glass finds by laboratory-based specialists as well as careful descriptions of stone, clay and other finds. Aerial imagery and remote sensing techniques revealed settlement activity and anthropogenic changes in the landscape. A remote-controlled flying system newly introduced in the highlands of the Indonesian archipelago allowed for the development of large-scale mapping and thus helped in the understanding of the spatial context of the geoarchaeological environment of the region.

Bukit Gombak is part of a community (*jorong*) of the same name in the district (*kecamatan*) of Lima Kaum in the regency (*kabupaten*) of Tanah Datar, part of the province of West Sumatra. Tanah Datar, which means "flat land", and refers primarily to a fertile highland plateau that covers a total area of 1,336 km^2 south of the volcano Gunung Merapi at an average altitude of 420 m (see Map 1). The capital of the regency, Batusangkar, lies in the southeastern part of this plain. It is located along the Selo, the principal river of the region, the southern reaches of which cross the mountains before turning eastwards and joining the Batang Hari River in the broad lowland plains. The Selo is the only river-based transport route to Sumatra's east coast, though it is not an easy one. Other routes

MAP 1

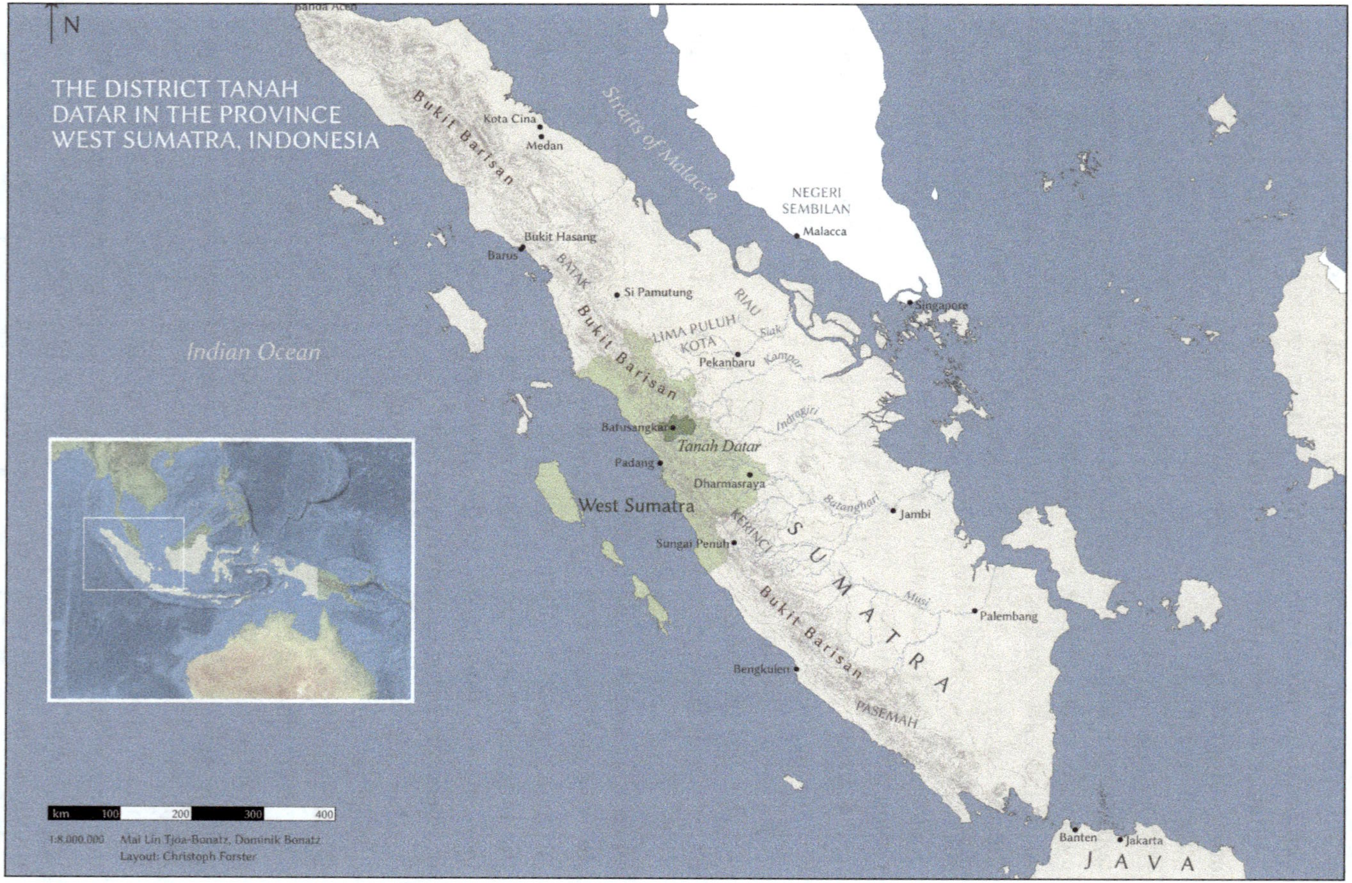

The Tanah Datar district in the province of West Sumatra, Indonesia

Source: Mai Lin Tjoa-Bonatz and Dominik Bonatz; lay-out: Christoph Förster.

lead to the nearby west coast of Sumatra, the eastern lowlands, and the north, passing through deep ravines and over steep passes in the Barisan Mountains, a difficult but passable range whose highest volcanic spurs rise to almost 3,000 m in addition to Gunung Merapi (2,891 m), Gunung Singgalang (2,877 m), and Gunung Sago (2,271 m).

The region has exceptionally fertile soils, gold and other metals, and forest products including beeswax, honey, different species of wood, aromatics and ivory, providing a distinctive microclimate for the development of early societies. As a legendary land of gold and the original homeland of the Minangkabau (see Chapter 3), it is of immense importance for understanding the cultural history of the modern period.

The resources of the highlands were highly regarded in the international maritime trade and decisive for the region's political-economic systems. For the first time in a historically detectable way during the fourteenth century, these dynamics brought the highlands of West Sumatra into a network of supra-regional trade that brought glass beads, porcelain, and stoneware from China, other parts of Southeast Asia, and West Asia into the highlands. The circulation of these items is discussed in the context of the development of local traditions changes arising from state formation under Adityavarman. Material culture remains at the settlement sites under investigation indicate long-distance exchange relations, and the international trade wares reveal that maritime connections of an early globalized trade linked the interior highland region of Sumatra with both coastlines. The interdependence of the uplands and the lowlands influenced highland society, but archaeological finds indicate that the highlands remained autonomous and did not form part of the state system of the lowlands, where political entities such as the emporium of Srivijaya-Melayu or Dharmasraya of the late thirteenth and fourteenth centuries on the upper Batang Hari River in Southeast Sumatra were the most important political and economic powers at that time.

Many socio-economic changes have been identified in the societies of Southeast Asia during the "age of commerce" in the fifteenth century. Anthony Reid (1993) identifies six fleets sent by the Chinese emperor as trading expeditions to the Indonesian archipelago and the Indian Ocean in the early fifteenth century as the starting point of this new era. Challenging this chronology, archaeological materials from West Sumatra show that socio-political and economic complexity in the fourteenth century made possible intensified maritime trade in the next century, when wet-rice agriculture became established, local iron production became more important, and political centralization and territorial consolidation took place. It seems, therefore, that the shift towards new economic modes in the highlands began before 1400.

The establishment of a capital in the highland region of Tanah Datar under Adityavarman, far from any seaports, has been the subject of extensive scholarly discussion (Miksic 1987, pp. 9–10; 2015, p. 36; Reichle 2007; Kulke 2009, pp. 233–37). Adityavarman, a high official of royal descent in the East Javanese Majapahit court (1292–1527), founded the first identifiable monarchical polity in the Sumatran highlands. This period is a particular focus of the present book because it led to various changes in the socio-political, economic, and cultural landscape of the region. It is viewed against the background of written records of Adityavarman's reign and new archaeological data. However, the evidence also raises questions about the extent to which structures of rule as well as other economic and symbolic influences that developed out of external traditions, fit into existing local structures of settlement and society.

The "Tanah Datar Project" began with a hypothesis that Adityavarman's reign marked a turning point for the Sumatran highlands and the research sought archaeological traces of his rule to provide a point of reference for examining early state formation. This research then moved to broader questions about prehistoric conditions and historical consequences, as well as the formation of a Minangkabau ethnic identity.

The core of this project consisted of excavations at two mountain sites, Bukit Gombak and Bukit Kincir, carried out by Dominik Bonatz, Johannes Greger, and Annika Hotzan-Tchabashvili and reported in this volume. Bukit Gombak was a central place in Adityavarman's kingdom, and provides evidence of the organization and material development of this political entity. Surveys in the Tanah Datar plain provided evidence of other settlements that could be examined in relation to each other and to sites from earlier and later periods, and used to sketch out the settlement history of Tanah Datar from prehistoric times to the pre-colonial period.

Chapter 1 outlines the history, methods, and objectives of the research project. In Chapter 2, Benjamin Vining describes survey methods and Johannes Greger discusses the excavation procedures, addressing the spatial aspects and political implications of the archaeological evidence. Chapter 3 begins with the discovery of a prehistoric findspot and documents the excavations at the plateau of Bukit Gombak, the potential royal centre of Adityavarman, and the hill top of Bukit Kincir, which was an iron-working site. These twin mounds are connected by a burial ground at the lower part of Bukit Kincir. Functionally both habitation sites are closely related but each has distinctive characteristics, including artefact types and proportions. An analysis of intrasite spatial adds information about the consumption of imported luxury goods and a differentiated economy. Chapter 4 deals with find groups and single finds relating to material culture. The sites at Bukit Gombak and Bukit Kincir contain material relating to household activities, trade, and manufacturing, underlining a differentiated habitation pattern. Items of foreign origin indicate that international trade was an essential part of this society. Bukit Kincir also served as a burial place, with stones erected as grave markers and for ritual practices. A prehistorical tradition of erecting stones connected with burials appears to have continued during Adityavarman's reign.

Evidence that Bukit Gombak and the adjacent Bukit Kincir form the oldest royal seat in the Minangkabau area, with continuous settlement from the fourteenth to seventeenth centuries, challenges local historiography. It is a fundamental belief of Minangkabau oral history, supported by colonial sources of the late seventeenth century, that the ruling family of Pagaruyung was accorded a higher status than other rulers because it was the oldest and most prestigious kingdom of West Sumatra. It has obtained wealth as supplier of gold, forest products, and especially rice, which was rare in the entire island in the early colonial times. Archaeological finds raise questions about the claim that Adityavarman founded the royal court of Pagaruyung. Rather, it seems that the supremacy of leadership in the political realm of West Sumatra was constantly contested by competing lineages. Archaeological evidence indicates that Pagaruyung was a settlement site during the time of Adityavarman but less important than Bukit Gombak, and that the lineage of Pagaruyung only seized power when Bukit Gombak diminished in importance during the late seventeenth century.

***

This study could not have been completed without the support of numerous individuals and institutions and their help is gratefully acknowledged. After a preliminary survey in 2008, archaeological research on West Sumatra was undertaken between 2011 and 2014 by the Freie Universität Berlin (FU Berlin) under the direction of Dominik Bonatz, with funding from the Deutsche Forschungsgemeinschaft (DFG, German Research Foundation). Fieldwork in 2011 and 2012 was carried out in cooperation with the Pusat Penelitian dan Pengembangan Arkeologi Nasional (PUSLIT Arkenas, National Research Centre for Archaeology) in Jakarta, Balai Purbakala dan Cagar Budaya (BPCP, Centre of Antiquities and Cultural Property) in Batusangkar, Balai Arkeologi Sumatera Utara (Archaeological Centre of North Sumatra) in Medan, and the École française d'Extrême-Orient (EFEO, French School of Asian Studies) in Jakarta, under a research permit from Kementerian Riset dan Teknologi Republik Indonesia (RISTEK, Ministry of Research and Technology of Indonesia). Surveys and excavations ran for eight weeks in March and April 2011 and 2012 with teams of up to 60 people. A final period of fieldwork was carried out over two months in mid-2014.

The BPCP in Batusangkar made archaeological material and sources from the region accessible, supported by Budi Istiawan. Geoarchaeological surveys and area mapping were conducted by Wiebke Bebermeier of the Institute of Geographical Sciences, FU Berlin, and Benjamin Vining of the University of Arkansas. In addition, other participating institutions were the Hochschule für Technik und Wirtschaft Berlin, the National Museum of Cambodia Phnom Penh, Universitas Indonesia, and the University of Adelaide. During the 2011 field season, assistance was given by Baskoro Tjahyono. In the same season Arlo Griffiths (EFEO) directed an epigraphic research project. The "Tanah Datar Project" is grateful that he provided access to the paper estampage of the inscriptions of Adityavarman and gave helpful advice. He aims to publish the corpus of inscriptions separately. The reading of these epigraphic records is beyond the expertise of the authors of this book so that this material for historical reconstruction is still awaiting a reappraisal. Archaeologists who directed fieldwork teams were Veronique Degroot, Johannes Greger, Annika Hotzan-Tchabashvili, Lucas Partanda Koestro, Andri Restiyadi, Maresi Startzmann, Kilian Teuwsen, and

Arne Weiser. Mai Lin Tjoa-Bonatz identified the ceramics and small finds. Special thanks go to Rizky Fardhyan, Terrylia Feisrami, Anissa Oruzgan, Tres Sekar, and Belinda Natsya Worung from Universitas Indonesia who participated in the archaeological work, as well as Ham Seihasarann and Khom Sreymom from Cambodia who joined the estampage process of the inscriptions. Thanks goes to Annika Hotzan-Tchabashvili for editing the excavation plans. Follow-up funding from the DFG and a visiting fellowship at the Nalanda-Sriwijaya Centre, ISEAS – Yusof Ishak Institute in Singapore made possible the completion of the work for the present book.

Special thanks go to Uli Kozok who introduced us to the region in 2008. The members of the "Tanah Datar Project" would also like to express sincere gratitude to Hermann Kulke and John Miksic who visited the excavations and the ceramic laboratory in 2012. Gratefully acknowledged are Miksic's critical identifications of the ceramics and his enduring advice. Valuable assistance on the excavated lithic material was provided by Johannes Moser of the Kommission für Archäologie Außereuropäischer Kulturen (KAAK, Commission for Archaeology of Non-European Cultures), and on the ceramics by Edmund Edwards McKinnon and Tai Yew Seng. The study of the glass finds was kindly assisted by Alison Carter, Laure Dussubieux, and James Lankton. The excellent drawings of Dayat Hidayat from the Balai Arkeologi Bandung were most helpful to understanding the artefacts. Małgorzata Daszkiewicz and Gerwulf Schneider of Topoi, FU Berlin and ARCHEA, Warsaw carried out archaeometric ceramic analyses. Dating studies were undertaken by the Curt-Engelhorn-Zentrum Archäometrie (MAMS). Curators from numerous museums in Germany, the Netherlands and Switzerland made available their ethnographic collections for comparative studies. The "Tanah Datar Project" members appreciate the efforts of curators who gave access to their collections: Francine Brinkgreve, Dietmar Grundmann, Richard Kunz, Petra Martin, and Roland Platz. Special thanks also go to various scholars who have provided literature and insights in their respective fields of expertise including Jane Drakard, Lydia Kieven, Marijke Klokke, Gauri Krishnan, Wibke Lobo, Brigitte Majlis, Anthony Reid, and Andreas Reinecke. Most helpful were the comments of anonymous referees.

Last but not least, thanks also go to those who have helped to make this book a reality: Paul and Adam Kratoska for helping with copy-editing, Ng Kok Kiong for accepting the book on behalf of the ISEAS – Yusof Ishak Institute and Agus Rubiyanto at the Indonesian embassy in Berlin for additional funding.

Mai Lin Tjoa-Bonatz,
September 2019

NOTE

1. Dates are provided in CE and are generally unmarked. CE and BCE are noted only if absolute dates are provided.

ABOUT THE CONTRIBUTORS

Dominik Bonatz is Professor of Ancient Near Eastern Archaeology at the FU Berlin, Germany. He has an MA and PhD in Ancient Near Eastern Archaeology from the Johann Wolfgang Goethe Universität Frankfurt am Main, Germany. He wrote his PhD thesis on Iron Age funerary monuments in the Syrian-Anatolian region, Turkey, and has a strong interest in ancient West Asian visual arts. In the highlands of Sumatra and on the island of Nias he has studied dispersed megalithic remains. His research covers the history of images and monuments, state formation, political spaces in ancient societies, and critical approaches in archaeology.

Johannes Greger is a research assistant at the FU Berlin, working on the archaeological project "Telling Stones – Megaliths on Sumatra" with a focus on the object life-cycle of the megaliths. He has an MA in Near Eastern Archaeology and Philology and participated in the excavations and surveys in Tanah Datar and the Mahat valley in Indonesia between 2011 and 2014. His main interests are critical perspectives in archaeology and archaeological interpretation, theories of the cultural turn, and phenomenologies of material cultures. He is co-editor of the journal *Forum Kritische Archäologie*.

Annika Hotzan-Tchabashvili is a Research Associate at the Institute of Near Eastern Archaeology, FU Berlin, Germany. She has an MA in Prehistoric Archaeology, East Asian Art History, and Near Eastern Archaeology from the FU Berlin, Germany, and has taken part in excavations in Syria, Russia, Georgia, and Iraq. She worked as a research assistant for the "Tanah Datar Project" in 2011–14. Her main interests are landscape archaeology, migration, and interaction in prehistoric societies.

Mai Lin Tjoa-Bonatz is Curator of the Golden Lotus Foundation Singapore. She has a PhD in Art History from Technische Universität Darmstadt, Germany, and an MA in Art History, Archaeology, and Southeast Asian Regional Studies from the Johann Wolfgang Goethe Universität in Frankfurt am Main. She was a Visiting Fellow with the Nalanda-Sriwijaya Centre at the ISEAS – Yusof Ishak Institute in Singapore and served as a research assistant for excavations conducted on Sumatra, Indonesia in 2003–8 and 2011–14. Her main interests are architecture, maritime cultural heritage, gold jewellery, settlement and missionary history in Southeast Asia.

Benjamin Vining is an Assistant Professor of Anthropology at the University of Arkansas-Fayetteville in the United States. His research and teaching focuses on using geospatial methods, including remote sensing and GIS, to model interactions between archaeological cultures and environments. He has an MA and a PhD in Archaeology from Boston University, and previously held faculty positions in the Institute for the Environment at Tufts University and the Department of Anthropology at Wellesley College.

1

RESEARCH HISTORY, METHODS, AND OBJECTIVES

1.1. Research History (*Mai Lin Tjoa-Bonatz*)

In the early decades of the nineteenth century, colonial officials took an interest in the antiquities in the West Sumatran highlands (Anonymous 1855; Raffles 1991), inspiring epigraphic works on Adityavarman's inscriptions by philologists and archaeologists (Kern 1917*a*; 1917*b*; Machi Suhadi 1990; Casparis 1992; Djafar 1992, pp. 12–21; Budi Istiawan 2014; Bambang Budi Utomo 2007, pp. 51–82). Apart from Frederic M. Schnitger's reports (1937, pp. 13–15; 1964, pp. 167–72) on Buddhist remains connected to Adityavarman and the megaliths in the valleys of Mahat and Sinamar in the regency of Lima Puluh Kota, scholars have prepared brief inventories of the antiquities found in the region, including Tanah Datar (Krom 1912; Bronson et al. 1973, pp. 13–14). Since 1977 the regional conservation body BPCB (formerly BPPP) in Batusangkar, working under the authority of the Ministry of Culture, has been locating, documenting, and protecting heritage sites that were previously unrecorded and largely unknown. However, the rich data in their constantly updated heritage inventory has not yet been systematically examined to understand spatial patterning in the ancient landscape of Tanah Datar.

The first Indonesian archaeologists to work in the region were interested in the megaliths in Mahat. In 1984 the PUSLIT ARKENAS and the Indonesian Directorate for the Preservation and Protection of National Heritage carried out a series of short-term archaeological projects and restoration work on stone monuments, concentrating on the Lima Puluh Kota regency. This work produced confidential reports (Yuwono Sudibyo 1984; Tim Peneliti Tradisi Megalitik Sumatera Barat 1984; 1985).

For a long time, the best systematic attempt to record and interpret the archaeological monuments, finds, and inscriptions in Tanah Datar and its neighbouring regency to the north, Lima Puluh Kota, was a series of articles by John Miksic (1985*a*; 1986; 1987; 2004; 2009) based on his fieldwork as well as external sources. He focused on megaliths (locally called *batu tagak*) and their relation to similar stone monuments on the Malay Peninsula in the states of Negeri Sembilan and Melaka in Malaysia. Miksic (1985*a*, p. 79) created the description of kris-hilt shaped megaliths, erected stones which are mostly rectangular but are curved at the top so that they resemble the hilt of a kris (see Figures 1.1 and 1.2).

FIGURE 1.1

Erected stone with mirrored spirals from Bawah Parit, Lima Puluh Kota regency

FIGURE 1.2

Erected stone with mirrored spirals, foliage and triangles originating from the Mahat valley, Lima Puluh Kota regency, now in the Museum Nasional Indonesia, Jakarta (no inv. no.)

Although it is obviously only a descriptive term using a design feature of an artefact that was later introduced in the area, it highlights a regionally characteristic shape. His study of archaeological remains from Tanah Datar and Lima Puluh Kota, also referring to some inscriptions of Adityavarman, included finds of settlement remains and art such as ceramics, stone objects, sculptures, and brick fragments. In 1985, Miksic (1987, p. 9) explored Bukit Gombak, but did not report any archaeological finds. He was the first (Miksic 1987, p. 21) to conclude that Bukit Gombak could have been a central settlement site during the time of Adityavarman, later reassured by Hermann Kulke (2009, p. 242).

Between 1985 and 2010, various Indonesian teams carried out excavations and surveys in the regencies of Solok and Lima Puluh Kota that focused on megalithic grave markers and cave sites deemed to be prehistoric (Uka Tjandrasasmita et al. 1985; Marsis Sutopo 1991; Rambung and Budi Istiawan 1998; Triwurjani 2010). Laboratory analyses proposed dates for the megaliths that ranged from the second millennium BCE to the tenth century CE. ^{14}C samples of human skeletal material taken from the burials in Bawah Parit and the Mahat valley in the Lima Puluh Kota regency yielded widely differing dates (see Figures 1.1–1.2): for Bawah Parit, 1550±100 BCE, 1050–450 BCE, and 120–180 BCE; for Guguk Nunang, CE 970±120; and for Sati, CE 580±170, CE 220±140 (Triwurjani 2010, p. 108). The reliability of these dates thus requires further investigation. More systematic archaeological studies in Lima Puluh Kota regency are needed to get more accurate information about the age of the megaliths and clarify their social and functional context (Bonatz 2015; 2019, pp. 416–22).

In Tanah Datar, one grave site with human skeletons was excavated at Gunung Bungsu (Marsis Sutopo and Bagyo Prasetyo 1994), but in the absence of scientific dating methods their rough assignment to the pre-Islamic period remains fairly broad. From 2010–11 excavations under the direction of Budi Istiawan discovered a goldsmithing site at Ponggongan in Tanah Datar, probably of the sixteenth or seventeenth century (see pp. 59, 71–74). However, the results of these small-scale excavations were not integrated with the broader settlement history of the region.

The BPCB's list of monuments in Tanah Datar, accessible only at their Batusangkar office, is impressive, but like the other archaeological investigations has a number of missing details. First, none of the finds or sites in Tanah Datar definitively predates Adityavarman. Second, aside from the monuments dedicated to Adityavarman, consisting of 22 inscriptions, and other metal and stone artefacts (see Chapter 2.2) connected to him, it is difficult to link other remains or sites unambiguously to his reign. Third, no attempts were made to investigate possible habitation sites despite this region's central importance to the understanding of sociocultural developments in highland Sumatra.

In response to these gaps in the research, the following chapters on the "Tanah Datar Project" correlate surveys and large-scale excavations, and reconstruct historical processes from archaeological evidence. This full description extends preliminary excavation reports (Tjoa-Bonatz 2013*a*; 2013*c*).

1.2. Megalithic Complexes in the Highlands of Sumatra (*Mai Lin Tjoa-Bonatz*)

Sumatra is the second largest island of the Indonesian archipelago, covering 434,000 km². From north to south the island reaches 1,650 km in length, but its widest point from east to west is only 350 km. Located along the waterway linking the Indian and Pacific Oceans, it is situated at the western entrance of the Indonesian archipelago, where sailing boats had to await the turn of the monsoon winds. Archaeological and written evidence reveal that maritime routes ran along both the west and the east coast of Sumatra (Tjoa-Bonatz 2018). On this long but narrow island, the highland areas lie along the Barisan Mountains, which stretch almost uninterrupted from Aceh in the north to Lampung in the south, and are the watershed between the wide plains of the east coast and the narrow lowland strip on the west coast (see Map 1). The mountains were formed through tectonic folding caused by subduction of the Indian Ocean plate under the Sunda Shelf, resulting in the formation of two parallel ranges characterized by widespread volcanic activity. The western range of mountains is more or less continuous, with elevations averaging about 2,000 m, while the eastern one is more segmented, with elevations ranging from 800 to 1,500 m. Between the two ranges lies a tectonic depression, referred to as the Semangko Graben or Median Graben, which forms a series of highland rift valleys. For at least 3,500 years ago, settlement cores with diverse cultural identities have developed within the fertile valleys of this mountainous area (Bonatz et al. 2006; Tjoa-Bonatz 2012). These valleys are considered the original homelands of several Sumatran ethnic groups (Miksic 1985*b*, p. 425). The Minangkabau are one of the largest highland communities on the island today, but their ethnogenesis is unclear.

Megaliths are the outstanding archaeological feature of the Sumatran highland region. They primarily occur in four regional clusters, each with a distinct formal appearance: in the Batak highlands of North Sumatra; in Lima Puluh Kota and Tanah Datar in West Sumatra; in the highlands of Jambi including the regencies Kerinci, Serampas, and Sungai Tenang; and on the Pasemah plateau in South Sumatra. Miksic (1987, pp. 1–2) suggested that most, if not all, megalithic complexes on Sumatra can be dated to CE 1000–1500, but new findings suggest a wider dating span, and that culturally very different populations used megaliths. The presence of megaliths, firmly fixed stone monuments with some bearing anthropomorphic images, indicates sedentary living connected with territoriality and the symbolic marking of space. Whether the spread of the megalithic phenomenon generally indicates a multi-local process of sedentarization, and whether processes of a Neolithic can be inferred in the highlands, are disputed issues, and the difficulties of dating the various megalithic complexes makes them difficult to resolve (Bonatz 2009).

There is convincing archaeological evidence that the Pasemah highlands are associated with pre-Srivijaya polities, and the iconography of the sculptured stones show a Dong Son style drum and other metal artefacts made within the first few centuries of the first millennium AD (Guillaud et al. 2009, pp. 416–20; Bonatz 2009, p. 60; Manguin 2009, pp. 442–43). Comparable, though not necessarily contemporaneous, processes can be assumed for the Jambi highlands, where more secure dating indicates a starting point for the erection of megaliths in this region around CE 1000. The tradition persisted for roughly 300 years and then ceased. Excavations were carried out at two megalithic sites, Pondok in Kerinci and Bukit Batu Larung in Serampas, while systematic surveys mapped other megalithic sites and archaeological sites in these regions. For the megaliths, it has been possible to document clear connections with permanent forms of settlement and other remains of material culture associated with the late Melayu-Srivijaya period (Bonatz et al. 2006; Tjoa-Bonatz 2009; Bonatz 2012, pp. 58–65). New elements of material culture also appear in this context, the most noteworthy being bronze items such as Dong Son style drums (including miniature ones), an arm protector and a flask found near Lake Kerinci, but these bronze items might have been brought to the highlands of Jambi long after they were manufactured, because in the tenth century a motif reference to the bronze drums can be seen in local pottery of a jar burial site in the vicinity of a megalithic site (Tjoa-Bonatz 2012, p. 25). The exact time of the arrival of these metal artefacts in the highlands is therefore ambiguous and their use for dating creates a circular argument, but it seems clear that upstream-downstream networks exchanged metal objects.

For the Tanah Datar region, the tradition of erecting stones began in prehistory and continued during the time of Adityavarman (see pp. 79–85, 120–27). Although different scenarios for megalithic sites on Sumatra can be constructed, in West Sumatra marking territoriality with stones and that the emergence of social complexity are associated with intensification of trade in international commodities and metal exchange with the lowlands.

1.3. Settlement Archaeology and State Formation (*Mai Lin Tjoa-Bonatz*)

The scarcity of locally written sources for early Southeast Asia encourages archaeologists to use archaeological evidence to assess cultural, socio-political and economic interactions. Compared to other parts of the world, settlement archaeology emerged relatively late as a research focus in Southeast Asia, first appearing in the 1970s. Concepts of settlement patterns and their centres developed by geographers and historians provided the basic analytical framework for defining Southeast Asian settlements (Lombard 1970; Reid 1980; Wheatley 1983).

Theories on the formation and transformation of complex societies for island Southeast Asia that emerged from a slowly extending empirical database in archaeology display two main tendencies: an effort to understand settlement systems in non-western contexts, and a growing dissatisfaction with unilinear evolutionary models.[1] Researchers have focused on diachronic studies, particularly relating to long-distance exchange (Nishimura 1988; Christie 1995; Junker 1999), and used indigenous concepts to define settlements (Miksic 1989*a*, pp. 7–12) or to refer to environmental conditions (Miksic 1999; Bacus and Lucero 1999). These studies used various decisive factors to establish development sequences and explain the emergence of social complexity within a specific micro-regional setting. In the last decade, settlement studies have continued to identify themes of change in an interdisciplinary discourse and develop cross-cultural perspectives (Wade and Sun 2010; Miksic 2013). Methodologically, archaeological investigations involving excavations and systematic regional surveys, along with ethnohistorical or written sources, are the most promising ways to analyse settlement history.

For island Southeast Asia, archaeologists have mainly focused on sites in coastal areas with foreign records and monumental architecture or inscriptions. Implicit in this focus is a preference for sites with "spectacular" discoveries. Archaeology in Sumatra has mainly concentrated on the north and the southeast. On the northeast coast, three important trading sites have been excavated. Kota Cina dates from the eleventh to the mid-thirteenth centuries (Miksic 1979; Edwards McKinnon 1984; Miksic 2000, pp. 110–12; Perret et al. 2013), Aru from the seventh to sixteenth centuries, and Kota Rentang from the twelfth to sixteenth centuries (Damanik and Edwards McKinnon 2012). Along the northwest coast, French-Indonesian teams have investigated the Barus area, a trading centre for camphor and gold from the second half of the first millennium (Guillot 1998; 2003; Perret and Heddy Surachman 2009). More recently these teams shifted their focus to the highlands of North Sumatra, discovering settlement remains at the religious site of Padang Lawas dating from the mid-ninth to the thirteenth centuries (Perret 2014).

Archaeological data from various coastal sites on Sumatra provide evidence for the maritime trade fuelling the spread of trading centres over the first millennium CE. In Southeast Sumatra, for example, small settlements at Kota Kapur on the island of Bangka, Air Sugihan, and Karangagung offer insights into earlier sites and push the settlement horizon of Sumatran port sites back to CE 220–440 (Koestro et al. 1998; Manguin 2004, pp. 287–88; Agustijanto 2012).

The most intensively studied state system in Southeast Sumatra is the trade-based emporium of Srivijaya. Originally centred around Palembang from the seventh to the eleventh centuries, its centre shifted to the Jambi region called Melayu-Srivijaya from the eleventh to the fourteenth centuries. In both locations, the control of international maritime trade and efforts to centralize authority blended with Hindu-Buddhist ideology and supported the process of state formation. The description of Srivijaya's polity has evolved from ideas of kingship through "Indianization". Not understood as imitation but the transfer of knowledge, art and political concepts as response to the local context within the Indo-Pacific world through maritime connections has not lost its significance in scholarly discussion (Gauri Parimoo Krishnan 2016). Similar to "galactic" polities in mainland Southeast Asia, Srivijaya has been canned a "mandala polity" characterized by a centre with satellites at the peripheries (Wolters 1982; Tambiah 1977; Kulke 1993). Jan Wisseman Christie's (1990, 1995) notion of the late emergence of the Srivijayan state stems from a paradigm of comparison with better researched areas on Java, Bali, and mainland Southeast Asia. Pierre-Yves Manguin (2000; 2002*a*) later reconceptualized this model based on his extensive archaeological research in the region. Manguin adopted the term "city-state" for early polities based on maritime-trade that drew on the resources of a wide hinterland such as Srivijaya.

Although the temple complex of Muara Jambi in the Jambi region has yielded a wide range of remains such as sculpture, written material, and imported artefacts that date as early as the ninth century, the settlement areas have not yet been the subject of substantial archaeological investigations. Archaeological accounts of settlement debris from the eleventh to the thirteenth centuries along the lower Batang Hari River attest to the existence of numerous settlements during the Melayu-Srivijaya heydays (Miksic 2013, p. 117). Various types of Minangkabau dwelling architecture inscribed on bricks have been documented at Muara Jambi, probably dating from the tenth to the twelfth centuries (Tjoa-Bonatz et al. 2009; 2013*b*, pp. 70–71; Griffiths 2011, p. 164). Similarities in building style might reflect early contacts between upland and lowland, and probably migration from the highlands to the Southeast Asian plain.

Heterogeneity in conceptualizing political power has been posited for Southeast Asia (White 1989; Miksic 2000). This view proposes multi-linear and agent-oriented definitions for the development of social complexity, and contrasts coastal cities in island Southeast Asia operating as trading ports with heterogeneous, multi-ethnic societies with inland, agrarian-based centres such as the states of Bali and Java, which had divine Hindu-Buddhist rulers and "hydraulic" societies built around wet-rice cultivation.[2] This model emphasizes on social relations, creating relatively short-term but nonetheless dynamic networks. Similarly, polities on Sumatra have been described as "amorphous" or "volatile" due to a lack of structural features in their local representations, such as topography and territory (Manguin 2002*a*; Colombijn 2003). These perceptions of a "weak" state need to be considered against the Orientalist assumptions about the instability of Asian regimes.

The perception that control over people rather than land was key for political power neglects the element of territoriality. The research described in this volume reinvestigates this issue in the settlement system and state formation in West Sumatra. Recent analyses of royal scripts, treaties, and state myths from the highlands have revealed valuable information on spatial relations and boundaries that clearly indicate the importance of territory (Colombijn 2003, p. 513, fn. 14; Drakard 2008–9; Teh Gallop and Neidel 2009; Hunter 2015, pp. 318–20; Druce 2017, pp. 22–23). Following these ideas, the research focuses on using archaeological evidence to interpret the cultural and socio-political landscape and the symbolism of spaces and places in settlement history. The erection of stone monuments in the highlands endowed space with value, so do the inscribed stones of Adityavarman that represent territoriality and structural features of his realm as explained in the following chapter.

No independent states developed on the west coast or in the interior of Sumatra in the early modern period apart from the Minangkabau kingdom, which scholars agree, fulfilled the minimal functional definition of an early state.[3] Thomas Hunter (2015, p. 364, fn. 3) is persuaded that Victor Lieberman's (2003) "charter state" best describes the political form of Adityavarman's kingdom because public inscriptions presenting state ideals and practices support a centralized form of state organization, and the writing blended Sanskrit with local vernaculars. However, these characteristics run counter to certain traits of political fragmentation for which we have more information in the early modern period, including the hereditary status of competing clan heads, the existence of a triumvirate that espoused strong royalist rhetoric, and corporate bodies in the villages that built strong alliances and may have operated as a kind of autonomous village republic (Kahn 1993, pp. 71–72; Colombijn 2003, pp. 509–12, fn. 9). The goal of the "Tanah Datar Project" is to delineate archaeologically recognizable features of the Minangkabau state.

1.4. A Highland Perspective (*Mai Lin Tjoa-Bonatz*)

In contrast to the scholarly interest in the coastal areas, little research has been carried out in the Sumatran highlands (Bonatz 2012). This neglect is partly due to a perception of the uplands as a marginal domain and partly to a division of scholarship. While historians and archaeologists have been preoccupied with state formation and urbanization in the coastal areas, the highlands have been the preserve of prehistorians and anthropologists. The consequences of partitioning cultural landscapes as a disciplinary paradigm obscure the intrinsic connection between these landscapes. Although addressing the highland of mainland Southeast Asia, the focus on the nonstate-centric history of mountain areas, now often referred to as "zomia", is an important shift in the historical perspective to accommodate the "world of peripheries" (Scott 2010).

In recent decades archaeological research on Sumatra started to shift from its earlier focus on harbours and coastal sites to consider inland areas. In the highland regions of Kerinci, Serampas, Sungai Tenang, and Pratin Tuo at the western border of Jambi province, a dense settlement system that formed in the early second millennium has been documented (Bonatz et al. 2006; Tjoa-Bonatz 2009). Despite their geographical isolation, highland communities have long maintained political and economic ties to both the eastern lowlands and the west coast of the island. Early highland involvement in international trade is indicated by the presence of archaeological material of foreign origin such as the bronze artefacts or stone beads found in Pasemah and the highlands of Jambi (van der Hoop 1932; 1940; Calò 2013). Upland histories reveal a regular connection to the lowlands (Bonatz et al. 2009).

This interaction between the highlands and the lowlands was the focus of Bennet Bronson's (1977) influential river-based "dendritic model", which builds on Frederick L. Dunn's (1975, p. 100, figure 7.1) socio-geographic account of foragers in Malaya to explain systems of exchange in Southeast Asia. Bronson's approach helps to explain settlement dependences as well as their socio-economic and cultural relations. Waterways facilitated communication, trade, and transport links between coasts and the interior. Accordingly, a hierarchical riverine settlement pattern—similar to branches of a tree and the source of the name of this model—developed with the primary centre at the river mouth, connecting overseas suppliers and consumers with intermediate collecting nodes and ultimately to upriver sources of trading goods. Manguin (2002*b*, pp. 77–78, figure 1) and Miksic (2009, pp. 79–80, figure 4-1) have changed the model in fundamental ways (see Figure 1.3). At Muara Jambi the primary centre was at least 75 m inland, and at Palembang 90 m inland, and "forest producer" in the mountain areas are added to what becomes a three-tiered hierarchy. Finally, the revised model captures the way riverine systems use mountain passages and trans-insular routes to compete for trading opportunities. To assess these spatial relationships, archaeologists have explored ancient footpaths within riverine systems as means of socio-economic communication in various regions of the highlands (Edwards McKinnon 2009; Neidel 2009).

The topography of the island of Sumatra island is important for assessing spatial relationships from a highland perspective. The mountains are no longer understood as a natural barrier limiting the scope of seaborn commerce because passages allow trade to penetrate the total island space, providing connections to the Straits of Melaka, the Indian Ocean, and beyond. Although in the latest river-based model, shown in Figure 1.3, locations are correlated, and defined within vertical relationship in tiered hierarchies relative to river transport and according to distance from the sea, the highlands are accorded greater flexibility in these hierarchies by virtue of direct access to the primary trade nodes on the east coast and interrelationships between dentric systems on the west coast. This accommodates interactions of varying degrees of complexity. From an upland perspective, the relationship of greatest local importance shifts to changing opportunities for trade. Hence, their relevance of primary and non-primary distinctions

1. Research History, Methods, and Objectives 13

FIGURE 1.3

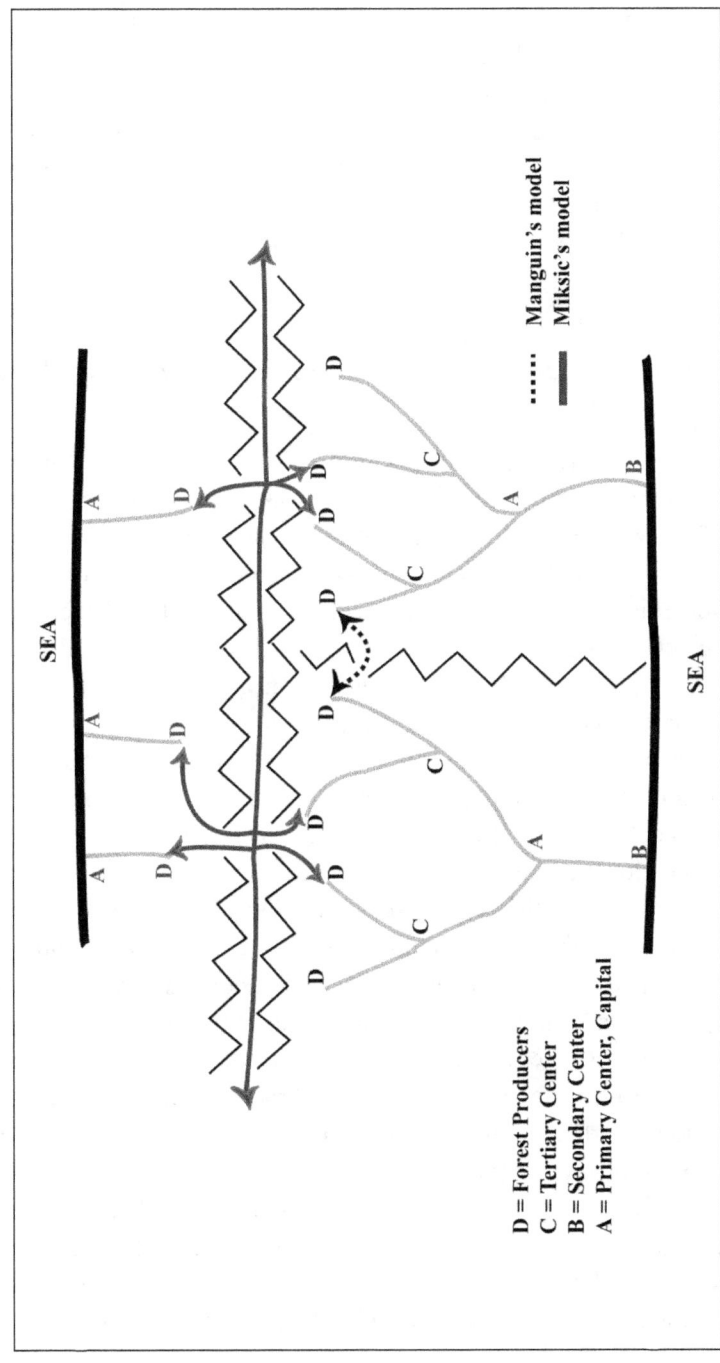

The "dendritic model" of Bennet Bronson from 1977

Note: The horizontal zig-zag line represents the Barisan Mountains and the light grey lines the connecting rivers.
Source: Updated by P.-Y. Manguin (2002b, pp. 77–78, figure 1) and J. Miksic (2009, pp. 79–80, figure 4-1).

between trade nodes will be defined accordingly. Ethnohistoric and archaeological studies indicate that the upriver centres are the collector of valuable interior forest resources as well as discrete producer for commodities in the river-based trading system and therefore played a significant role in the regional economy (Junker 1990; 1999, pp. 65–71). Research on the highland kingdom of Adityavarman identifies these assumed hierarchies and opens a new path for addressing archaeologically its significance to riverine trade systems.

1.5. The "Age of Commerce" and the Fourteenth Century (*Mai Lin Tjoa-Bonatz*)

Many fundamental changes can be identified in the societies of Southeast Asia during the fifteenth century. This period was characterized by Anthony Reid (1993) as the "age of commerce". He assumes that after a huge Chinese trading exploration was launched, a new global economy based on maritime trade emerged. The importance of the fifteenth century as the starting point for the modern period of Southeast Asian history is not denied (Wade and Sun 2010). However, when archaeological materials are brought into account, a key question that arises is whether this shift occurred as a sudden event which marked a sharp discontinuity with the former times or as a gradual change towards new economic modes that already existed before the 1400s (Miksic 2010, p. 385).

The archaeological material at hand to test this hypothesis in island Southeast Asia is rather limited. In the archipelago, only a few settlement sites of the fourteenth and fifteenth centuries, e.g., in North Sumatra, Western and Eastern Java, Singapore, Riau, Brunei, Sarawak, Sulawesi, and on Negros Oriental in the central Philippines, have seen archaeological publication.[4] Among them, academic attention once again has tended to be confined to coastal areas where the finds of imported ceramics, which provides evidence for international trade relations, are generally more frequent than in the uplands. Despite these regional studies, very little comparative work with a wider regional scope has been done throughout the archipelago, apart from Miksic's (2013) study on the regions bordering the Straits of Malacca. There are various reasons for this interregional neglect. First, comprehensive excavation reports, which include statistical breakdowns of artefact density by number and weight, are scarce. Second, surface collections in combination with large-scale excavations are rarely pursued by local teams, although surveys are a useful and cost-effective method to analyse settlement pattern. Third, many Indonesian excavation reports, which are published by the regional archaeological offices, are not accessible to a wider audience and are incoherently stored at the central library of the national archaeological office at PUSLIT ARKENAS, yet to be found online. It is hoped that the material presented in this in-depth study can serve as the basis for further comparative studies of the fourteenth or fifteenth century habitation in Southeast Asia.

The restrictions on foreign overseas trade implemented by Ming (1368–1644) government policies caused a severe shortage of Chinese ceramics during the first half of the fifteenth century, followed by a second moderate decline from about 1520–67. This shortage of export ware from China has been called the "Ming gap" and was first recognized at land sites in Brunei (Harrisson 1958). At that time, a sudden increase in imports of mainland Southeast Asian ceramics can be seen. Roxanna M. Brown (2009) set up a sound chronology of ceramic trade wares[5] for this time period which demonstrated that larger quantities of Chinese blue-and-whites were only exported in the second half of the fifteenth century at wreck sites. Evidence for this phenomenon largely comes from shipwreck cargoes as there has not been sufficient research on land sites. The excavations at Bukit Gombak show international trade networks since the fourteenth century including trade ware of the middle Ming period. These materials deserve particular attention (Tjoa-Bonatz forthcoming). They are best explored in the context of an early commercial boom which was established in the late fourteenth century and consolidated into a thriving maritime trade during the fifteenth century.

1.6. Documentation Techniques

1.6.1. Surveys and Aerial Images (Mai Lin Tjoa-Bonatz)

The fieldwork in Tanah Datar involved extensive surveys and various documentation techniques. To re-construct the historic landscape, we explored the relationship between ancient remains and the landscape.

Stone inscriptions, habitation debris, burial sites, public installations such as monuments, and meeting places marked by stone structures constitute promising material data defining socially important spaces in the past. Guided by the BPCB heritage inventory, from 2004, our surveys re-investigated the archaeological data from Tanah Datar and analysed spatial features based on distributional, relational, and directional patterns. Mapping, grouping, and connecting historic sites made clear the geophysical setting where they are located, which locations were favourable for human settlements or trade, and what constraints were imposed by geographical irregularities. Both the distribution of sites and the relational characteristics of the state were analysed. Their orientation to larger features, e.g. mountains, rivers, or earlier cultural layers gives additional clues into the settlement history. However, owing to limited data from dated sites, the profile of the archaeological sites over time needs further investigation.

During fieldwork in 2012, the "Tanah Datar Project" employed a remote-controlled, autonomous flying system, an octocopter, to generate large-scale numeric maps, orthophotos, and digital surface models. An unmanned aerial vehicle equipped with a digital camera allowed us to take aerial photos at a combined temporal and spatial resolution from heights of up to 100 m (see Figures 3.2–3.4). Pictures taken from a height of 60 m provided an exact spatial resolution of about 2 cm.

This method of acquiring aerial imagery allowed for large-scale mapping that supported archaeological fieldwork. The geophysical data informed the larger spatial context of the excavations, particularly when positioning find groups according to their distribution pattern. Aerial photos also helped with the reconstruction of the region's geo-archaeological environment. For example, the path of an ancient water channel at the source of Bapahat, which Adityavarman claimed, was traced to its origin (see pp. 51–53 and Figure 2.27). Moving beyond the constraints that limited the areas that could be excavated, the aerial documentation identified additional promising excavation sites on the mound of Bukit Gombak. An unexcavated area near the edge of the north-western part of the hilltop shows evidence of anthropogenic changes through the existence of rectangular structures under the topsoil, evidence that the mound was extensively covered by habitation.

1.6.2. Geophysical Surveys (*Benjamin Vining*)

During the 2011 field season, an excavation was carried out to locate potential house foundations (post moulds) and other features of archaeological interest. A geophysical survey conducted during the initial weeks of this investigation covered 9,300 m² of the site. The survey employed a Geometrics G-858 cesium vapor magnetometer,[6] which is sensitive to changes in the structure and composition of subsoils, to scan the surface of area excavations and identify evidence of soil disturbance such as trenching and filling from antiquity.

Magnetometry records localized magnetic anomalies. As the method relies on changes in the amount of ferric minerals by natural and cultural processes, it is best utilized and interpreted in concert with complementary geophysical methods and excavation. It is often necessary to rely on excavation results to interpret subsurface features over broader areas than can feasibly be excavated. Magnetic data provide additional information that can be used to plan further exploratory excavations.

The magnetometer is sensitive to minute changes in near-surface magnetism. These changes are typically due to thermoremnant magnetism from features or materials that have been heated above 500°C, including fire pits, furnaces, burnt structures, and fired brick. Magnetometry can also detect magnetic objects such as ferromagnetic metals and minerals. At Bukit Gombak, andesite cobbles relocated from river beds below the site as building materials and ferrous waste products were typical finds. Magnetometry also showed that the topsoil in certain locations was magnetically-enriched, creating detectable anomalies. Both magnetic objects and magnetized topsoils contrasted sharply with the highly-developed tropical oxisols underlying the site, which has lost any magnetic properties owing to oxidization of mineral iron into non-magnetic forms. The magnetometer survey used two sensors in a gradiometer mode to improve the detection of anomalies. Modelled magnetic fields determined an optimal sensor orientation (45° out of vertical) and transect direction (north–south). Standard grids were 30 × 30 m, or factors thereof, to accommodate the site's topography, and oriented with the excavation grid. Transects were spaced one metre apart and surveyed at an average velocity of 1 m per second. Gradients were measured on a 0.1 second cycle, for an average of one measurement every 10 cm along-transect.

Both modern features and archaeological sources can create anomalies. At Bukit Gombak, modern sources were identified at the surface and removed from plots of the magnetic data, with the exception of agricultural ploughing. Ploughing in recent decades has furrowed the topsoil, redistributing near-surface magnetic minerals across the site.

Recent agricultural use does not preclude identifying magnetic features of archaeological interest. Archaeological anomalies are apparently due to enhanced magnetism from pieces of eroded brick worked into upper soil horizons, andesite river cobbles transported to the site for building purposes, anthropogenically-modified soils (from possible rubification and other unknown processes), and individual

FIGURE 1.4

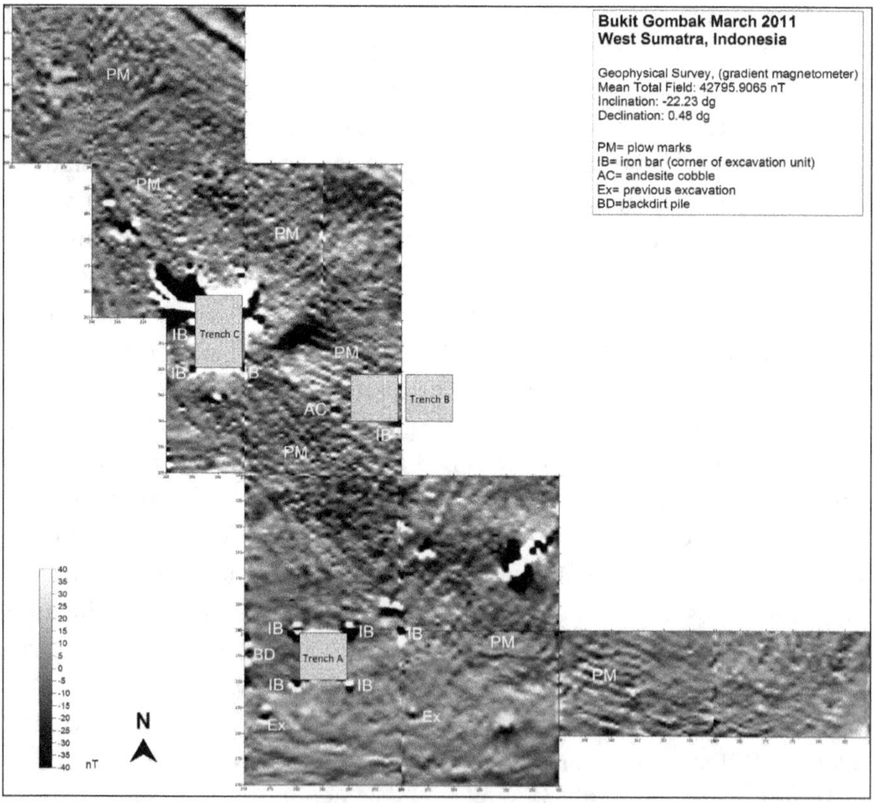

Magnetic anomalies (annotated) that correspond to modern features visible on the surface

Source: Benjamin Vining.

FIGURE 1.5

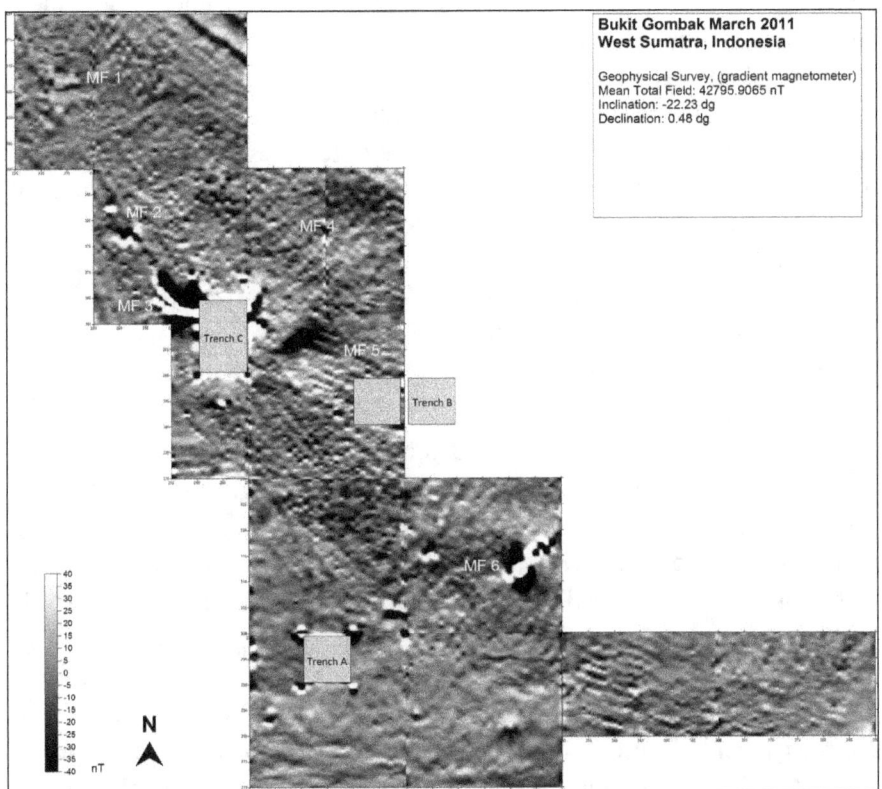

Magnetic anomalies without correspondence with modern surface features and which possibly are archaeological in origin
Note: Magnetic features are indicated by "MF"
Source: Benjamin Vining.

archaeological artefacts such as ceramic fragments, bits of iron ore, and ferrous objects. Archaeological anomalies can be grouped into a first class of well-defined and high-magnitude magnetic anomalies, and a second class of lower-magnitude and diffuse anomalies.

One noteworthy feature (designated MF3, magnetic feature) was large and extremely high-magnitude compared with typical archaeological features (see pp. 100–104 and Figures 1.4–1.5). The anomaly had a spatial extent of approximately 15 × 20 m, and a peak intensity of −1930±2050 n T. The anomaly is complex, with multiple dipoles. Magnetic features two and six are similarly well constrained and strong. Complex shapes also suggest that these anomalies are comprised of multiple, individually-magnetized objects. The strong linearity of MF6 is suspicious as it resembles modern utility lines that create regular and linear anomalies, but this does not rule out the possibility that it is archaeological. The complex shape, variable orientation of positive/negative dipole pairs, and large magnitude of these features indicate that the anomaly consists of large and highly magnetic objects and features. Excavation found several (around 20) large andesite river cobbles, commonly found in local riverbeds but anomalous in the well-developed soils of Bukit Gombak. Additionally, there were significant numbers of brick fragments, and sediments discoloured and contained ferrous clastic material such as iron prills and vitrified concretions. This feature may be industrial in nature.

The second group of features consisted of several areas of low-magnitude, diffuse anomalies typical of anthropogenic soils that develop through compaction and changes in composition during occupation. MF1 is an area of positive magnetism ringed by negative magnetic poles. Similar anomalies at Pulau Majapahit, Kota Rentang, in North Sumatra were found to correspond to living floors made of compacted sandy sediments that contrasted magnetically with the surrounding natural soil (Edwards McKinnon et al. 2012, pp. 72–74). MF5 is an area approximately 10 m in diameter of positive and negative soil anomalies, partially disturbed by ploughing. This feature may also indicate an anthrosol (archaeological sediment), and its proximity to MF3 is noteworthy. MF4 is a similar area of diffuse soil anomaly, but this feature is considerably more diffuse, poorly defined, and consequently is equivocal. Magnetometry was successful at identifying anomalies that reflect both residential and potentially industrial activities.

1.6.3. Excavating in a Minangkabau Community (*Johannes Greger*)

The modern topography of Bukit Gombak has been strongly affected over the last 30 to 40 years by agricultural activities on its slopes and on the plateau. Terracing on the upper slopes, ploughing, and planting trees have continuously altered the ground and cultural layers near the surface have subsequently become mixed up. When excavations began in 2011, there were only three empty school buildings on the eastern slope. In 2013, after the completion of our excavations, more buildings were

1. Research History, Methods, and Objectives 21

erected in the area. This construction work also affected large areas of the northwest plateau, where it was still possible to carry out excavations in 2011 and 2012 (Trench B). Despite these modern topographical alterations on Bukit Gombak, the conditions for excavations remained favourable in 2011. Most areas of the wide, 5.13 ha settlement plateau were partly covered by thick bushes or high grass (*alang alang*) used to graze cattle. It was therefore possible to plan excavation areas (called trenches) in all desired areas of the settlement plateau and, hence, to aim for a systematic archaeological exploration of the settlement layers near the surface.

To measure the excavation trenches and excavated finds, both Bukit Gombak and Bukit Kincir were divided into a grid of 10 × 10 m squares. The designations of the individual squares (PQ) followed the south–west coordinates, the first value being the north-value, the second the east-value. Parallel to this work, an updated contour plan of Bukit Gombak and Bukit Kincir was drawn, which also provided the basis for a 3D model of Bukit Gombak (see Map 3.1, Figure 3.3) that illustrated natural and geographical features of the research area.

During two excavation campaigns from 7 March to 16 April in 2011 and 5 March to 6 April in 2012, eleven trenches (A, B, C, D, E, F, K, M, N, S, T) covering a total area of 1035.5 m² were excavated, removing 346.85 m³ of material on Bukit Gombak (see Table 1.1). In addition, survey finds were added (collected in Z). On Bukit Kincir nine further trenches were opened, which are distinguished between the 304.25 m² settlement site (O, P, R) and the 486 m² burial ground (G, H, L1–3, Q). The area that was excavated was approximately 2.49 per cent of the total estimated area of the settlement plateau. The 78,155 m² settlement area consists of Bukit Kincir's hill top (9,859 m²), the burial site (16,995 m²), and the plateau of Bukit Gombak (51,301 m²). The twin mounds cover 295,140 m².

The organization of the excavation trenches distinguished the findspots according to contexts, where a context (C) is generally defined as the smallest findspot unit arising from natural and anthropogenic deposits. During our excavations, however, a context often had to be defined as an artificial unit, because it was not possible to distinguish different deposits stratigraphically. Throughout the excavated areas, all

TABLE 1.1
Distribution and Density of Sherds Retrieved at the Excavated Sites of Bukit Gombak, Bukit Kincir, and Tanah Lua

Bukit Gombak	Trench	Size of Trenches (m)	Surface Area (m²)	Volume Excavated (m³)	Weight of Sherds (g)	Weight of Sherds (m³)	Number of All Sherds	Quantity of Sherds (m³)	Number of Diagnostic Sherds	Earthenware	Ceramics
Core area	B	2 × (9 × 9)	162	65.41	16,589	253.62	2,416	36.94	325	233	92
	C	2 × (9 × 9)	162	84.09	26,766	318.3	6,280	74.68	499	378	121
	D	2 × (9 × 9)	162	44.79	14,800	330.43	4,163	92.95	293	143	150
Extended settlement area	A	9 × 9	81	49.06	915	18.65	311	6.34	31	4	27
	E	9 × 9	82	36.76	890	24.21	259	7.05	10	5	5
	K	4.5 × 9	40.5	11.42	4,105	359.46	918	80.39	63	38	25
	N	9 × 4	36	5.74	4,415	769.16	871	151.74	170	151	19
	S (spring)	6 × 6, 30 m²	66	2.41	390	161.82	140	58.09	8	4	4
	Z (survey)	—	—	—	—	—	25	—	28	17	11
House site	F	9 × 9	81	9.2	600	65.22	146	15.87	23	6	17
	M	9 × 9	81	36.93	905	24.51	246	6.66	44	14	30
	T	9 × 9	81	16.31	280	17.17	58	3.56	32	24	8
Total			1,033.5	362.12	70,655	2,342.55	15,833	534.27	1,526	1,017	509

1. Research History, Methods, and Objectives

Bukit Kincir (Settlement)	Trench	Size of Trenches (m)	Surface Area (m²)	Volume Excavated (m³)	Weight of Sherds (g)	Weight of Sherds (m³)	Number of All Sherds	Quantity of Sherds (m³)	Number of Diagnostic Sherds	Earthenware	Ceramics
	O	9 × 9	81	34.05	2,405	70.63	390	11.45	40	34	6
	P	L-form	142.25	63.63	2,795	43.92	824	12.95	63	62	1
	R	9 × 9	81	41.36	6,400	154.74	1,297	31.36	107	107	–
Total			304.25	139.04	11,600	269.29	2,511	18.06	210	203	7

Bukit Kincir Burial Site	Trench	Size of Trenches (m)	Surface Area (m²)	Volume Excavated (m³)	Weight of Sherds (g)	Weight of Sherds (m³)	Number of All Sherds	Quantity of Sherds (m³)	Number of Diagnostic Sherds	Earthenware	Ceramics
	G	9 × 9	81	32.5	365	11.23	59	1.82	3	1	2
	H	9 × 9	81	19	965	50.79	165	8.68	6	4	2
	L	3 × (9 × 9)	243	103.28	740	7.15	173	1.67	14	12	2
	Q	9 × 9	81	31.7	190	5.99	26	0.82	8	7	1
Total			486	186.48	2,260	12.12	423	2.27	31	24	7

Tanah Lua	Trench	Size of Trenches (m)	Surface Area (m²)	Volume Excavated (m³)	Weight of Sherds (g)	Weight of Sherds (m³)	Number of All Sherds	Quantity of Sherds (m³)	Number of Diagnostic Sherds	Earthenware	Ceramics
	A	8 × 12	96	32.32	–	–	–	–	–	–	–
	B–F, Z (survey)	5 × (2 × 2)	20	11.57	4,365	377.27	874	2.03	89	89	–
Total			116	43.89	4,365	377.27	874	2.03	89	89	–

archaeological finds were embedded in a humus layer of 25–30 cm beneath the grass cover. Although the finds had been disturbed due to the agricultural activity, traces of settlement activities could still be detected. Beneath this "cultural layer" was a layer of loamy-sandy material that changed to tufa (volcanic igneous stone) in the deeper layer. At no point was it possible to carry out a stratigraphic excavation encompassing several settlement levels due to rapid geomorphological decomposition in the wet-tropical climate of this region and the use of organic building materials such as wood or bamboo. The reconstruction of ancient settlement patterns, activities, and developments is mainly based on the findings of archaeological objects and installations from disturbed levels of finds that cannot be stratigraphically distinguished from each other. No bones or other organic materials remain because the soil is highly acidic (pH 4.2),[7] so reconstruction of the ancient settlement landscape had to be supplemented by additional survey finds, aerial photography, geomagnetic survey, and historiography.

Excavations on Bukit Gombak and Bukit Kincir were carried out with the support of 30 local assistants on average, consisting of farmers from the neighbouring community of Bukit Gombak and the community of Pagaruyung on the other side of the Selo River. Both groups are connected to the *koto piliang* political tradition (see p. 32). The field workers were all male and they discouraged active participation by women, but women often knew more about the region than the men. Minangkabau society is matrifocal and some of the women were landowners or tenants, and were less reluctant than their male partners to explore difficult terrain.

Although none of the workers had previously taken part in an archaeological excavation, they proved to be skilled at uncovering excavation trenches and finds. Their principal tool, a mattock with a flat blade (*cangkul*), is used every day in the field to precisely dig, cut, and scrape the ground (Tjoa-Bonatz 2013a, figures 6–7; see Figure 3.5). The workers declined to be assigned to specific tasks according to skill, and opted for equal pay regardless of each worker's specific duty. A strong sense of egalitarianism fostered a harmonious atmosphere during the day-to-day excavation work. The only tension that arose was with two people who claimed to own the land of the excavation ground. They were neither employed on the excavation nor related to any of the workers. With visible unease but tacit acceptance, the workers and our Indonesian colleagues acquiesced to their demands to rent the land for the duration of the excavations.

The wives, children, and other family members of the workers frequently visited the excavation. Some women sold drinks and snacks, so the excavation site regularly hosted cheerful picnics. Numerous groups of schoolchildren and their teachers as well as journalists from the regional and national press came to the excavation site, especially during the first campaign in 2011 (Chaniago 2011; Rinaldi 2011; 2012*a–b*). On a local level, apart from offering an unusual form of employment, our excavation prompted interest because of widespread awareness of the importance of King Adityavarman to the history of the Minangkabau. In this respect, the results of the excavations were disappointing for the local people as they uncovered none of the treasures commonly associated with rulers, namely the legendary golden riches, impressive temple buildings, or monumental art that are typical for other parts of Indonesia.

More attention should be paid to the influence of archaeological work on the local population.[8] Unlike in North America, where archaeology is institutionally linked with anthropology and therefore influenced by theories that stress the importance of human factors, many other schools of archaeology seem generally to assume that archaeology deals only with objects and not with living people. Two examples related to newly discovered places illustrate the impact of archaeological research on the locals.

The first is connected to the discovery of a largely silted and overgrown spring on the western slope (Trench S). According to local information, the spring was used until 1985, but since then had become overgrown and largely forgotten. News of its rediscovery in 2011 spread quickly and prompted many local people to visit. What attracted the people was not just curiosity about the rediscovery and archaeological activities, but also the appealing charm of a hidden spring site (see Figure 3.12). The aura of this place soon became tangible and, through the stories of the few locals who still remembered it, became part of everyday reality. In the language of the Minangkabau, the site of the spring is called *Luhak Kandikia*. *Luhak* means spring, while *kandikia* or *kandike* denotes the bark or pieces of a tree used for cleaning silver. The auspicious character of the place was further emphasized by the legend of a female spirit said to live in the tops of the trees at the edge of the spring who had the ability to seduce unmarried men if they fell asleep in the area. The workers at our excavation extended the length of the midday break to avoid the spring during this time. The reawakened magic of the spring lasted through the early part of 2011 when the excavations were being carried out. On the return of the excavation team in 2012, however, the site was largely overgrown and no longer visited. Although archaeological work had briefly called attention to this auspicious locale, it quickly faded back into obscurity.

The second example is connected to the burial site on Bukit Kincir. In the last week of the excavation in 2011, rumours spread among the excavators about "mysterious stones" on the densely forested neighbouring hill. They told us that spirits had erected them and, while there were many suggestions, little concrete information could be obtained. The first ascent up Bukit Kincir was more difficult than anticipated because, according to local residents, the presence of men would anger the female spirit who lived on the hill, and for this reason we had to reduce our initial expedition by half. Our guide Gustar,[9] husband of the owner of the Bukit Kincir site, had avoided the hill since childhood, and he only agreed to cooperate with the survey after his wife intervened. She suggested that her presence would appease the spirit, and she led the male team to the hill, where oval river stones were sticking out of the ground in the forest thickets. After several visits we located an area suitable for excavation, with numerous anthropogenic stone formations (see Figure 3.18–3.19). Our local excavation helpers expressed enormous discomfort about excavating this "mystical place". The same team that had worked frolicsomely on Bukit Gombak before behaved reverentially here, and the discovery of another stone formation below the surface layer in Trench G deepened their fear of spirits. A misty cloud cover fell over the Bukit Kincir one morning in 2011 as the archaeological team took their second break, and when it was time to return to digging the pits in Trench G, the local excavation helpers refused to continue work on Bukit Kincir because they were too concerned about harming the spirits.

The discussions continued all morning and finally some of the younger workers agreed to continue excavating, but they demanded to work in short shifts to minimize contact with ghosts. Despite these concerns, the spirits proved more merciful than expected and the excavation yielded amazing results (see Chapter 3.3). During the second year of the excavation, the stone field became a centre of attention and the formerly awesome stones of Trench G were used to build a fireplace (see Figure 1.6). The wood left over from clearing the top of Bukit Kincir was then bundled and carried off by local women who wanted to continue logging the dense forest. After an excavation is completed any trenches are normally covered over but in 2011, to our surprise, the landowner's family asked us not to fill in the pits in the grave site of Bukit Kincir because they could be used as pitfalls for boar hunts.

FIGURE 1.6

Fireplace was set up on the excavation site

The local people did not avoid Bukit Kincir due to the presence of a graveyard. Rather, knowledge about the place's former use had been lost over the years and been replaced by other cautionary stories such as that of the female spirit. Through archaeological work, the way local people viewed the place underwent a fundamental change. Our excavation made the ground usable, and people filling the hill with life during our second round of excavations in 2012. This archaeological intervention was the profanation of a site, going against the beliefs of the local people. In 2014, during a short visit of the site, we found that the fauna and flora had quickly recaptured their realm, but the mystic character that had surrounded Bukit Kincir for generations was gone.

This change made us more aware of the responsibilities and consequences of archaeological work. Apart from the archaeological material that was retrieved, a further consequence of the two campaigns was an elevated awareness within the local community about their heritage. Five of the excavation helpers became photographers and tourist guides in the Pagaruyung palace heritage museum in Batusangkar. It is hoped that other archaeological projects will foster similar local interest in the archaeological reconstruction of history. Before our excavation project, archaeological knowledge was not a part of the local Minangkabau culture, which is grounded in oral tradition. The two years of field research in Tanah Datar were not only a curiosity in the everyday life of the region but also developed a longer-term local awareness of scholarly work, which should lead to cooperation with the local educational and cultural institutions.

NOTES

1. For an overview, see Miksic (2006, pp. 149–51) or the update by Perret et al. (2013, pp. 74–75).
2. For pre-colonial state-models of Bali, see Hauser-Schäublin (2003), and for Java see Christie (1995, pp. 272–76).
3. Colombijn (2003, p. 504); see Christie (1995, pp. 237–38) for a review of theoretical descriptions viable for early Southeast Asia, in which the basic characteristics are a centralized socio-political organization, fixed territory, minimum population, stable surplus, and a legitimizing ideology.

4. See the overview in Miksic (2006, pp. 148–50; 2010, pp. 392–96, fn. 11), more reports in Edwards McKinnon et al. (2012); and Damanik and Edwards McKinnon (2012).
5. The term "trade ware" refers to the most commonly exported utilitarian ceramics found in the region in contrast to "export ceramics" which denotes imperial ware of high quality design and refined forms, specially made for the export market (Brown 2009, pp. 29–30).
6. Because of equipment malfunction, no data from an A GSSI SIR-2000 Ground Penetrating Radar with a 900 MHz antenna were collected beyond the initial trial.
7. Analyses were performed by the Institute of Geographical Sciences, FU Berlin.
8. Westerlaken (2011); cf. studies in Latin America (Kendall 2005; Herrera 2011).
9. I would like to thank Gustar and his family as well as the excavation helpers: In, Yarli, Cokoik, Feri, Gustar, Adrius, Samsiwar, Jon, and Luzi.

2

EARLY HISTORIES
Historiography and Archaeological Surveys

Mai Lin Tjoa-Bonatz

2.1. The Minangkabau and Adityavarman

Chronicles and Myths of Origin

The *Manangkabwa* enter the historic record in the *Nagarakrtagama*, an epic text written in Java in 1365, in which they are listed among the 24 overseas vassals of the East Javanese Majapahit court "under the territory of the Malay lands" (Prapañca 1995, canto 13, 1). The list, in which most of the Sumatran place names can be localized, describes numerous polities stretching along the river systems in South, Central, and North Sumatra starting from the southeast coast, including Dharmasraya in the hinterland of Srivijaya along the Batang Hari River, and extending to the northwest coast of the island. The realm of the Minangkabau is the only highland polity mentioned. This reference has been taken as evidence of Javanese suzerainty in Southeast Sumatra, but as the chronicle was written for the Majapahit ruler Hayam Wuruk

(1350–89), it is actually a far-reaching imperialistic proclamation of the part of the Javanese court.[1]

In 1405, the Chinese became aware of the thriving inland polity of the Minangkabau when they started differentiating the political landscape on Sumatra, and Chinese envoys sent imperial proclamations to the 米囊葛卜 *Mi-nang-ge-bu* (Wade 2005). Chinese appreciation of an inland polity and prospect for international trade created further economic opportunities for the highlands. Minangkabau has been understood as a political entity engaged in international diplomatic and trade-based activities since the second half of the fourteenth century.

In the middle of the fourteenth century, Adityavarman became the progenitor of the Minangkabau monarchy. There are many legends connected to the origin of the Minangkabau, some of which include Adityavarman or could be associated with the Javanese king. The name "Minangkabau" consists of two words: *minang* (victorious) and *kabau* (water buffalo). The most popular explanation of this name is found in the historical chronicle *Hikayat Raja Pasai*, which is believed to have been written in the fifteenth century. It tells the story of a mighty Javanese prince who "came in a boat loaded with valuables" intending to annex the Minangkabau country.[2] A fight between two water buffalos determined who would rule. While the Javanese chose a large animal, the locals chose a baby buffalo and fixed iron spikes to its nose. When the two buffalos faced off, the baby ran to the big buffalo trying to nurse and slashed its belly with the iron spikes. The big animal died and the Javanese lost. This story shows the importance of the buffalo for the Minangkabau and tells of an unequal conflict in which an outsider contested the leadership of the community. It differs from the founding myths in many highland communities, which were often trade-based or seafaring tales and featured a prominent foreigner. The idea of prosperity was connected with the image of a foreign ship fully laden with rich merchandise, or a captainship where a shipmaster endowed with exceptional powers became the founder of a community (Manguin 1991).

The traditional Minangkabau chronicles (*tambo*) present Adityavarman as a king who came as an outsider into a well-established system of leadership dominated by clan alignments and lineage elders. He bifurcated the political traditions (*laras*)[3] into an autocratic orientation called *koto piliang*, literally chosen words, and a more egalitarian one called *bodi caniago*, literally valued character. According to a local story, the creators of these two traditions were two brothers, Datuk Ketemanggungan and Datuk Perpatih Nan Sebatang, who quarrelled about the leadership. Only the former, who stands for the *koto piliang* tradition, recognized the royal status of the newcomer, Adityavarman. Their quarrel about legitimacy raised questions about political organization, jurisdiction, and inheritance. Inherited property was passed down through the matrilineal line, a tradition defended by Datuk Perpatih Nan Sebatang.

The *tambo* describe Adityavarman as an ambitious ruler in a time of political instability or economic weakness. Whether his achievements were due to military strength or the fact that he married into the ruling family,[4] these accounts confirm that the Minangkabau did not lack political organization. It is likely that in this family- or clan-bound system, the *koto piliang* and *bodi caniago*, confederations provided one of the primary dynamics of state development through peer polity interactions.

Another origin story mentions Alexander the Great, a common element in many regions influenced by Islam (Taufik Abdullah 1972, pp. 183–84; Dobbin 1975, p. 78; Drakard 1999, pp. 168–69). In this account Alexander's three sons sailed to different destinations, one to the east, one to the west, and the final one, said to represent the ancestor of the Minangkabau people, landed on "Perca", the island of Sumatra, at the top of the volcano Mount Merapi. From here, the Minangkabau heartland—Tanah Datar, Agam, and Lima Puluh Kota—became populated. In one variation, the ancestor Suri Maharajo Dirajo, who descended from the volcano, bears a title similar to those Adityavarman used in his inscriptions (Kozok and van Reijn 2010, p. 136). All three ascribed their rights of leadership to sacral power. Another account, which is believed to include Hindu ideas, adds the destruction of a *naga*, a giant serpent called Sikatimuno, by Sang Sapurba who then became the ruler of the Minangkabau. He used his sword, called Si Mandang Giri, to slay the serpent (Hill 1960, pp. 199–200; Drakard 1999, pp. 239–40; 2008–9, pp. 135–36, ft. 2).

These orally transmitted stories have been modified through the centuries, and must be treated with caution. However, most versions of these accounts on the origin of the Minangkabau agree on the following points: first, a foreigner contests leadership and emerges as the paramount leader; and second, connections exist with regions beyond Sumatra, reflecting early coastal interactions probably through trade.

Artefacts Connected to the Founding Myths

Artefacts, some of considerable age, have been kept as heirlooms or *pusaka* over the centuries. Among them are imported ceramics, weapons, beads, glass, metal ware, and even a golden crown said by Alfonso d'Albuquerque (in 1511–13) to have come from Alexander the Great (Drakard 1999, p. 240). Some items are "creatively asserted" in official Minangkabau letters and in oral traditions beyond the island of Sumatra (ibid.). The king of Pagaruyung still holds other pieces directly related to the above-mentioned origin stories.[5] These heirlooms were formerly exhibited in the *istana* (palace) of Pagaruyung until a fire destroyed the palace in 2007, after which they were returned to the king of Pagaruyung until they could be displayed in the rebuilt palace.

Among these *pusaka* owned by the king of Pagaruyung, a hollow head approximately 5 cm in height is said to represent the decapitated head of the giant serpent called Sikatimuno (see Figure 2.1). Frederik D.K. Bosch (1931, p. 210, figure 47*b*) assumes that the smiling or

FIGURE 2.1

Head Sikatimuno, heirloom of the king of Pagaruyung

laughing head is made of gypsum or some kind of baked clay and dates it to the Majapahit period. The refined workmanship of the fleshy face with slit eyes, a finely chiselled pageboy cut and an open mouth wide enough to see the teeth and tongue—suggest it is non-local and of old but unknown age. It might be a Buddhist image from East Asia.

A gilded dagger called Si Mandang Giri (Kiri or Curik) is said to have killed the serpent. It is 36 cm long with a double-edged, straight blade that broadens towards the hilt (see Figure 2.2). Bands of clouds spread in a crescent shape across the base of the blade, the part resting against the hand. Scrolls decorate each facet of a baluster-like shaped hilt. A deity is depicted on each side of the blade, a stout male figure and a female with long dishevelled hair. Each is standing with slightly

FIGURE 2.2

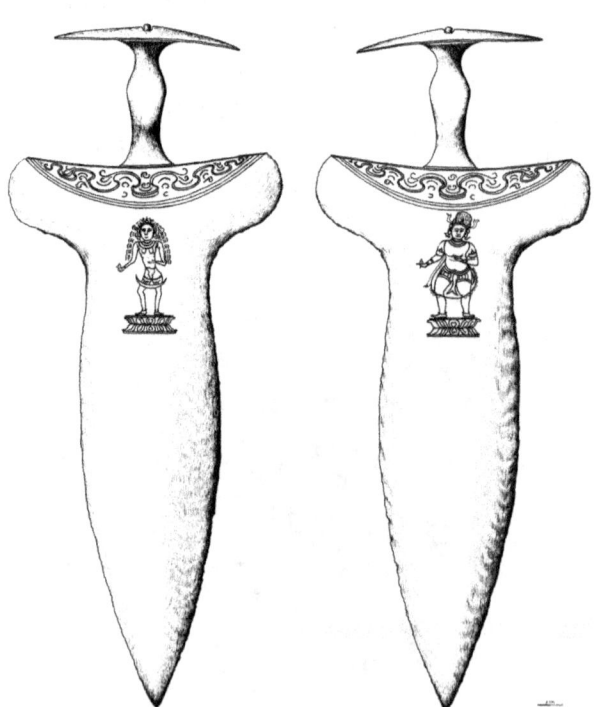

Dagger Si Mandang Giri depicting a male and female Buddhist deity, fourteenth century, heirloom of the king of Pagaruyung

spread legs on a double lotus cushion, wearing a short dress,[6] jewellery, and holds a *vajra* or thunderbolt in the raised left hand and another object in the bent right hand—characteristics typical for wrathful deities in late Buddhism.[7] A garland hangs across his hips and a crescent above hers. Scholars support Bosch's assumption (1931, pp. 210–14) that the iconography of the figures and the ornamentation are indicative of the East Javanese period of the fourteenth century but not all agree with him that "Bhairawa and Bhairavi" represent Adityavarman and his wife. Claudine Bautze-Picron (2014, p. 114) contends that both deities display attributes of a wrathful Indian Buddhist Mahakala. Regarding the female deity, she admits that these goddesses do not follow an established iconography in visual arts and, as a result, does not label her. The shape of the dagger may reflect older models if compared to a depiction on the inscription stone of Hujung Langit in Lampung from the tenth century.[8] Daggers showing deities are rare,[9] and the Pagaruyung dagger may represent the oldest preserved dagger depicting deities on the blade.

Throughout the Hindu-Buddhist period, rulers and high nobles possessed paraphernalia made from precious metals to display their status, and use them in ceremonies. They are a persuasive way to visualize history and serve the idea of royal authority. It is likely that this dagger came to the highlands during the time of Adityavarman, either with his entourage or as his personal possession.

Adityavarman's Connection to Java

Adityavarman left 22 inscriptions on Java and Sumatra, namely in East Java, Dharmasraya, and Tanah Datar,[10] and is connected with some of Indonesia's most impressive sculpture. However, the inscriptions are not yet fully translated and where translations exist, the metaphorical wording has resulted in various, often contradictory interpretations, making him one of history's most intriguing figures. Sometimes only circumstantial references help to identify names and explain the eulogistic phrases about the monarch.

Adityavarman is one of the few royal figures in Indonesia's history who connect Java and Sumatra during the heyday of the Majapahit period. Controversies exist about his lineage, but most authors agree on a connection to the East Javanese court. The Javanese chronicle *Pararaton*, an idealizing, therefore less reliable record from the sixteenth century, describes an expedition that returned from Melayu in 1292 bringing two princesses, Dara Petak and Dara Jingga, to Java. The latter became the mother of the king of Melayu, called Sri Marmadewa or King Matralot (Phalgunadi 1996, pp. 113, 115). Scholars generally connect this account to the lineage of Adityavarman but have offered different interpretations. First, it has been taken as straightforward evidence for his mixed parentage or at least for his predecessor having descended from a Sumatran princess.[11] Second, it is evidence of his rule over Melayu. Third, the most cautious interpretation, is that it offers general proof of dynastic relations between the courts of Java and Melayu (Machi Suhadi 1990, p. 230; Kozok and van Reijn 2010, p. 1, ft. 2; Miksic 2015, p. 32).

Adityavarman's connection to Java is clearly stated on the back of a statue of Manjusri (109 × 84 cm) from the Jago temple in East Java dated to the year 1343.[12] The statue, currently part of the Hermitage collection in St. Petersburg, Russia, describes Adityavarman as one of the most influential figures at the Majapahit court. Descended from a Javanese queen, possibly the ruling queen Tribhuwanottungadewi (r. 1329–50), he was one of the leading officials of the Majapahit dynasty (Lunsingh Scheurleer 2008, p. 295). Both inscriptions, one at the front and one at the back, refer to Adityavarman, although there are epigraphic differences and Old Malay in the script, presumably used by a Sumatran writer.[13] The one in front, which was "squeezed in", states that a religious official called Siwanatha consecrated the image in that year. Pauline Lunsingh Scheurleer (2008, p. 296) has argued convincingly that the statue was carved in the Singosari period (1222–92), which means that the inscriptions were added at least two generations later. The image represents a copy of northeast Indian statues of the Pala style. Like others, she believes that it was a cult image from the Jago temple in East Java (Reichle 2007, pp. 196, 198). This assumption emphasizes that, first, Adityavarman used stone slabs bearing existing cult images to commemorate his act of re-instalment; that, second, he was based in Java in 1343 or earlier; and that, third, the earliest he could have arrived on Sumatra was between 1343 and 1347.

Adityavarman in Dharmasraya

Adityavarman is connected to two stone sculptures found in Dharmasraya, one of the key sites around the upper Batang Hari River. Epigraphical evidence from the late thirteenth and fourteenth centuries indicates the existence of a major power centre in this region.[14] Both the Javanese poem *Nagarakrtagama* from 1365 and the legal code of the Tanjung Tanah manuscript, likely written between 1379 and 1387 in Kerinci, refer to Dharmasraya as a political entity and also mention its "illustrious Emperor" (Prapañca 1995, canto 13, 1; Hunter 2015, p. 300). Archaeological investigations since 1995 have revealed the existence of brick sanctuaries, Chinese ceramics, and statuary at Rambahan,[15] the temple complexes of Awang Maombiak, Tabek Bintungan, Siguntur, Pulau Sawah,[16] and Padang Roco (Budi Istiawan 2012; Miksic 2015, pp. 45–47). Evidence from these archaeological remains leads to the conclusion that Dharmasraya not only denotes a place with a large ceremonial centre, but also a thriving polity during the twelfth to the sixteenth centuries, between the downriver centre at Muara Jambi and the mountainous area upriver.

At Padang Roco (literally "sculpture field"), which is also known as Sungai Langsat, a large stone slab (163 × 139 cm) of Amoghapasa Lokeswara and his pantheon was found (see Figure 2.3). Its base, however, was retrieved 7 km upriver. Because there is no evidence to show that the sculpture was moved or when a move might have occurred, all arguments remain speculative.[17] The statue bears three Sanskrit inscriptions. According to the first inscription on the front, it originated in East Java and was sent to Sumatra in 1286 to be erected at Dharmasraya by the last Singhasari king, Kertanagara (r. 1248–68). Scholars who have connected this action with an expedition sent by the East Javanese court to Sumatra in 1275 have also seen the inscription as a proof of Java's domination over the region (e.g., Krom 1931, pp. 335–62). Others have suggested a more peaceful interpretation, seeing it as a way of forming alliances against a Chinese invasion (de Casparis 1985; Miksic 2016, p. 268). The second inscription on the backside of the Amoghapasa statue re-dedicates this image to Adityavarman in 1347. The third inscription has never been translated and may shed more light on the meaning of this imagery.

FIGURE 2.3

The statue of Amoghapasa was brought to Dharmasraya in 1286 and re-consecrated by Adityavarman in 1347, now in the Museum Nasional Indonesia, Jakarta (inv. no. 6469)

The rededication mentions that Adityavarman was "restoring the previous situation" for the benefit of *malayapura*.[18] Natasha Reichle (2007, p. 129) relates this passage to the re-consecration of an old image whereas Miksic (2015, pp. 31, 47) speculates that it alludes to renovation work on a rectangular brick sanctuary, a terrace of 20 m × 20 m, which Schnitger (1937, p. 2) claims was enlarged by 85 cm. If not taken metaphorically, it stresses Adityavarman's appreciation of antiquities and the use of existing monuments to make leadership claims. This replacement of older structures is also expressed in two of his Tanah Datar inscriptions, in Ombilin and Batu Papahat (see pp. 51–53, 69–70). That *malayapura* and not Dharmasraya is mentioned is taken as a reference to his palace, based on the assumption that Melaya represents "the area ruled by a king" and "*pura*", the palace, whereas Dharmasraya denotes a specific ceremonial centre (Miksic 2015, pp. 31, 34). *Malayapura* reoccurs in the Gudam I inscription (also called Pagaruyung IV)[19] in Tanah Datar, where it is thought that a former palace of the Minangkabau kings stood (see pp. 60–61, next to the person in the centre of Figure 2.5). Adityavarman was honoured as a monarch (*mahārājādhirāja*) who, together with another high functionary identified as *deva-tūhan prapātih*, has "acquired wealth and gold" (see p. 72). The paramount title *mahārājādhirāja* for Adityavarman, continuously used in other inscriptions in Tanah Datar,[20] was either chosen due to diplomatic rhetoric between the reigning monarch(s) in Southeast Sumatra with regard to the Majapahit court, or to a local preference for longer titles without assuming a ranked hierarchy (Kulke 2009, p. 234; Hunter 2015, pp. 301–4). The Amoghapasa is used to legitimize Adityavarman's rule by evoking Buddhist imagery to connect him to a Javanese lineage and to extol his merits.

At Padang Roco, a free-standing statue 441 cm tall, the largest in Southeast Asia, was found near the village of Sungai Langsat at Jorong Sei Langsek, Kenagaian Siguntur, Kecamatan Sitiung (see Figure 2.4). The stone figure stood on a high plateau overlooking the point where the Pingian River flows into the Batang Hari.[21] This spot was an important communication node linking the eastern lowlands and highlands with West Sumatra, and Chinese porcelain from the Song and Yuan dynasties was retrieved there (Miksic 2013, p. 188). Carved in high relief, a male figure with bulging eyes stands atop another human figure interpreted as an ascetic (Reichle 2007, p. 172). The standing image is bejewelled and wears a tall headdress in which a small figure, generally identified as Amithaba, is seated holding a knife and a skull bowl. Skulls are also found on the short skirt and the pedestal. Although there is no direct written evidence, the statue has generally been connected to Adityavarman due to his esoteric Buddhist religious affiliation, and a smaller

FIGURE 2.4

The Bhairawa statue associated to Adityavarman from Sungai Langsat, Padang Roco, now in the Museum Nasional Indonesia, Jakarta (inv. no. 6470)

Source: Kulke 2009, figure 10-1. Image Archive "Lotos" Film.

statue with the same iconography found at the temple of Jago.²² Until recently, the statue was assumed to be a portrait-figure of Adityavarman (Kulke 2009, p. 229). However, Marijke Klokke (1994) argues that it is not a likeness because the attributes and gestures are ritualized. "Deification image" better expresses the complementary unification of an image that represents a deified mortal and a Hindu or Buddhist deity at the same time.

Reichle (2007, pp. 168–75, 204–9) identifies the gigantic sculpture as Bhairava, an apotropaic figure that serves as a boundary marker and as a symbol of the king's power. The idea that this image represents a mighty ruler is supported by a metonymous fourteenth-century reference to "the state of serviture [servitude] proper to the devotee of a deity, or the reigning monarch", which is represented by "placing one's head beneath the foot of the deity or monarch as a sign of respect and submission" (Hunter 2015, p. 338). Scholars agree on the coarse and terrifying character of the figure, and its iconography correlates with the sculptural traditions of other so-called daemonic deities documented in East Java and Sumatra.²³ Lunsingh Scheurleer (2008, p. 327) distinguishes images like guards made in the round, which are "coarse and terrifying", from deified royalties carved in high relief that are "refined and peaceful". The statue of Padang Roco has elements of both categories. Bautze-Picron (2014, pp. 113–14, 116, ft. 34, 45) emphasizes the iconographic distinctions in India between a Bhairava, a form of Shiva, and its Buddhist counterpart called Mahakala. This interpretation has lately been adopted by Miksic (2016, p. 146); other scholars are of the opinion that during tantric Buddhism syncretism was common in Indonesia.²⁴ Epigraphists reject speculations about orgiastic rituals formerly connected to it (Griffiths 2014, p. 241, ft. 144; Hunter 2015, p. 308). Thomas Hunter (ibid.) assumes that the statue played a symbolic role in psycho-sexual practices. Updated translations of Adityavarman's inscriptions should clarify this point. According to Miksic,²⁵ the fine-grained stone of the slab is not found in Sumatra but is common in Java. This observation coupled with Adityavarman's relatively short presence of no more than five years in Dharmasraya, his connection with East Java, and Javanese objects brought to his realm in Tanah Datar, all support the idea that the monumental Bhairava image was carved in Java. Mineral studies of the stone would help settle this issue.

Dharmasraya was an intermediate seat of Adityavarman's reign before he moved to the Minangkabau highlands. His role in the polity of Melayu-Srivijaya is still debated. Some scholars have taken the reference in the Rambatan inscription as proof that he represented the king of Melayu-Srivijaya and equated the names of other rulers with him.[26] It was therefore assumed that, under Adityavarman, the capital was transferred from Muara Jambi to Dharmasraya, and then to the highlands (Satyawati Suleiman 1977, p. 9; de Casparis 1989, pp. 922–24). Building on the same assumption, Leonard Andaya (2001, pp. 323–24; 2008, pp. 83–88) proposed that Minangkabau ethnicity evolved in response to the Javanization of Sumatra and is connected to an assumed Malay ethnic identity. There is not enough epigraphic and archaeological evidence to support this hypothesis, and based on the available sources it seems unlikely that the Melayu court was transferred to the highland (Miksic 2015, p. 38). The following sections elaborate on some of the counterarguments. While it is true that the trade connection to the Batang Hari was important to Aditavarman's highland kingdom, other geostrategic and socio-political alliances became equally important over time. The picture of the political landscape should become clearer when more archaeological and epigraphical evidence relating to the socio-cultural and political-economic ties between the coastal centre, its hinterland, and the highlands becomes available.

The following sections discuss the growing complexity of the formative period of Adityavarman's kingdom: a ruler who represents the symbolic centre of the polity marked by inscriptions, control of the immediate hinterland with an economy based on trade and exchange as well as wet-rice irrigation, metal production, and gold resources.

2.2. The Archaeological Context of Adityavarman's Inscriptions

The inscriptions associated with Adityavarman in Tanah Datar are carved on three stone types: generally on slabs, one on a rock and one on a mortar. The most numerous are irregularly shaped stelae and rectangular slabs with a raised upper outline, which was characteristic of burial stones probably dating back to prehistoric times in the region. Most of the inscriptions are written in Sanskrit using the Kawi script, but one is in Grantha script and others are in Old Malay and Old Javanese.[27] The latter is found on a funerary or commemorative monument for a person called *tumaṅguṅ kuḍa vīra* who was either an immigrant or was descended from someone from Java (Griffiths 2012, pp. 2–5).[28] Five of the inscriptions in Tanah Datar bear a chronogram, a set of auspicious parameters for the *saka* era that allows them to be dated from 1347–75. The inscriptions deal with religious affairs and praise the merits of Adityavarman, but they also mention religious architecture (*vihara*) and other structures such as public works installations (gates, causeway, wall, water channel), cult images, and stone artefacts such as funerary and inscription stones (*śilalekha*).[29] They state that Adityavarman installed officials and religious dignitaries, including a teacher called *dharmadhvaja* in order to set up an administrative network and a centralized building programme for his state (Satyawati Suleiman 1977, p. 5; Budi Istiawan 2006, pp. 3–8; Kulke 2009, p. 239). The reference to structures, artefacts, and toponyms in his inscriptions allows some sites to be linked to them. The following section examines on the geo-archaeological features of his inscriptions, focusing on the eight which are still standing in their original place.[30]

The archaeological remains from the period of Adityavarman's reign in the highlands—stone inscription and statuary—are distributed over Tanah Datar and the adjacent regency of Solok. However, his royal sphere can be clearly defined because the artefacts and in situ inscriptions are concentrated within a limited area. Most were collected in the southern part of Tanah Datar in the district of Tanjung Emas along the Selo River, at or around the twin mounds of Bukit Gombak and Bukit Kincir between the villages of Pagaruyung and Saruaso (see Map 2.1). Fifteen inscriptions originate from sites along the Selo: two at Bukit Gombak, four on the west bank where Bukit Gombak is situated (including the lost inscriptions at Batu Papahat consisted of two faces and two from Kapalo Bukit Gombak), five at Ponggongan,[31] and two at Gudam. The final two are across the river, on its eastern bank at Saruaso.[32] Some of these inscribed stones, including those supposedly originating from Bukit Gombak, have been moved to Pagaruyung and Batusangkar, where they can be visited today.

MAP 2.1

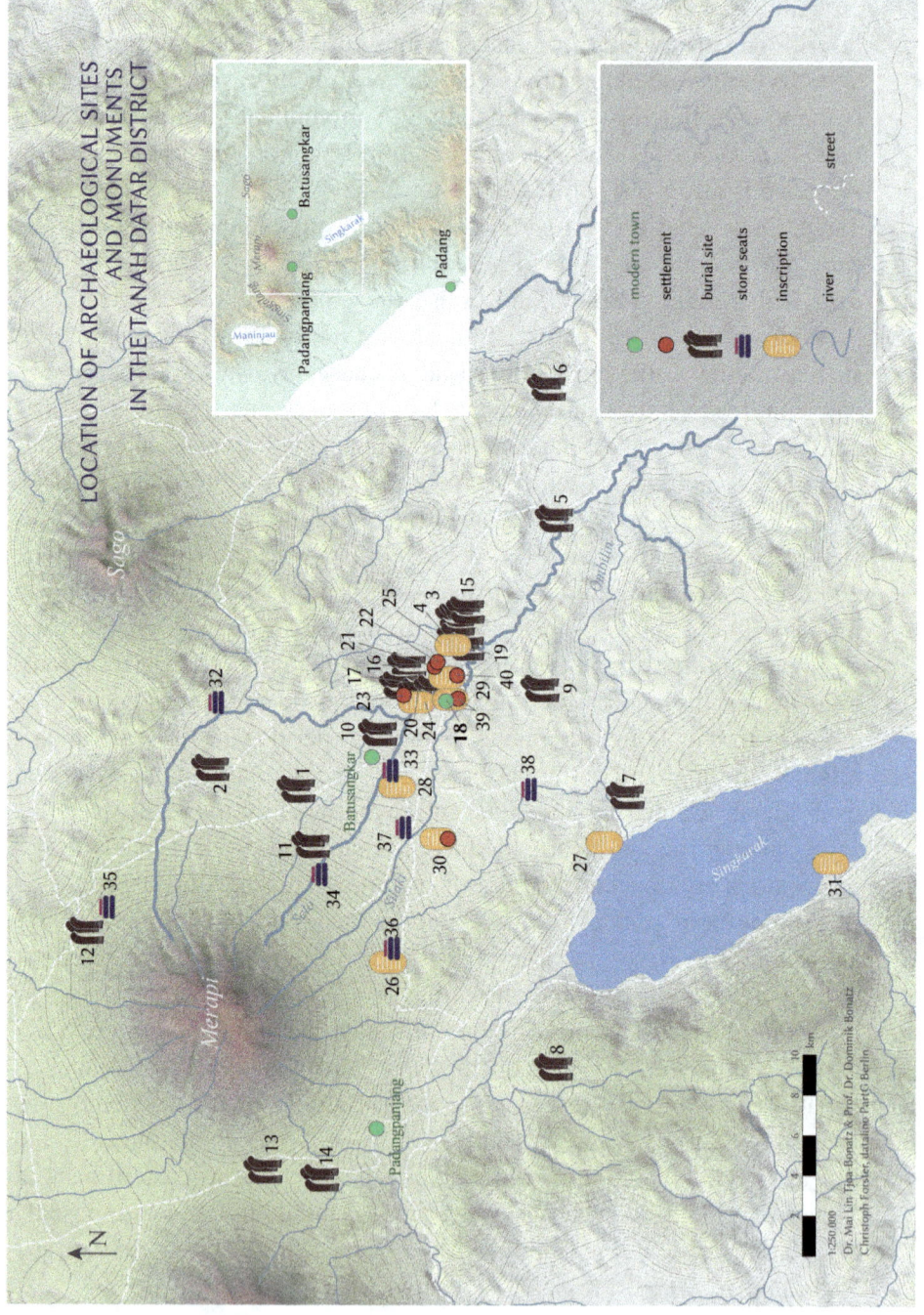

Archaeological sites and monuments in the district of Tanah Datar

A) Burial sites: Makam Tuan Titah (1), Makam Makhudum (2), Makam Indomo (4), Makam Tuan Kadhi (5), Makam Syech Ibrahim (6), Simawang (7), Gunung Bungsu (8), Talago Gunung (9), Makam Sultan Muningsyah (10), Makam Ninik Janggut Hitam (11), Koto Laweh (12), Makam Haji Miskin (13), Makam Tuanku Pamansiangan (14), Tambun Tuland (15), Makam Tuan Gadih (16), Ladang Rojo (17), Makam Raja-Raja Saruaso (19);

B) Settlements: Saruaso (3), Bukit Gombak (18); Bukit Ambuang (21), Bukit Sikupan (22), Biaro (23), Tanah Lua prehistoric site (40);

C) Inscriptions: Kapalo Bukit Gombak (20), Ponggongan (24), Saruaso (25), Pariangan (26), Ombilin (27), Kubarajo (28), Batu Papahat (29), Rambatan (30), Paninggahan (31), Bukit Gombak (39);

D) Meeting places and other stone remains: Medan Bapaneh Ateh Lago (32), Medan Bapaneh Koto Baranjak (33), Medan Bapaneh Sitangkai (34), Medan Bapaneh Gunung (35), Makam Panjang Tantejo Gurhano (36), Batu Batikam (37), Medan Balimbing (38)

Source: Mai Lin Tjoa-Bonatz, Dominik Bonatz; lay-out: Christoph Förster.

The mound of Bukit Gombak is at the southern end of the fertile plain of Tanah Datar, which is south of the volcano Mount Merapi near the Silaki and Selo rivers. To the east, Pagaruyung, the assumed traditional seat of the Minangkabau kings, is situated on the mountain slopes and separated from the two hills by the Selo River valley, which flows between Bukit Gombak and Pagaruyung into the Saruaso valley, where it provides the only natural gateway from the east to the high plains of Tanah Datar. Adityavarman's Batu Bapahat inscriptions at the base of Bukit Gombak marked this route (see pp. 51–53). At the southern foot of Bukit Gombak and Bukit Kincir runs the Silaki River, a small tributary of the Selo that must have been an important waterway leading to the north and a source of water for the settlements on Bukit Gombak and Bukit Kincir. The Selo and the Silaki enclose both hilltops within a narrow triangle. To the south and west of the two hills a long, steeply rising chain of hills forms the West Barisan range. Seen from the north, Bukit Kincir appears steep and inaccessible, but the long plateau of Bukit Gombak becomes visible from the east, revealing that it is well suited for settlement (see Figures 3.3–3.4).

Bukit Gombak: Concentration of Ancient Artefacts

Bukit Gombak is in the transition zone along the River Selo that gives access to the lowlands to the east and leads to the west. Apart from these geostrategic features, the proximity of Mount Merapi, the volcano that is regarded as sacred and power-filled because of its connection to the elements, particularly fire and water, makes this place the most significant settlement site in central Tanah Datar. Adityavarman's inscriptions contain several references to mountains, such as the mention of *mahameru* (literally, the great mountain) in the Gudam II inscription (also called Pagaruyung VII on the very left of Figure 2.5; de Casparis 1989, p. 923), which in the context of Sumatra refers to Mount Merapi, described in local accounts as the nucleus of the Minangkabau heartland (Taufik Abdullah 1972, p. 184). Physical elevation, such as a position on a status-giving hilltop, was a key element of political authority in Sumatra and Majapahit (Andaya 1993, pp. 30, 34; Kieven 2013, pp. 113–15).

The first survey of the "Tanah Datar Project", conducted in 2008 on Bukit Gombak, yielded a few surface finds of pottery, including sherds of Chinese porcelain from the Song dynasty (960–1279). The decision to excavate the site was inspired by finds apparently originating locally, including at least two inscription stones, an undecorated but worked stone and a headless female torso (Krom 1912, pp. 42–43, nos. 23–26; Miksic 1987, p. 9; see Figures 2.5–2.11). The longest inscription within the corpus, the Bukit Gombak I inscription (260 × 130 × 38 cm) from 1356, has 21 lines and mentions various building structures and officials (see the largest erected stone with a raised upper side in Figure 2.5). Above the lines of writing is a plano-double-convex shape with a wavy upper line surmounted by a triangle with three spiralled bands attached, an image also found on seven inscriptions probably issued by Adityavarman (see Figure 2.6).[33] On the Bukit Gombak II slab in the foreground on the right side of Figure 2.5, the image is enclosed by a band of *vajras* and an s-curved *om*,[34] which suggests a religious connotation. The meaning is unclear, but it seems to represent a royal symbol of Adityavarman called *asana* or *padma* (Vernika Hapri Witasari 2011, pp. 63–64). In 1917 J. Hendrik C. Kern documents that several inscriptions were paired, one erected vertically and another stone put horizontally so that they formed seats (Bambang Budi Utomo 2007, figure 2 on p. 63).

Miksic (1987, p. 8) mentions a spring on the southern slope of Bukit Gombak, and he assumes that a headless stone statue around 40 cm in height,[35] now located in Bundo Kanduan in Batusangkar, was originally set up at this spot (see Figures 2.10–2.11). The female torso has bent arms and supports her breasts with her hands. The long fingers are incised while the thumb is abducted. The breasts are perforated and the roughly worked back features a two-layered hole, 5–10 cm in diameter, designed to attach it to a water supply. It is a rather crude, locally made version of East Javanese female spout figures, similar to those at Belahan in East Java. The spring attached to the statue may have served as an ancient bathing site or an auspicious spot on the slope of Bukit Gombak. In Javanese written records and artwork, the symbolism of water, as water of life, refers to the elixir of immortality and is important for fertility and purification rituals (Kieven 2013, pp. 117–21). Water is an important subject in Javanese art, and is often linked to mountains. In Tantrism, water-related activities were visualized using female goddesses, either holding their breasts or holding a jar with spouts that represent the female element (Kempers 1959, pp. 70–71, figure 204). We may suggest a similar association.

FIGURE 2.5

Inscriptions of Adityavarman: the one dated to 1356 from Bukit Gombak (called Bukit Gombak I) is the largest erected stone seen on the photo of c. 1910

Source: National Archive of Indonesia, image code OD-1639.

FIGURE 2.6

FIGURES 2.7–2.8

Detail of the inscription Bukit Gombak I: Adityavarman's symbol

FIGURE 2.9

Three fragments of a Bodhisattva statue with long hair, Central Javanese Period (700–900): lotus base, badly restored, originating from Bukit Gombak, now at Bundo Kanduan in Batusangkar

Two fragments of the legs and upper body, originating from Bukit Gombak, now at the BPCP in Batusangkar
(inv. nos. 033/BCB/B/A/12/V/2008, 034/BCB/B/A/12/V/2008)

FIGURES 2.10–2.11

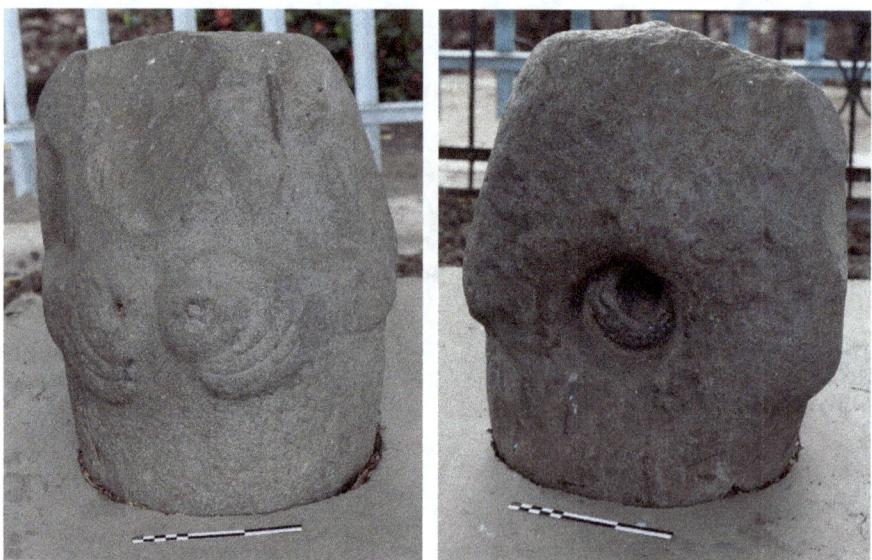

Female water spout and its backview, originating from Bukit Gombak, now at Bundo Kanduan in Batusangkar

A spring discovered at the southern slope of Bukit Gombak was investigated during the 2011 excavation. It was important not only as the water supply of the settlement but also, as the data suggests, for ritual use (see pp. 111–14, Trench S on Map 3.1).

From "Kapalo Bukit Gombak" originate also two inscribed stones which were moved and are thus also called Pagaruyung III and VI (190 × 66 × 15 and 100 × 36 × 46.5 cm).[36] The first seen in the foreground on the left of Figure 2.5 is dated to 1347 and the second is a commemorative or burial place, literally ash-deposit of Kuḍa Vīra, a Javanese official or of Javanese descent (Griffiths 2012, pp. 4–5).

The ancient names of the twin-mound are not known, and references to "Bukit Gombak" need to be treated with caution because this toponym is a general description of a rolling or undulating hill and is used by the local people for a larger, hilly area south of the high plains and west of the Batang Selo. In the past, Bukit Gombak was also called Bukit Dama (or Damar, meaning "resin hill"), which could suggest further geographical differentiation or renaming due to the vegetation found on the hill. On an 1887–92 map of the area, "Boekit Gombak" denotes a relatively large village situated in the plain along a principal road with extensive agricultural land, coffee plantations, and wet-rice fields to the north of "Bukit Koentjir" (today Bukit Kincir, see Figure 2.3). The prominent topography and archaeological remains suggest that Bukit Gombak was an ancient settlement centre or the potential royal seat of Adityavarman, a point further discussed on pp. 117–20.

Batu Bapahat and Wet-rice Irrigation

The importance of water regulation for wet-rice irrigation is expressed by two faces of an inscription found at Batu Bapahat water source "near the spot where the water appears"[37] (see Figure 2.12). The texts

FIGURE 2.12

The inscriptions above a water channel at Batu Papahat of 135(?) are lost

emphasize royal contributions to maintaining and restoring public installations over two generations and are presented as an achievement of the economic growth and well-being of the people. The names of two kings, Adityavarman and Akarendravarman, are mentioned alongside the date 135(?).[38] The inscriptions directly refer to the water source, although they have been lost, probably in the late 1990s, but the ancient channel can still be traced for 1.5 km (see Figure 2.13). From the water source, the channel still directs water to the eastern fields on the mound of present day Tanah Lua, well-seen from Bukit Gombak, before draining into the Selo River. A prehistoric site was discovered around the source, and the inscription probably marked the rice-growing core utilized by the court centre (see pp. 91–96).

FIGURE 2.13

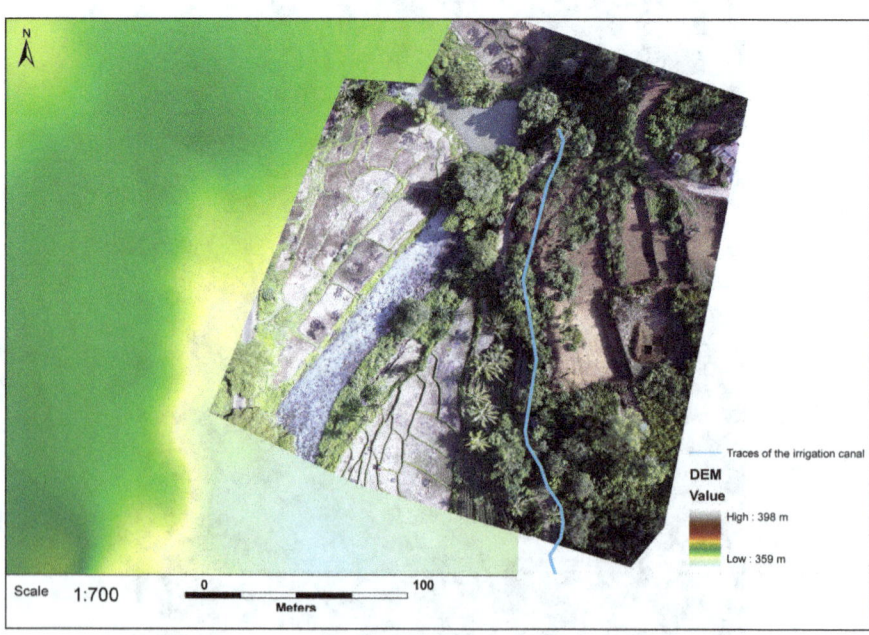

Irrigation channel built by Adityavarman
Source: Manfred Touch.

The control of water resources is frequently connected to a dynastic, territorial claim on agricultural land, and both are political issues. Water management was a central feature of state formation and royal rituals, as evidenced in Bali and Java since the eleventh century (e.g., Christie 1995; 2007). Irrigated rice cultivation produced an important staple food[39] and made the extraction of a permanent agricultural surplus possible. Centralizing this surplus created stronger and more densely populated heartlands. In discussing the construction of the channel, the inscription also documents the availability of corporate labour forces and allied subordinates under the royal lineage. Adityavarman aimed at developing a kingdom based on irrigated wet rice (*sawah*) cultivation.

The use of the South Indian script (Grantha) led Christie (1998, p. 262) to conclude that the inscriptions were bilingual, but Griffiths (2014, p. 222, ft. 41) rejected this argument because both used Sanskrit language. Others have taken the inscriptions as evidence of the presence of a Tamil-speaking community in the Minangkabau area (Schnitger 1937, p. 13; Perret and Heddy Surachman 2011, p. 170). However, in contrast with other hinterland regions in Sumatra, such as the northern Batak area where South Asian influences on the material culture and Tamil place names are apparent, no such influences have been found in the excavated material from Tanah Datar. It is likely that Tamil speakers came only for short periods of time, or that the Tamil community was too small to have left any substantial traces on the settlement.

Saruaso: Another Royal Site

At Saruaso, only a few kilometres downriver from Bukit Gombak, a mutilated Buddhist sculpture and two inscription stones were recorded when Thomas Stamford Raffles visited the Minangkabau highland in 1818 (Reid 1995, pp. 171, 173). The lotus base of the mutilated statue, which is around 50 cm in diameter, has been moved to Bundo Kanduan in Batusangkar, with the exception of two fragments 60 cm in height stored at the BPCP office Batusangkar (inv. nos. 33/BCEB/B/A/12//V2008, 3/BCEB/B/A/12//V2008, see Figures 2.7–2.9). The statue itself is made of a polished and finely grained red stone. A sash-like thread falls diagonally from the deity's left shoulder across the body and a single belt hangs on the hips above a long skirt. The figure, which was probably two-armed and sparsely adorned with jewellery, stands with straight legs on a lotus cushion, indicating that it represents a deity. One explanation of the statue is that it represents the Bodhisattva Awalokiteswara and was carved in the ninth to the eleventh centuries, while another suggests that the long hair spilling in straight locks on the shoulder indicates that the upper part of the figure represents Lakshmana, and the lower part belongs to a different female image.[40] However, reassembling the two broken parts and referring to the older reconstruction seen in a photo of 1890–1910 makes it clear that all three parts belong to a single statue. Marijke Klokke has proposed that the image is a Bodhisattva, "given the fact that Buddhism was important in Sumatra". This agrees with Schnitger's interpretation (1937, p. 13). Stone sculptures of standing Bodhisattva are rare in Java and there are few details for comparison with other images, but scholars[41] date it closer to the Central Javanese period than to the East Javanese period. If so, this statue is another antiquity connected to Adityavarman that originated in Java about 700–900 and was brought to Sumatra.

Among the inscribed stones, the inscription that is in situ lies on a settlement ridge high above the Selo River. The well-smoothed stone cube (133 × 110 × 75 cm), called Saruaso I, was placed near the former palace in the early nineteenth century (Reid 1995, p. 171). The inscription, dating from 1374,[42] was written on two adjacent faces of the cube, suggesting that the stone could be viewed from multiple angles (see Figure 2.14). It praises the royal qualities of Adityavarman and mentions the toponym *surāvāsa*, which also occurs in the Batu Bapahat inscriptions. *Surāvāsa* is eloquently praised with royal terms. The inscription further elaborates that the "divine king sits always on the high throne, eating and drinking in his hall of audience" (Hunter 2015, pp. 306–7). Similarities may be drawn to Thomas Dias' description in 1684 of a royal meeting with the king of Pagaruyung, who sat on an elevated throne in front of a royal audience (see p. 76).

The other stone, called the Saruaso II inscription, was re-purposed as a stepping stone for the nearby mosque, a point noted by Raffles in 1818, and has been moved to the Bundo Kanduan in Batusangkar (Reid 1995, p. 171). The front and the back of the rectangular slab

FIGURE 2.14

The in-situ inscription Saruaso I of 1374

(110 × 75 × 17 cm), which is slightly raised on the right side, concern Ananggavarman, who "pays homage to the inscription of stone [placed] before the entryway of the place [palace] of the Eminent Crown Prince" (Hunter 2015, p. 325). Most scholars agree that Ananggavarman was the crown prince under Adityavarman.[43] As some of Adityavarman's inscription stones are raised on the right side, this provides an important clue about what rock shapes were favoured.[44] The inscriptions provide information about their function, who they addressed and who were their recipients. The inscribed stones were visible symbols of royalty, placed in prominent public locations such as Saruaso where everybody who entered the royal residence would pass them. The Saruaso inscription also mentions certain rituals connected to royalty that were performed in front of the erected stones. They were thus understood as monuments.

At Saruaso, habitation remains were found such as stone tools of unknown date and context: a round mortar, a conical pounder, and two rocks with several circular depressions. The imported luxury ceramics collected by the survey attest to the same habitation horizon as Bukit Gombak, starting in the fourteenth century. The sherds include a large, misfired green-glazed Longquan dish with an undulating rim, probably from the fourteenth or fifteenth century, a small Swatow vase with a sandy base and blue-and-white painting from the sixteenth or seventeenth century, and some multi-coloured European, probably Dutch, stoneware from the nineteenth or early twentieth century.

A burial ground for the dignitaries of Saruaso located near the inscription stone points to the enduring socio-political importance of local leaders and their hereditary status (see Figure 2.15). Historical accounts continue to describe Saruaso as the second royal centre of the Minangkabau in Tanah Datar during the mid-1670s (Drakard 1999, p. 88, ft. 12; pp. 91, 125–26; Kozok and van Reijn 2010, p. 137). At the time, it was the second largest settlement in the West Sumatran highlands, with an estimated population of 4,000, and was four times larger than the royal palace "where the emperor lived" (Macleod 1906,

FIGURE 2.15

Burial ground of the kings of Saruaso

p. 1444). This provides an important clue about the multi-centred division of power in the Minangkabau area. In subsequent centuries, Saruaso retained its status as an important site within the royal sphere of the Minangkabau. The royal language of Adityavarman's inscriptions is said to be echoed in letters from the ruler of Saruaso in the early eighteenth century (Drakard 1999, p. 244; 2008–9, p. 163, ft. 124; p. 159, ft. 111). For Johannes G. de Casparis,[45] Saruaso represents the capital or a newly transferred palace site, but so far the references in the stone inscriptions along with the archaeological inventory and historical references only provide ample evidence that Saruaso was an influential and economically thriving settlement, and that it was connected to the monarchy since the end of the fourteenth century.

Between Saruaso and Pagaruyung lies Biaro, an archaeologically promising site because scholars connected the toponym with the Sanskrit word *vihara* for a monastery (Krom 1912, p. 36, no. 1; Miksic 1987, p. 21, figure 16). However, this place did not reveal ancient structures, and no datable artefacts were retrieved apart from sparse habitation remains marked by brick fragments (21 × 14 × 5 cm) and a stone burial marker (49 × 29 × 12 cm).

Ponggongan: Inscriptions Near "Firing Places"

Following the Selo upriver a short distance to the north of Bukit Gombak, another inscription stone is found in the middle of the rice fields at Ponggongan, which literally means "burning" or "firing places" (Krom 1912, p. 45, no. 36; see Figure 2.16).[46] A gold workshop has been excavated nearby, and the use of fire at this workshop may explain the name (see pp. 72–74, Figures 2.17–2.19). The flat and heavily weathered inscription stone called Ponggongan I (150 × 90 × 30 cm) is slightly raised on the upper right side. The inscription is too fragmented to read. An inscribed stone mortar called Ponggongan II or Pagaruyung VIII (52 × 49 × 30 cm) was collected at Ponggongan and later moved to Pagaruyung. It may have been used for pounding rice or other food stuff (see Figure 2.20). The inscription, which dates to 1375,[47] is found on three sides of a nearly cubic stone and mentions that the king of the gold land has established an abode.

FIGURE 2.16

The in-situ inscription of Ponggongan covered by a roof, today found in the middle of rice fields

Its shape, with its well-smoothed surfaces and clear-cut edges, contrasts with other stone mortars (*lumping batu*) commonly found in the region, which are rounded and roughly shaped.[48] They were a domestic implement of considerable importance in daily household activities, for the daily ponding of rice what was mostly conducted by women. Mortars may also have fulfilled ritual functions, for instance during harvest ceremonies, and have been re-used as house pillar supports, stepping stones, or mounting blocks for elephants, or markers for horse races (Miksic 2004, p. 200). The fact that a mortar bears an inscription highlights the importance of agricultural products, probably rice, to the economy at the time.

FIGURES 2.17–2.19

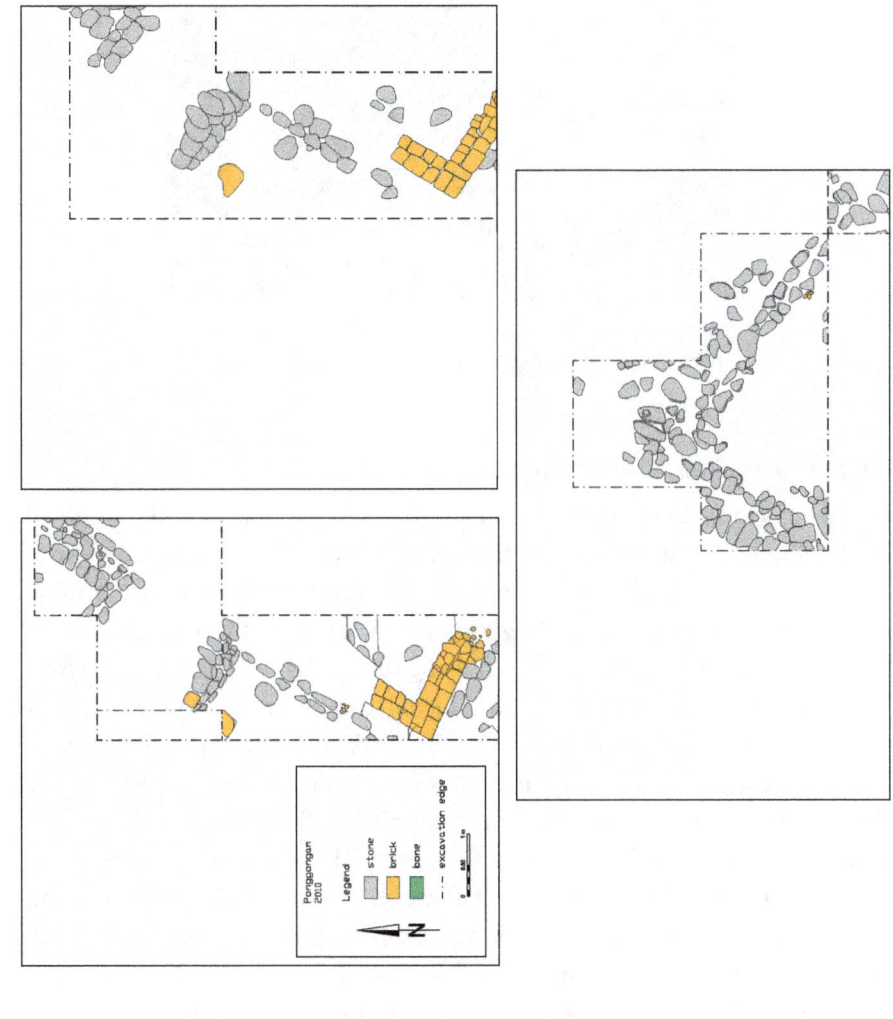

Excavation at a gold workshop at Ponggongan, sixteenth to seventeenth centuries: remains of a stone wall

Source: Budi Istiawan, BPCP Batusangkar.

FIGURE 2.20

An inscribed stone mortar of 1375, originating
from Ponggongan, now at Pagaruyung

Gudam: The Question of Succession

Further north at Gudam,[49] beyond the Selo River and directly south of Pagaruyung, lies a village of the same name where two inscriptions originate. The Gudam I inscription is highly eroded and no transliteration is yet available (also called Pagaruyung IV, see the third erected stone from the left of Figure 2.5). An irregularly shaped inscription stone found in 1818 "near the site of the former *kudam* or palace" and "partly buried in the ground" (Reid 1995, p. 171) is probably what is now known as the Gudam II inscription; it has been transferred to Pagaruyung, thus called Pagaruyung VII (left in Figure 2.5). The inscription was issued by Akarendravarman. He is either his predecessor or successor to Adityavarman, but there is no consensus on this point. De Casparis is of the opinion that at least he is an important figure,[50] but Griffiths (2012, ft. 9) assumes that Akarendravarman is Adityavarman's successor. Either way, the succession followed patrilineal rule. The inscription also mentions three community heads and four clans (*suku*).[51] Among them "Tuhan(s) in Pariangan",[52] Tuhan Parpatih, and a person called *biraparākramakuda*, a Javanese name, are acknowledged (Budi Istiawan 2006, pp. 19–22; Griffiths 2012, p. 5; Hunter 2015, p. 345). The first name is linked with a toponym on the west coast, the harbour of Pariangan (see p. 70); the second community head is also mentioned in the Rambatan inscription and reflects an Old Javanese title for a military or political advisor to the king.

A flat, three-tiered stepped stone of unknown purpose was also found in Gudam (Krom 1912, no. 31, see Figure 2.21 and the second stone from the right of Figure 2.5).[53] One side is incised and follows a stepped, geometric outline that may represent bamboo shoots, a frequently employed ornament on various artworks of the Minangkabau (e.g., the megaliths of the Mahat valley).

FIGURE 2.21

A three-tiered stepped stone of unknown
purpose from Gudam, now at Pagaruyung

Kuburajo: Stone Seats and Commemorative Stones

The Silaki River provides the second riverine connection from Bukit Gombak, this one towards the northwest leading to Kuburajo, where two adjacent stone assemblages have two inscriptions relating to Adityavarman. The first is a community grave with four stones, including a stone slab called Kuburajo I (108 × 36 × 13 cm) that is inscribed with 16 lines of Sanskrit letters (see Figure 2.22). The stone is rectangular with a raised upper-right side and, for this reason, was seen as a burial marker and kept together with other, similarly shaped stones.[54] The inscription refers to Adwayavarman, who is also mentioned in the Batu Bapahat inscriptions. According to de Casparis (1989, pp. 922–24), Adwayavarman was Adityavarman's father or predecessor.[55] The text containing this genealogical reference states that the king of the gold land comes from the lineage of the thunderbolt-bearer, i.e., Indra, the incarnation of Lokeswara (Kern 1917c, pp. 217–21). He might be thus a "founding father" (Budi Istiawan 2014, p. 34).

The second assemblage is a set of five stone seats, three of which are similar in size, rounded, embellished with a circular motif and surmounted by an ogival-shaped arch with a central groove (see Figures 2.23–2.25). The central one bears an inscription connected to Adityavarman. On the left side of the stone, many letters on the so-called Kuburajo II inscription

FIGURE 2.22

The in-situ inscription Kubarajo I
mentions Adityavarman

2. Early Histories: Historiography and Archaeological Surveys

FIGURE 2.23

Stone slabs are used as seats at Kubarajo, the central stone is the inscription Kubarajo II

FIGURE 2.24

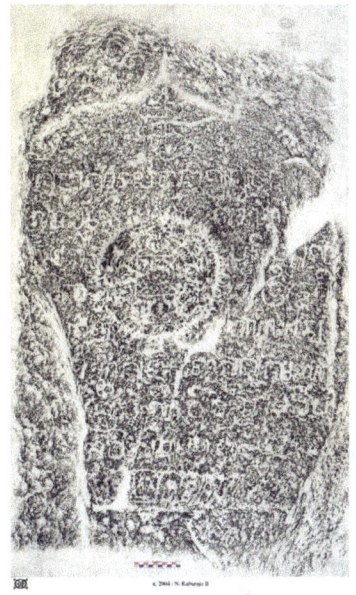

Paper estampage of the in-situ inscription Kubarajo II

Source: Estampage EFEOB-est.n2004.

FIGURE 2.25

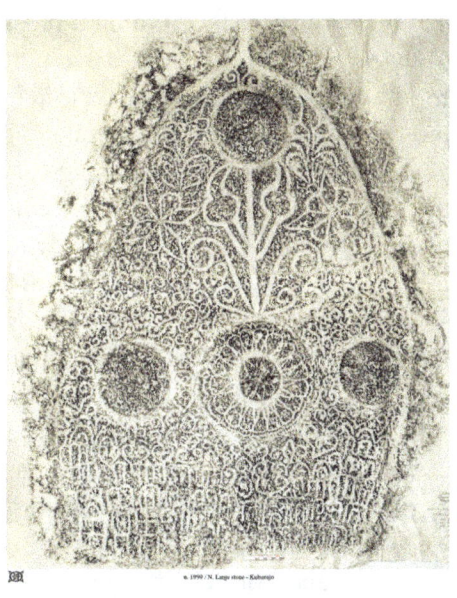

Paper estampage of the ornamented stone slab at Kubarajo

Source: Estampage EFEOB-est.n1999.

(152 × 93 × 84 cm) have been eroded, making the inscription difficult to read. The stone has a large disk with a square in its centre set above a lotus pedestal and surmounted by an ogival shape (see Figure 2.24). Miksic (1985a, p. 74; 2015, p. 40) interprets the disk as a solar motif with four *vajra* around it. I would argue that the disk instead represents a lotus blossom. Found above is the same symbol of Adityavarman, which is seen on the central top of the Bukit Gombak I inscription (see Figure 2.6). It emphasizes the importance of the Kubarajo inscription in the royal realm.

The adjacent stone (192 × 120 × 23 cm), the last in the row of stones in Figure 2.23 and the largest piece, has a central disc surrounded by a drop-shape that merges at the top into a central groove based on a triangular shape that expands into mirrored spirals or leave-shapes. This motif resembles ornaments found on megaliths in the regency of Lima Puluh Kota, e.g., at Ateh Sudu.

One face of the second largest stone (187 × 125 × 23 cm) is fully covered with a rich floral and geometric pattern in low-relief neatly outlined in strict symmetrical order with three disks in the centre (see Figure 2.25 and in the foreground of Figure 2.23). The central one includes an eight-pronged star forming a blossom with two circles of pointed and rounded petals. From here arises a blossoming flower stem with pointed fruits and triangular leaves intersected by mirrored spirals. The latter forms the basic motif of a scroll frequently used in Minangkabau artwork that is called "sleeping cat" (*kuciang tiduah*). More ornamental features can be recognized that seem to be of considerable antiquity and local origin: two eight-pointed stars including chevrons, spirals (*kaluak paku*) similar to fern tendrils, and a flower motif consisting of a diamond-shape supported by mirrored spirals. The last two motifs are frequently carved on burial stones in the Lima Puluh Kota regency at prehistoric sites such as Bawah Parit or in the Mahat valley (see Figures 1.1–1.2). This vegetal and geometric decoration is still used in more recent decorative Minangkabau arts such as woodcarving or textiles.[56] Various interpretations have been proposed for the motifs. Understood as a tree of life, the fern tendrils with open and closed volutes, male and female, stand for fertility and kingship (Sanday and Suwati Kartiwa 1984, p. 22).[57] For Budi Istiawan (2006, pp. 35–36), the number of leaves and blossoms implies numeric symbolism. He counts twelve and seven leaves and adds it to the three blossoms what may suggest the *saka* date of 1273 (1351 in the Gregorian calendar). For the Minangkabau, numerals have auspicious meaning such as three-, eight-, and nine-groupings (Josselin de Jong 1951, p. 153; Drakard 2008–9, p. 158, ft. 107). Although it is clear that the decoration was intentionally chosen to incorporate a local iconic basis, these interpretations still remain highly speculative.

Local ornamentation was incorporated in the design, but the overall composition seems to reflect other artistic sources. Miksic (1987, p. 19) suggests that the stone is part of Adityavarman's Javanese "classical tradition" because of the symmetrical arrangement around a central flower. The complex interwoven pattern of floral decoration is very different from the sparsely used singular ornaments on megaliths in the area and is probably derived from other crafts such as wood carving or textiles. The backside of wooden thrones in Southeast Asia is often richly ornamented in a relief that evolves from a central axis.[58] Written references to thrones of the Minangkabau royalty give no information on the material or the design used. Was local weaving already sufficiently developed at the time to create such complicated pattern? The export of silk from the region is documented in the early sixteenth century, leaving open the possibility that the cloth was of foreign origin (Mill 1970, p. 100). In Southeast Asia, radiocarbon dated textiles from India appear from the fourteenth century onwards, and Gujerati ceremonial cloths with geometricized floral design and mordant-dyed paint on resist-dyed cotton have been found in island Southeast Asia (Guy 2007, pp. 42–45). A reference from the early sixteenth century proves that this kind of cloth was imported into the Minangkabau area, although we do not know with certainty that these trading networks existed earlier. Tomé Pires explains that two kinds of cloth were traded in the region, writing that "Kling and Gujarat cloth [...] is valued throughout the island, and red cotton cloth is valued most in Menangkabau" (Pires 1944, p. 152).

In assessing the function of the stone assemblage, scholars have suggested several interpretations of the toponym Kuburajo. One is that it refers to the king's grave (*kubur raja*) and represents the burial place of Adityavarman. Another is that it refers to the site of a king's palace or fort (*kubu rajo*), and a third is that it refers to a no man's land between two opposing clans (Satyawati Suleiman 1977, p. 5; Miksic 2004, p. 203; Kozok and van Reijn 2010, p. 154, ft. 87). Adityavarman's inscriptions provide no evidence about the burial place.[59] The site, a narrow ridge above a pond, seems too small for a royal settlement. The third explanation better suits the orally-transmitted tradition that the stones were ceremonial seats for the three Minangkabau kings, a triumvirat of Raja Adat, the "king of the customary law", Raja Ibadat, the "king of religion", and Raja Alam, the "king of the world" (Miksic 1985a, p. 74). It remains highly speculative, but the upper central groove with the ogival-shape found on these stones may have featured in rituals, such as pouring water over the stone so that the content of the stones is consumed by those taking part, attesting to their allegiance. This kind of oath stone is known from early Srivijaya, in the late seventh century in Southeast Sumatra, and one such stone was found upstream from Batang Hari (Manguin 2009, p. 448, figure 19-1).

This setting is central to the question of megalithic continuity and the adaptive use of motifs transferred into a political context during the time of Adityavarman or shortly afterwards. The stones clearly constituted a set, and at least one is connected to Adityavarman. Hence, during his lifetime or shortly thereafter, members of the ruling elite erected these stones to create a political space for council meetings and possibly rituals of allegiance. The tradition of meeting places with stone seats probably began in the late fourteenth or early fifteenth century and became standard for communal space in the Minangkabau region in subsequent centuries (see pp. 79–82). The combination of local elements, Buddhist symbolism, and adaptations of complex design patterns from other genres into stone carving implies that stone was the preferred material for communal arenas, and featured pure iconic symbolism. Merging various artistic ways and traditions seems to have been typical during the time of Adityavarman.

Rambatan: Place for Rest and Worship

The comparatively flat inscription stone (130 × 60 × 10 cm) at Rambatan, in the regency of the same name, is smooth on all sides (see Figures 2.26–2.27). The inscription is dated to 1369.[60] Some parts on the left edge of the stone have flaked off. The stone was originally found near five large rocks beside a fishpond a hundred metres south of its present position.

FIGURES 2.26–2.27

The in-situ inscription at Rambatan and its paper estampage
Source: Estampage EFEOB-est.n2001.

This site may be associated with a place of worship, that is, Buddha's footprint as mentioned in the inscription (Budi Istiawan 2006, p. 40). Griffiths reads it as a place for rest for travellers, "people who come here, having come here after traveling on the way, and having taken rest even for a moment".[61] The importance of a resting place becomes obvious when referring to the fourteenth-century Tanah Luah code of Kerinci and other legal texts from Southeast Asia that encourage hospitality for travellers by granting passage and providing food (Kozok and Waruno Mahdi 2015, p. 93).

Discoveries at the site included small- to large-sized imported dishes with base diameters of 8–18 cm, and a high density of undecorated earthenware sherds, firm evidence that the stone was located within an ancient settlement. Datable objects recovered by the survey include Thai and Chinese ceramics such as heavy, olive green glazed bases for bowls or dishes, among them two with incised flowers from the Yuan dynasty (1279–1368), indicating that the site was contemporaneous with Bukit Gombak and connected to the long-distance trading routes.

Pariangan on the Way to the West

From Rambatan, two overland routes branch off from the plain of Tanah Datar toward the west coast. Both are marked by inscription stones. The northernmost path is marked by a stone inscription in the village of Pariangan, in the regency of the same name (see Figures 2.28–2.29). The triangular rock (260 × 160 × 160 cm) is on a mountain spur at 837 m and located above the Batang Air, which drains into the connecting

FIGURES 2.28–2.29

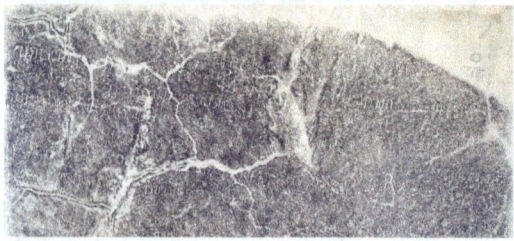

The in-situ inscription on a rock at Pariangan and its paper estampage

Source: Estampage EFEOB-est.n2003.

Ombilin River. When viewing the five lines of the inscription, which are mostly illegible apart from the name of Adityavarman,[62] one faces Mount Merapi, an auspicious setting. It is the only example among the in-situ inscriptions where the original orientation has not been changed,[63] but the inscription has not been translated.

Ombilin and Paninggahan Near Lake Singkarak

The second route crosses Lake Singkarak, an important communication link that extended the socio-political space of Adityavarman's polity to the west. In the early nineteenth century, walking from Pagaruyung to the lakeshore took five and a half hours (Raffles 1991, p. 361). The footpath passed an inscription stone at the village of Ombilin in the Rambatan regency, on the eastern shore of Lake Singkarak. The inscription, on two faces of a rectangular slab[64] (93 × 64 × 32 cm), mentions dilapidated structures that Adityavarman refurbished (see Figures 2.30–2.31).[65]

FIGURES 2.30–2.31

The in-situ inscription at Ombilin facing the Singkarak Lake, *c.* 1910

Source: Tegu Hidayat et al. (2010), p. 25, image code DP 20217; Estampage EFEOB-est.n2024.

The restoring of older structures is reminiscent of similar undertakings mentioned in the Amogaphasa inscription.

On the southwest shore of the lake, an inscription at Paninggahan in the Junjung Sirih district of the Solok regency, marked the connection across the lake. The inscription on this well-rounded stone (91 × 66 × 21.5 cm) refers explicitly to the hydronym.[66] The connection with the Ombilin inscription lies in the importance attached to crossing the lake, a geopolitical claim that emphasized geostrategic and trade benefits of Adityavarman's kingdom. At Paninggahan, a river allowed travellers to descend to the coast where the harbour of Pariaman, like Tiko and Barus, was one of the main trading centres of the Minangkabau. A reference to "Tuhan(s) in Pariangan" relates to "the three heads of the community"[67] in the Gudam II inscription and highlights the importance of this harbour for the highland kingdom during Adityavarman's time. Indian, Chinese, and Arab ships used the route along the west coast of Sumatra (Tjoa-Bonatz 2018). In the early fifteenth century, Chinese court documents mention the Minangkabau along with two other places on the west coast of Sumatra, although most of the ports named lay along the more heavily frequented route on Sumatra's east coast along the Straits of Malacca, used by ships on their way to South China (Wade 2005). According to an early sixteenth-century Portuguese source, two or three ships from Gujerat came to the west-coast ports annually to trade (Pires 1944, p. 161). Written records also mention a large highland lake in the Minangkabau region that was bordered by many settlements and provided a rich supply of food as well as facilities for sailing craft (Hess 1931, p. 76; Pires 1944, p. 165). Although it is not known which of the numerous lakes is addressed here, the reference notes that it was placed under the jurisdiction of the three kings of the Minangkabau, making its geopolitical and socio-economic importance clear.

Conclusion

The stone memorials of Adityavarman were incorporated into complex social practices linking them to human interaction, landscape, and ideology. The religious context of the inscriptions is clearly Buddhist. Their archaeological context suggests that they were all produced within

2. Early Histories: Historiography and Archaeological Surveys   71

a similar trading culture and that at least three of the inscriptions in Tanah Datar were located within settlements, with some standing next to royal buildings or religious places. All were written on locally available stone that was often roughly worked. Inscriptions were placed on a grinding stone or a rock, but most were found on upright slabs of rectangular shape, no more than 260 cm tall. Their content included proclamations, markers for religious and public establishments, and funerary or commemorative messages. The last of these functions was a longstanding tradition of the region, and stones used for this purpose were rectangular with a raised upper part, typical of burial stones from the early first millennium found in the northern region of the Minangkabau area. Stones of this shape were used for four inscriptions that are probably connected to royal places.

The in-situ-inscriptions were found within a close network of aligned settlements, a contiguous and compact territory that maintained socio-cultural and commercial links to the coastal regions. Objects recovered by survey at these sites include imported wares that suggest a habitation horizon from at least the fourteenth century. Projecting the sites onto a relief map of the area, the connections between them along waterways and footpaths become obvious (see Map 2.1). The rivers were the major channels for trade and communication, while footpaths through forested areas linked the waterways. The sites filled various roles within the network, including agricultural or ritual centres, resting places, and trading nodes along the footpaths.

Connections with the mountainous hinterland from both the west and east coast were well established in the fourteenth century. Trading routes likely shifted over time depending on commercial opportunities. The goods sought by Chinese, Portuguese, and Indian traders of the early fifteenth and sixteenth centuries included gold, manufactured wares such as silk, and jungle products including rhinoceros horn and certain kinds of wood or wood extracts such as lakawood, eagle-woods, benzoin, and camphor (Pires 1944, p. 161; Mill 1970, p. 100). Later exports included iron and pepper. From the Minangkabau heartland, the west coast could be reached in one to two days and the east coast in ten days (Reid 1995, pp. 40–41). The information about routes and distances necessary to cross Sumatra gave the Minangkabau a geographical image of their island, and this kind of geographic memory, addressing toponyms and hydronyms in particular, is found in Adityavarman's inscription and in the geostrategic setting of the stones, with further references occurring later in written records (Drakard 2008–9).

2.3. Gold Processing

Several of Adityavarman's inscriptions state that he was the sovereign of the land of gold. The expression "Land or Earth of Gold" is mentioned in the Bukit Gombak I and II, Kuburajo I, Paninggahan, and Ponggongan II inscriptions. The land or island of gold is well-known in Indian sources (as *suvarnabhumi* and *suvarnadvīpa* respectively), corresponding to Sumatra and possibly Java or Kalimantan as well. In Adityavarman's inscriptions such as that at Kubarajo, Kern (1917*a*, p. 219) understands Kanakamedini ("the Golden Earth") to be a toponym synonymous with Suvarnadvipa (Sumatra), but if denoting a specific geographic region on Sumatra, Adityavarman's inscriptions highlight his goal of controlling the gold-exporting region, and particularly Tanah Datar (Kulke 2009, p. 243).

The court official *Deva Tuhan Parpatih*, who appears in the Rambatan and Gudam II inscriptions, was responsible for conveying the ruler's orders to his subjects (Kern 1907, pp. 169, 173–74), but it is not clear if he handled setting up the gold trade and could take credit for the resulting prosperity, or if he simply grew wealthy from it. His somewhat grandiose name was taken from Javanese political vocabulary, leading some scholars to comment on possible influences from Javanese political models. However, this title alone is not enough evidence to suggest that the government was a Javanese polity. Others argue that it is more of a localized Javanese term because it combines both Malay and Javanese words (Kern 1907, p. 169; Dobbin 1983, p. 62; Drakard 1999, p. 22).

From the early sixteenth century, various European writers identified the Minangkabau region as the place of origin for Sumatran gold (Hess 1931, p. 76; Dobbin 1983, p. 61; Drakard 1999, pp. 25–29). Gold is widely distributed throughout the Minangkabau area in bedrock and placer deposits. These deposits have been exploited historically both by mining and panning. Gold mining and sedimentary gold powder found in rivers were recorded in colonial writing as early as the early sixteenth century (Pires 1944, pp. 164–65). Today and possibly in earlier times, a wooden pan is used to separate lighter particles from the denser gold or silver particles in flowing water. Panning still takes place in the rivers which drain to the southeast of Tanah Datar, e.g., along the Sungai Lasi (Sartono 1984, figures 2–3). By the nineteenth century, there were at least 158 mines near Bukit Kandong in the Solok district, south of Tanah Datar, some of which reached a depth of 50 Dutch ells, about 41 m (Couperus 1856, pp. 123, 125). In the seventeenth century, gold was mined on Bukit Gombak and Saruaso (Kroeskamp 1931, p. 56). Still in the early nineteenth century, gold mining was pursued around Pagaruyung on Simawang hill (Raffles 1991, p. 361). Today the gold extracting areas are in the regency of Lima Puluh Kota, where early twentieth-century Dutch goldmines are re-exploited by small-scale mining groups, whose workers include migrants from Java or Irian Jaya.

Archaeological evidence for gold processing in Tanah Datar comes from the excavation of a gold workshop at Ponggongan, probably from the sixteenth or seventeenth century.[68] Excavations in 2010 and 2011, directed by Budi Istiawan of BPCP Batusangkar, uncovered building structures at a slope of 415 m (see Figures 2.17–2.19). The walls, which were of brick and stone, measured between 50 and 60 cm. The length of the bricks varied between 21 and 40 cm, but all seemed to be standardized to a width of 20 cm and a height of 6 cm. Several corner edges of solid walls reveal the existence of separated spaces. The excavation discovered 23 objects, including high-tempered earthenware such as jar fragments featuring a loop or horned handle and a roughly potted crucible (see Figure 4.7: A). The shape and its small diameter of the crucible of 6 cm makes it likely that it was used for melting gold.[69] Two sherds belonging to two different small blue-and-white bowls showed characteristics typical of the late Ming or rather early Ching period and were undoubtedly imported.[70] One has floral decorations and the other a band of alternating circles and colons.[71] Two grindstones of non-siliceous material were used: one as a grinding or hammering instrument with a 10 cm long plano-convex section and the other as a grinding slab with a circular depression 5 cm in diameter at its centre.[72] These tools support the conclusion that the site was a gold workshop.

Gold is often associated with regional place names in Tanah Datar. Oral accounts report that gold was retrieved from both the Pendulangan Lobo stream and the Selo River (Raffles 1991, p. 359). A map from 1887–92 labels the Selo River as "Soengai Amas" meaning Golden River (see Map 2.3). Although the river is deep and quick flowing, gold can be panned because sand banks and rows of stones disrupt the flow of water. It is not known if the stones were placed there by humans. Place names across the river from Saruaso allude to gold (e.g., Sungai Emas village and Tambang Emas hill). In the seventeenth century, the trade in gold, alongside other agrarian and metal resources such as iron tools including weapons, appears to have been key to the region's economic growth (Kroeskamp 1931, pp. 14–16). The supply of gold in Tanah Datar started to dwindle around the end of the eighteenth century (Dobbin 1983, p. 66).

2.4. The Royal Court Pagaruyung Seized Power in the Seventeenth Century

The Court of Pagaruyung

After the death of Adityavarman and his successor, the supremacy of the leading family was contested, and conflicts arose among competing lineages across the Minangkabau region. These quarrels caused a severe decline in trade in the 1580s, and it only recovered after 1619 (Andaya 1993, p. 49). The 1670s and 1680s, when the Pagaruyung lineage seized power in Tanah Datar, brought changes to the organization of the Minangkabau kingdom. In 1685 a claimant to the Pagaruyung throne holding the high-ranking title *yang dipertuan sakti* (who has spiritual power) fled to Palembang (Andaya 1993, p. 115).

The presence of occupational debris at Bukit Gombak supports the conclusion that it remained a settlement site until it fell into obscurity, probably at the same time Pagaruyung became politically important in the late seventeenth century. Neither archaeological nor inscriptional evidence from the fourteenth century indicate any association of Adityavarman's royal line with that of Pagaruyung.

The earliest western reference to Pagaruyung is in Dutch records from 1641, where the word identifies an area along the Sinamar River between

Buo and Kumanis at the eastern fringe of Tanah Datar. Local histories support the idea that the dynasty moved from there to central Tanah Datar, suggesting that in 1680 Radjo Alif divided his realm among his three sons, who became rulers at Sungai Taro', Saruaso, and Pagaruyung (Josselin de Jong 1951, p. 101). Scholars agree that the shift from the east of the Minangakabau area to central Tanah Datar took place because of rivalry among different branches of the royal family (Reid 1995, p. 153; Drakard 1999, pp. 33, 65, 103).

These dynastic fluctuations explain why members of the Pagaruyung royal family were living in the Buo-Kumanis area when Thomas Dias, a Portuguese VOC (Dutch East India Company) representative, met the Minangkabau king in 1684 at a place he called Pacu (today Paku) on the Kampar Kiri River. His account of meeting the king, whom he calls "Rajo Malijo" (Raja Malayo), in "Paggar Oejem" (Pagaruyung) provides rare insights into the workings of the royal court in the late seventeenth century (Barnard 2013, p. 20). The number of royal followers he describes is remarkable. A delegation of 500 men received the foreigners, who were then guarded by 400 men on royal order. The first reception with the king's two sons was

> accompanied by about 4,000 men and the royal splendour of music instruments, plus very many *caitoquas* [sunshade and] parasols trimmed with gold and silver and other royal emblems, came to us to fetch the letters and gifts. The prince accepted the letter and laid it in a golden dish which he bore in his own hands. The great ones of the realm carried the gifts on silver dishes, while salutes were loosed from their firearms, and [they] escorted me to the palace staircase. Here the prince bore the letter to his father while I waited below with the great men (Barnard 2013, p. 23).

Dias passed through three gates before reaching the king's chamber. The first was heavily protected by a hundred guards but the second had only four guards and the last one only two, who were standing "with their unsheathed swords in their hands" (Barnard 2013, p. 25). A throne and a Persian carpet ("Al-Qatif carpet") furnished the royal chamber, where the king was surrounded by his council members and religious representatives called *hajis* (Barnard 2013, p. 26). The king presented Dias with royal gifts and a treaty. The gifts were set on a silver dish and included a "yellow standard and a weapon inlaid with silver resembling a halberd [...] as well as a ring of *tembaga suasa* [gold-copper alloy]" (ibid.). A succession of spaces leading to the interior council hall of the king, the elevating of the palace accessed by stairs and an elevated throne produced distance between the king and any visitors. The possession of various commodities, some imported from far away, demonstrated wealth and potency, and the king had metal goods and precious materials in the form of weapons, dishes, and jewellery. The visual power of these objects and other royal symbols conveyed the king's authority (Colombijn 2003, p. 512).

Tanah Datar in the Sixteenth and Seventeenth Centuries

During the fourteenth century, the highland valley around Tanah Datar became an expanding agro-ecological landscape based on irrigated wet-rice, causing the population to increase. In the middle of the fifteenth century, significant numbers of Minangkabau began to migrate to other parts of Sumatra and to the Malay Peninsula, settling there in what are now the states of Negeri Sembilan and Melaka where they also erected megaliths on burial places (de Casparis 1980, p. 5; Miksic 1987). In the late fifteenth century, pepper cultivation brought an economic boom, and early sixteenth-century Portuguese documents mention the Minangkabau by name along with their king, their trading goods, and trading partners (Pires 1944, pp. 152, 161–62, 164).

International maritime trade intensified along the Straits of Melaka after Melaka fell to the Portuguese in 1511, and the port was an important trading outlet for the Minangkabau during the sixteenth century.[73] After the VOC signed the Treaty of Painan in 1663 with rulers of the west coast states at Indrapura, the ports at Tiku, Padang, Painan, and Pulau Cinko became trading bases for the Dutch East India Company. In 1666 Padang was made the VOC administrative centre for the region and became the base for Dutch investigations of the Minangkabau (Drakard 1999, p. 68).

Population figures from the seventeenth century show 1,060 settlements in the Minangkabau area and a population of 8,000 for Pagaruyung (Haan 1897, p. 355; Miksic 1989*a*, p. 16). Maps of Sumatra dating from 1724–46 describe the Minangkabau state, the "Ryk van Maningcabo" (see Map 2.2), in the hinterland of Pariaman and Padang, with a dense

MAP 2.2

West Sumatra in 1724
Source: Details from François Valentyn (1724–46).

MAP 2.3

Scale: 1:10,000
Tanah Datar in 1887–92
Source: Topographisch Bureau te Batavia 1887–92, Blad 55 and 83 combined.

settlement pattern spread across the flat valley floors at the base of the mountains. Place names indicate the number of village (Kota) associations in the area: De 50 Kotas, De 20 Kotas, De Derthien Kotas, Sambilan Kota or Lima Kotas (the 50, 20, 13, 9, or 5 villages). These dense village clusters contrast with both the dendritic pattern of settlements along the rivers of the broad eastern plains and the shorter stretches of small towns lined up in "comb patterns" along the narrow west coast (Colombijn 2003, p. 514). River arteries or footpaths provided access into the hinterland. At Padang, the foothills ascend steeply around 10 km from the coast. The main upland route along the Anai gourge—probably the same western route used in the time of Adityavarman—passes the villages of "Batipoe" (now called Batipuh), "Semabor" (now Simabue), "Padang Pondjang" (now Padang Panjang), "Priangan", and finally "Sankar" (today's Batusangkar) in the heartland of Tanah Datar. Batipuh, and the adjacent villages of Sumpur and Bunga Tanjung, were relatively large trading communities in 1730, with as many as 4,000 resident merchants (Dobbin 1983, p. 70). These figures support Miksic's assumption (1989*a*, pp. 16, 21) that the highlands, particularly in western Sumatra, were one of the most densely populated areas in pre-colonial times (see Map 2.3).

2.5. Memories in Stone: Council Meeting Places and Burial Sites

Most of the early settlements in Tanah Datar were on hilltops. Some of these pre-colonial settlements have been abandoned but others are still occupied. Various ancient settlements are marked by stones signifying the location of meeting places and burial sites.

Council Meeting Places

The founding myth, which concerns a quarrel between Datuk Ketemanggungan and Datuk Perpatih Nan Sebatang for leadership, features on a stone monument (55 × 45 × 20 cm) at Batu Batikam, literally the pierced stone (see Figure 2.32). According to the legend, Datuk Perpatih Nan Sabatang used his mythical kris to make a hole in the stone that remains visible today (Taufik Abdullah 1972, pp. 185–88). The unworked stone is

FIGURE 2.32

The pierced stone at Batu Batikam near Pagaruyung that has allegedly been pierced with a mythical kris

found on a slope at a height of 633 m, only 3 km from Kuburajo. The hole might symbolize fertility but it could simply have been functional, allowing the stone to be carried more easily (Schnitger 1964, p. 172; de Casparis 1980, pp. 8–9). The stone mainly serves as monument of the Minangkabau orthogenesis. It is located in the centre of three open squares used for council meetings (locally called *medan nan bapane* or *balai-balai*). The rectangular squares are bordered by an alignment of stones; for example, the central square is surrounded on each side by 23 stone seats (see Figure 2.33). The upright stones are irregular in

FIGURE 2.33

Stone seats for council meetings at Batu Batikam near Pagaruyung

shape, but the ground is neatly paved. The two other squares are slightly larger, creating additional open space. Including the graves in the western section, the meeting space covers an area of 1,800 m². The branches of old Waringin trees arch over the squares, providing shade.

At Balimbing, in Rambatan district, another square marked by erected stones provides a reminder of a former space for communal meetings in the village centre. It was designed for the clan gatherings of three lineage groups: the Sumabur, Kampai, and Bodi. A recently refurbished community house is on the northern side of the square, and five stone platforms at its southern side mark the burial site of Sumabur members, whose status was higher than members of the other two clans, who were buried outside the village.

In the mountain village of Pariangan, a large, 629 m² stone structure connects the burial site with the communal meeting ground, creating a unique installation. Two layers of stone form a rectangular platform on which stones with a curved upper part are installed, representing a long grave according to local tradition. Eight stone seats flank the northern side. On the southern side, another grave mound with three stones is linked to Datuk Tantejo Gerhano, an honoured builder who is probably buried here.

Open stone spaces for council meetings are examples of communal architecture within the habitation core.[74] The shorter sides are reserved for communal features used to honour members of the community, such as stone seats or graves for distinguished figures, a council building or a symbolic marker of the Minangkabau ethnogenesis. The varying dimensions of these ancient spaces make it possible to estimate communal needs. Village affairs were decided by a council of male lineage heads who represented their respective matrilineal kinship groups (*suku*). Although village heads from the original settler lineages were accorded a higher status and were more influential, decisions were made by consensus.

Burial Sites

Collective inhumation cemeteries are part of the ancient landscape of Tanah Datar. The largest burial ground, at Simawang in Kota Gedang in the district of Rambatan, is 2,550 m². It contains 237 mostly unshaped stones of various sizes and shapes, which may imply status distinctions. The largest of the stones found at the mountain peak is 210 cm long and 65 cm wide. The megaliths are spread across a mountain ridge 550 m high that overlooks Lake Singkarak to the southwest. It probably represents a burial site of prehistoric or at least pre-1400 century, but no exact dating is available for this site (see Figure 2.34). No settlement which can be connected to this burial site has yet been discovered, and it might have served a dispersed, maybe still sedentary community as a collective cemetery. A common place for burials would have strengthened social bonds among individuals, families, and lineages who considered the region as their original home, and would explain why the site occupies a dominant position in the landscape. It establishes a permanent link between the community, their ancestral dead, and the land they claimed. The unshaped stones are ambiguously oriented towards the

FIGURE 2.34

Simawang, the largest burial ground in Tanah Datar, contains 237 stones of various sizes and shapes

west/northwest, which could either be to face Mount Merapi in a pre-Islamic burial tradition, or to face Mecca after Islamization. The BPCP's heritage inventory in 2002 vaguely suggests that the site may date to the pre-Islamic era, post-dating the eighteenth century. Although the earliest conversions to Islam were connected with the court in the late fourteenth century, when it was claimed that one of the three Minangkabau kings had converted to Islam almost fifteen years prior to 1512 (Pires 1944, p. 164), Islam only spread throughout the population in the eighteenth century.

An excavation at one of the early burial sites at Gunung Bungsu in the Batipun Selatan district produced no evidence of Islamic transformation, indicating that the site predates the eighteenth century (Marsis Sutopo and Bagyo Prasetyo 1994). Within an area of 1,250 m², 273 stones are erected next to the earth graves. The graves are orientated in a north-south direction with the heads directed towards Mount Merapi in the north. The bodies are laid in a supine position. However, the head of one of the bodies was turned towards the west, with one arm folded to the crotch and straight legs, while another was found with crossed legs. Earthenware sherds, among them carinated vessels with handles, point to the performance of burial rituals at the site. The fact that no burial goods accompanied the inhumation and the similar dimensions of the undecorated and knee-high stones suggests an unstratified society. The excavated three burials, though small in numbers, support the conclusion that burying the dead was not pursued in a standardized way.

Survey finds from two settlement-based burial grounds at *Makam Tuan Kadhi*[75] and Ladang Rajo in the Emas district between Batusangkar and Pagaruyung attest to continuous use of the sites from as early as the fourteenth century until the nineteenth century without any apparent Islamic influence. At Ladang Rajo unshaped stones were erected next to those with a curved upper part and column-like stelae with rounded tops like a head cover. Surface finds from Ladang Rajo included sherds of small celadon bowls dating to the thirteenth or fourteenth century, some with floral incisions in the fond and others with chrysanthemum on the interior and petals on the exterior wall,[76] in addition to blue-and-white ware with floral painting from the late Ming or Ching dynasty. The latter is from 1644–1912 (see Colour plate 1: F–G).

Collective burials in the settlements continued after the eighteenth century, but the graveyards shifted to sites in walled compounds. People were buried in lined graves pointing towards Mecca beneath low stone mounds, sometimes in individual graves and sometimes collectively. The grave mounds were marked by two upright stones placed at the head and the feet of the deceased. Despite these changes, the tradition of burials that were marked with two small, pointed, and unworked stones remained unaltered from earlier times. More elaborate graves featured a larger stone at one end that was often with a curved upper part, and a smaller, undecorated stone at the other. These two stone types can be seen at the large, 1,400 m² burial ground called *Makam Tuanku Idomo*, which is reserved for the *Idomo* lineage, the royal family of Saruaso (see Figure 2.13). Later gravestones become more figurative, featuring easily identifiable status-symbols such as pillars crowned by a turban-like head-cover with a kris in low-relief as part of the pillar. This iconography was employed for dignities holding the title of *daduk*. Examples of this may be seen in another graveyard in Saruaso, which was designated for leading figures elected by the clans of Padang Ganting, Sungai Tarab, and Sumani. The type of burial does not seem to have been affected by the sex of the individual.[77]

Miksic (2004, p. 203) speculated that erecting megaliths increased during the time of Adityavarman, and that they overlapped with the inscriptions. New archaeological material (see pp. 96–102) and evidence from the excavation of the burial ground (see pp. 102–27) support this hypothesis. These permanent structures were also supported by socio-cultural changes introduced by Adityavarman. The commemoration of ancestors within the settlement and the differentiation of burials by status suggest that hereditary status was an important factor in the formation of communal leadership and organization. However, communal space was not evaluated along a social hierarchy alone. Egalitarian principles contributed to the socio-political organization of Minangkabau villages and structured their spatial arrangements during the early modern period. How much autonomy a village democracy had, cannot be determined for the early period of the Minangkabau kingdom, but there is epigraphical and archaeological evidence of Adityavarman's legacy acknowledging communal articulation.

NOTES

1. De Casparis (1989; 1992); Andaya (2008, p. 59) contra Miksic (2015, p. 31).
2. Hill (1960, pp. 171, 207); Sjafiroeddin (1974, pp. 32–33) mentions a Javanese army.
3. Both traditions, also interpreted as federations or political parties, still coexist today (Taufik Abdullah 1972, pp. 185–86; Sjafiroeddin 1974, pp. 51–56; Dobbin 1975, p. 84).
4. Sjafiroeddin (1974, p. 51) assumes that Adityavarman married the youngest sister of Datuk Perpatih Nan Sebatang.
5. A sword and a kris called Carabun, which is decorated with mirrored bands of scrolls, also belong to the king of Pagaruyung. Its anthropomorphic hilt illustrated in Bosch (1931, pl. 46, 49*b*, *d*) has been lost.
6. Satyawati Suleiman (1977, p. 4) characterizes the costume as a "pubic tassel in the form of a sickle". For Bosch (1931, p. 212), it is a pair of trousers.
7. Some attributes are much too small and not precisely rendered to recognize them so that I got the impression that they were more or less interpreted

along analogy, e.g. the object in their left hand is seen as skull, bowl, or skull-bowl, his right hand holds a *vajra* or a weapon with a *vajra* handle (Satyawati Suleiman 1977, p. 4; Reichle 2007, pp. 6–8; Bautze-Picron 2014, p. 114, ft. 34), to the garland are attached bells or heads (Bosch 1931, p. 212; Bautze-Picron 2014, p. 115, ft. 41).

8. See Damais (1960, p. 282, figure 17); Reichle (2007, p. 207, ft. 106). A dagger with a similarly shaped blade appears on a panel of the fifteenth-century Sukuh temple on Java.
9. Cf. later periods in India (Bautze-Picron 2014, p. 115, ft. 44) or a kris from Cirebon/Java of 1850 that depicts scenes from the Mahabharata (Brinkgreve et al. 2010, p. 135, no. 60).
10. The total suggested by scholars varies. This number is from Arlo Griffiths, personal communication, March/April 2011.
11. According to a typescript "Adityavarman and Jambi" by de Casparis, available at the Kern Institute in Leiden. See also de Casparis (1992, pp. 928–29).
12. The English translation of Bosch's article of 1921 is provided by Kozok and van Reijn (2010, pp. 139–43).
13. Miksic (2015, pp. 32–34) resumes up the discussion of the Dutch scholars Bosch and Kern.
14. It was already in contact with downstream centres as early as the seventh or eighth century (Manguin 2009, pp. 450–51).
15. At Rambatan (also called Bukit Braholo) brick structures were excavated in 2006 (BPPP 2006).
16. Two excavation campaigns at the temple of Pulau Sawah II uncovered Chinese greenware and blue-and-white sherds from the twelfth to the sixteenth centuries (Marsis Sutopo 1996–97; Budi Istiawan and Tegu Hidayat 2001, figures 43, 45, 46).
17. Andaya (2008, p. 89) has wrongly assumed that the statue was transported to Saruaso. It was moved to the Museum Nasional Indonesia, Jakarta (inv. no. 6469).
18. This was after the English translation of Kern (1907) in Kozok and van Reijn (2010, pp. 149, 153).
19. I have chosen the reference names of the inscriptions in Tanah Datar according to the places they were originally found and not their present locations.
20. Namely, the Gudam II inscription (also called Pagaruyung VII), Bukit Gombak I inscription (also called Pagaruyung I), and Bukit Gombak II inscription (also called Pagaruyung II). See Budi Istiawan (2006, pp. 3–11, 19–22).
21. See historic images of the site (National Archive of Indonesia, image code OD-7584–6). The statue is now located in the Museum Nasional Indonesia (inv. no. 6470).
22. De Casparis' assumption (1992, p. 239) that the statue was commissioned by Adityavarman's predecessor Akarendravarman has not been taken up by other scholars (such as Reichle 2007, pp. 166–209; Lunsingh Scheurleer 2008, p. 295).

23. Among them are Dvarapala, guardian figures found in the Sumatran highlands in Padang Lawas that date from the ninth to the thirteenth centuries (Reichle 2007, figures 5.10, 5.20; Perret 2014, pp. 46–55). A locally-made relief on a megalith with iconic references to a Dvarapala was found in the Jambi highlands, dating from the twelfth to the fourteenth centuries (Tjoa-Bonatz 2009, pp. 202–3).
24. Fontein (1990, p. 167); Hedi Hinzler cited in Eggebrecht and Eggebrecht (1995, cat. no. 105); Reichle (2007, p. 250, ft. 25); Miksic (2016, p. 268).
25. Personal communication, 1 December 2016.
26. See the Chinese records in Wolters (1970, pp. 37–38, 57–58, 75). However, these records deal with a time long after Adityavarman had moved to Tanah Datar. Similarly, the assumption that he was on Bali is based on mistaken correlations, but is still cited in Sjarifoedin (2011, pp. 184, 186).
27. It is a "supralocal form of Old Malay" (Griffiths 2014, p. 239).
28. See the translation of the short Kapalo Bukit Gombak II inscription (also called Pagaruyung III) in Griffiths (2012, pp. 2–5).
29. Cf. the Saruaso I or Bukit Gombak I inscriptions (full reference list in Bambang Budi Utomo 2007, pp. 64–65, 78–79).
30. Two Sanskrit inscriptions in the regency of Pasaman, in northwest Sumatra, are outside the regional scope of this chapter and are therefore not considered: one from Tanjung Medan (Museum Nasional Indonesia, inv. no. MN1 7851) and the in-situ one at Lubuk Layang (Setianingsih 2005; Bambang Budi Utomo 2007, p. 84; Griffiths 2014, pp. 221–22, ft. 40, p. 236, ft. 125). The inscription of Lubuk Layang does not mention Adityavarman but is crucial in the interpretation of a possible successor called Bijayandrawarman. See the discussion in Hunter (2015, pp. 324–28).
31. Including a small cube also called Pagaruyung V, which is the fourth erected stone from the left of Figure 2.5, two fragments from Ponggongan, stored at the BPCP in Batusangkar (inv. nos. 213/BCB/A/12, 003 (1977) = 214 (2008)), the stone in situ and the mortar (see Figures 2.16, 2.20). Krom (1912, p. 44, no. 34) mentions an incised stone with a geometric motif from Ponggongan that was sent to the Batavia Museum but is not recorded in the Museum Nasional Indonesia in Jakarta.
32. Krom (1912, pp. 41–45); locals remember that one inscription originated from Saliawak at the confluence where the stream Simbodi flows into the Selo and another one from the river Cintingi south of the Bantang Malanga before it flows into the Selo. Investigating these sites, neither archaeological remains nor potential settlement sites were found.
33. These are the inscriptions of Gudam I, Bukit Gombak II, Kubarajo I and II, Rambatan, Saruaso II, and a fragment stored at BPCP Batusangkar (inv. no. 003 (1977) = 214 (2008)); full references of the first six stones in Bambang Budi Utomo (2007, pp. 58–60, 66, 77, 81–82).
34. Cf. Roth (1986, p. 250, pl. no. 1).

35. The actual size is not known because the statue is embedded in concrete.
36. More literature in Bambang Utomo (2007, pp. 67–68, 71).
37. According to a typescript by de Casparis, available at the Kern Institute in Leiden.
38. Ibid.; Bambang Budi Utomo (2007, p. 56); Arlo Griffiths, personal communication, 21 May 2012.
39. The fourteenth-century Tanjung Tanah manuscript from Kerinci first mentions using rice to pay debts, which underlines the dominant position of rice in the highlands during that period of time (Kozok and Waruno Mahdi 2015, p. 101).
40. Miksic (1987, figure 9; personal communication, 14 July 2016) refers to the interpretation made by Satyawati Suleiman (1977, p. 3, pl. 5) that the figure may represent Awalokiteswara.
41. Marijke Klokke, personal communication, 16 September 2016; Gauri Krishnan, personal communication, 9 September 2016. I am also thankful for additional stylistic remarks by Wibke Lobo and Lydia Kieven.
42. This is based on the reading of the chronogram and other dating elements (according to a typescript by de Casparis, available at the Kern Institute in Leiden; Kern 1917*b*, p. 261). Others have suggested 1375 (e.g., Budi Istiawan 2006, pp. 26–28; Hunter 2015, p. 306) and de Casparis also mentioned 1370 (?).
43. Such as de Casparis in a typescript, available at the Kern Institute in Leiden; Budi Istiawan (2006, pp. 29–32); Hunter (2015, p. 325).
44. The shapes of the inscriptions Kuburajo I, Bukit Gombak I, and Ponggongan I are similar.
45. According to a typescript by de Casparis, available at the Kern Institute in Leiden.
46. By 1890–1910, it was no longer part of a habitation setting; see the photo of the National Archive of Indonesia, image code OD-1642.
47. The date is proposed by Arlo Griffiths, personal communication, March/April 2011. The chronogram has been differently read as 1315 or 1316, which is far from the horizon of Adityavarman (de Casparis 1989, p. 927; typescript by de Casparis, available at the Kern Institute in Leiden), and 1368 (Budi Istiawan 2006, pp. 23–24).
48. Yuwono Sudibyo (1996–97); cf. five mortars stored at the BPCP Museum in Batusangkar (no inventory numbers except for one: inv. no. 217/BCEB-B/A/12/e/II/2008). In comparable flat stones used to crush rocks at gold working sites, the depression is shallower and wider than those of mortars for foodstuffs (Sartono 1984, figure 1; Miksic 1988, figure on p. 10).
49. This denotes the area that belongs to Raja Alam, also called Batu Patah or Batu Ampil, one member of the Minangkabau triumvirate (Josselin de Jong 1951, p. 101). The place name is also found on the map from 1887–92 (see Map 2.3).

50. According to a typescript by de Casparis, available at the Kern Institute in Leiden.
51. Ibid.
52. Ibid.
53. The stone was moved to Pagaruyung along with the other inscriptions from Bukit Gombak, Kepala Bukit Gombak, and Gudam documented on the historic photo of the National Archive of Indonesia (image code OD 1639).
54. The lower third of the stone broke after 1953 (compare the photo of 1890–1910 in the KITLV Leiden, image code DP 20198). The bottom right section of the stone, including the last line of the inscription, flaked off later, either in 1991, when the site was refurbished by the Batusangkar conservation office, or in 1988 during an attempt to steal the artefact (*Pelita*, 19 July 1988, p. 7).
55. Kern is uncertain whether the name in the inscription refers to Adityavarman's father or to Adityavarman himself (see the English translation given by Kozok and van Reijn 2010, p. 156). Later scholars have tended to conclude that he was the father or at least "the founding father" (Satyawati Suleiman 1977, p. 5; Budi Istiawan 2014, p. 34; Miksic 2015, p. 39).
56. The same motif is used as a central decoration on grave markers at Batu Giriang-Girian in the Akabiluru district. Spirals covering the surface of similar stones, for instance at Koto Gadang and Balai-Balai Batu (Miksic 1987, pp. 29, 31), can be traced back to prehistory and are present on several megaliths at Balubus in the district of Guguk Ninang, a site dated to 970±120 CE (Triwurjani 2010, p. 108). Spirals also outline the stones with a curved upper part at Kototinggi in the Suliki Gunung Emas district or at Lareh Kuning in the Harau district.
57. There are figurative meanings connected to plants which are particular Minangkabau expressions, e.g., a stake for a betel plant which means a "person serving as host" (Waruno Mahdi 2015, p. 214).
58. Brigitte Majlis (personal communication, July 2015) kindly provided woven comparisons and drew my attention to wooden thrones, which are only preserved from later periods.
59. References in Kozok and van Reijn (2010, p. 154, ft. 87).
60. According to a typescript by de Casparis, available at the Kern Institute in Leiden.
61. Arlo Griffiths, personal communication, March/April 2011.
62. Ibid., see also Krom (1912, p. 41, no. 17).
63. The others are covered by a protective roof and set in newly made foundations by the BPCP Batusangkar; their original placement may have been altered.
64. Today the inscription faces the lake but this might not be the original orientation. In 1818 the stone was lying among other rocks along the shore, within the reach of the water (Reid 1995, p. 174). In a photo taken in 1890–1910, the shorter side of the stone is vertical, which means that the script was not

written horizontally and standing upside down (National Archive of Indonesia: image codes DP 20217, DP 20218).
65. Krom (1912, p. 47, no. 42). Arlo Griffiths, personal communication, March/April 2011.
66. Arlo Griffiths, personal communication, March/April 2011.
67. Arlo Griffiths, personal communication, 6 December 2016.
68. This dating is proposed due to the small number of excavated Chinese sherds. However, it cannot be ruled out that the site could be older but no ceramics from this period were found.
69. John Miksic (personal communication, 27 March 2012) provided this convincing interpretation. Today, these vessels are still produced in the region and are pinched on one side to facilitate pouring.
70. Ed Edwards McKinnon, personal communication, 20 January 2013.
71. Cf. bowls dated to 1821 (Nagel Auctions: Tek Sing Treasures 2000, pp. 226–29).
72. Cf. pre-colonial tools for grinding gold ore in Bengkulu (Miksic 1989*b*, figure on p. 31).
73. Dalboquerque (1963 [1518], vol. III, pp. 142, 161); van der Meulen (1974, p. 13, ft. 45) citing João de Barros from the year 1560.
74. Photos of 1890–1910 in Tegu Hidayat et al. (2010: image codes DP 20202, DP 20203, DP 20204, DP 20205, DP 20206, DP 202159).
75. The name of the gravesite can probably be connected to Tuan Gadis, a virgin queen of the Minangkabau. Raffles (1991, p. 359) met her in 1818.
76. Cf. a Longquan bowl from the thirteenth or fourteenth century (Dupoizat 2009, pl. 9.6b).
77. Local residents reported that the same type of gravestone was used for both sexes at the *Makam Tuanku Indomo* at Saruaso.

3

EXCAVATIONS

Dominik Bonatz

3.1. The Prehistoric Settlement Site of Tanah Lua (*Dominik Bonatz*)

During the archaeological survey carried out in 2011, numerous sherds of pottery, a polished stone axe, and other stone objects were found on a slope below Pagaruyung overlooking the Selo River valley, an area that had been terraced shortly before the time of the survey (see Figure 3.1). The coarse construction of the pottery and the discovery of an axe suggested that the site was older than those at Bukit Gombak and Bukit Kincir. It faces Bukit Gombak, which stands beyond the narrow riverbed of the Selo River, and its prominent location helped attract archaeological interest (see Figure 3.2). Only 50 m below the site, a spring called Bapahat flows out of a cliff that rises steeply over the river (see Figure 2.12), and for this reason the area is called Tanah Lua, "Land of the Spring".

In 2012, excavations began in an 8 × 12 m area (Trench A) on a natural terrace (see Figure 3.2). To the east, the area was bordered by the rising slope. To the west there was a sharp drop off where the ground had been terraced. Objects collected here in 2011 had been found in

FIGURE 3.1

The prehistoric site of Tanah Lua

FIGURE 3.2

Aerial view of the prehistoric excavation site of Tanah Lua

Trench A appears in the left (north), Trenches B–F in the right (south) of the excavation area. In the foreground runs a modern channel, which seems to follow the path of the ancient irrigation system mentioned in the nearby Batu Bapahat inscription.

a dark layer of earth beneath more recent layers of humus. The layers are clearly visible in the eastern profile section of the terrace wall. The excavations in Trench A were intended to provide information about how far this older cultural layer continued, and whether it contained further finds and traces of settlement activities.

The excavations confirmed the order of the natural deposits seen in the large profile section of the terrace wall. After a dark, black humus layer 15–20 cm thick was a compact, reddish-brown, clay-like layer of earth. After 1 m the clay layer changed to yellowish-brown, sandy, and very compact dirt. There was little to find in the humus layer, while the layer of earth beneath it yielded only a few sherds of very rough ceramic and a small number of obsidian flakes found in the southern area of the trench. No anthropogenic traces were observed. These meagre results led us to shift our investigation to the southern part of the natural terrace, where there had been no modern disturbances (see Figure 3.2). After clearing the thick vegetation, we laid out five new excavation squares in a row, each measuring 2 × 2 m (Trenches B–F). Trenches C and D as well as Trenches E and F were combined during the excavations by removing 1 m wide strip of ground between them. All five trenches together covered a total area of 116 m², and excavated 44 m³ of material (see Table 1.1). Although a settlement site was discovered around the southwest corner of the area, the trenches could not be extended as further excavation was blocked by trees and thick underbrush. Estimating the total area of the natural terrace and taking into account the section to the northwest destroyed by modern terracing, the area of the settlement was roughly 4,000 m².

The clay layer was excavated in three artificial excavation layers in order to document any increases or decreases in the number of artefacts (C-0002, -0003, -0004). The amount of pottery discovered increased below the humus layer (C-0001) before decreasing in the lowest earth layer (C-0004). The sherds of coarse pottery collected across all the trenches presented a uniform picture both in typology and wares (see Figures 4.1, 4.10. A–C). A total of 89 sherds were collected. The pottery is brittle and red, a rough fabric with a large quantity of relatively big white inclusions used as temper. The pottery that was collected mainly consisted of jars with everted rims, among which a thick-walled wide mouth jar had the greatest diameter of around 50 cm.

TABLE 3.1
^{14}C-dating and TL-dating for Bukit Gombak (BG; Trenches A–D, M), the Settlement Site (Trenches O, P, R), and Burial Site (Trenches G, L) on Bukit Kincir (BK), and Tanah Lua (TL)

Lab. No. (MAMS)	Site	Trench	^{14}C-sample	TL-sample	Age (Cal 1 Sigma 1)	Age (Cal 2 Sigma 2)
13928	BG	A	BG-0010	–	cal AD 1418–1434	cal AD 1410–1440
13919	BG	A	BG-0013	–	cal BC 748–428	cal BC 753–415
13917	BG	B	BG-0512	–	cal AD 1451–1608	cal AD 1446–1617
113208	BG	B	–	BG-0526	930±110/350 BP	–
13927	BG	C	BG-1023	–	cal AD 1413–1429	cal AD 1405–1438
13922	BG	C	BG-0093	–	cal AD 1665–1950	cal AD 1662–1951
13923	BG	C	BG-0067	–	cal AD 1407–1425	cal AD 1330–1436
13924	BG	C	BG-0069	–	cal AD 1643–1661	cal AD 1529–1795
13925	BG	C	BG-0078	–	cal AD 1643–1661	cal AD 1529–1796
15657	BG	M	BG-0305	–	cal AD 1416–1433	cal AD 1408–1440
15666	BK	O	BG-0738	–	cal AD 1662–1950	cal AD 1653–1951
122967	BK	O	–	BG-0732	1090±600 BP	–
15656	BK	P	BG-0658	–	cal AD 1452–1613	cal AD 1446–1620
15655	BK	R	BG-1360	–	cal AD 1650–1793	cal AD 1644–1950
13918	BK	G	BG-1209	–	cal BC 1876–1741	cal BC 1883–1693
15654	BK	L	BG-0222	–	cal AD 1190–1252	cal AD 1170–1258
122965	BK	L	–	BG-0265	200±65 BP	–
122971	BK	L	–	BG-0269	470±200/460±70 BP	–
15658	TL	C	BG-0760	–	cal BC 762–553	cal BC 774–539

Note: Very early TL-date and the three early ^{14}C-dates do not seem applicable.

A few thin-walled, open vessels were documented, including a beaker and some bowls. Some vessels were covered by a knobbed lid. The decoration on the pots is simple and generally consists of fine paddle and anvil marks or a slip. One slipped sherd features a pattern of parallel incisions. In addition, numerous obsidian debitage was found (see Figure 4.14: H–I) along with a retouched, bilateral, obsidian flake with damage to its proximal-medial edge (see Figure 4.14: I).[1]

In attempting to date the samples, thermoluminescence analysis yielded no results, but a single wood-charcoal sample from context C-0003 in Trench C provided a calibrated date of 762–553 BCE (Sigma 1) or 774–539 BCE (Sigma 2) (see Table 3.1). Thus, we were able to obtain an approximate age for the site that was in accord with the total absence of imported Chinese pottery and the presence of stone artefacts. The date also confirmed the working hypothesis that Tanah Lua was a prehistoric settlement, probably from the first millennium BCE. Unfortunately, no other traces of settlement activities were discovered.

The results match the findings from another prehistoric settlement in the highlands of Sumatra. Excavations at Bukit Arat, located in Serampas to the south of Lake Kerinci, brought to light simple earthenware sherds along with a large quantity of obsidian artefacts and flakes. Bukit Arat is thought to be an early settlement site from around 1400–900 BCE that specialized in obsidian working (Bonatz 2012, pp. 42–54). In contrast, the relatively small yield of obsidian around Tanah Lua makes it difficult to infer any craft specialization. Nonetheless, a parallel can still be drawn with Bukit Arat in relation to the character of the finds, especially in the manner of production. So far, they are the two earliest dated sites in the Sumatran highlands in which pottery has been recorded.

As explained in Chapter 1, no sites have been identified in Tanah Datar that predate Adityavarman. Therefore, the prehistoric site of Tanah Lua must be from the period when sedentarization began in the highlands. The concentration of finds at a single location and the use of pottery indicate that local groups settled here for periods of time but, as no traces of residential architecture such as postholes were found, it is unlikely that the site was a permanent settlement. Early subsistence in the highland rainforests was likely a form of swidden agriculture or shifting horticulture that primarily produced tubers such as taro or yam. This type of agriculture, which was linked to hunting and fishing, demanded a mobile existence that can still be found in the Sumatran highlands (Bonatz 2009, pp. 64–65). The area around Tanah Lua offers sufficient opportunities for wide-ranging horticulture through slash-and-burn practices and swidden agriculture. Furthermore, the location of the site above the river valley and near the spring is ideal for water provision, fishing, and observing and tracking game. The acidic soils of the region do not preserve bone, so it is not possible to draw any inferences based on osteology about early types of subsistence. The same is true for botanical remains, and the plant species that were used cannot be identified. Rice-growing, typical of the region today, would have developed significantly later.

The results yielded by the excavations in Tanah Lua confirm the presence of an early settlement group at the southern edge of the fertile highland plains of Tanah Datar. This group was active in an area where the first highland kingdom later took shape, and which constitutes the centre of the ethnic identity of the Minangkabau. The Minangkabau trace their origin to Gunung Merapi, which lies at the northern end of the high plains (see Chapter 2.1), and Tanah Lua does not feature in any origin myths. It does, however, reveal that later developments did not take place in a landscape devoid of people.

3.2. Adityavarman's Royal Centre? The Settlement Site on Bukit Gombak (*Dominik Bonatz*)

The twin hills of Bukit Gombak and Bukit Kincir cover an area of 29.51 ha at the base (see Map 3.1). The slopes of Bukit Kincir rise steeply from 350 m at the base to 430 m at the peak; Bukit Gombak is slightly shorter at 420 m. Only three core areas high up on these hills are suitable for settlements. The first potential settlement area is the largest plateau on Bukit Gombak. It covers an area of 5.13 ha and rises gently from east to west and from north to south (see Figures 3.3–3.4). To the west, a gap at 400 m separates Bukit Gombak from Bukit Kincir. The second potential settlement area is at the northwest crest of Bukit Kincir and has 1.7 ha of usable land. The third area is the steeply rising crest in the southeast and covers 0.99 ha. The following excavation trenches are grouped according to their locations from west to east.

3. Excavations

MAP 3.1

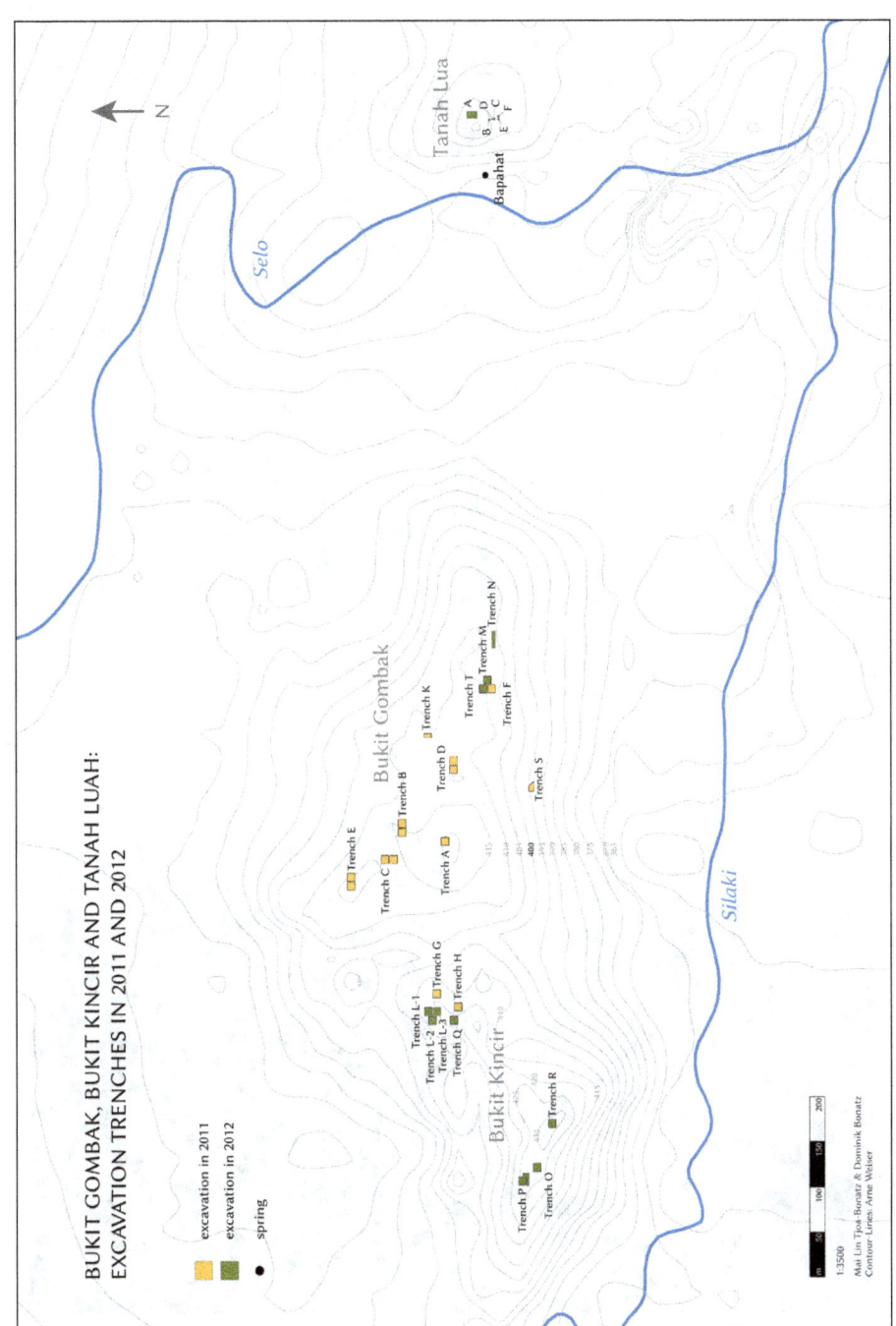

Topographical plan of Bukit Gombak, Bukit Kincir, and Tanah Lua showing the excavated areas in 2011 and 2012
Source: Mai Lin Tjoa-Bonatz, Dominik Bonatz; contour-lines: Arne Weiser.

FIGURE 3.3

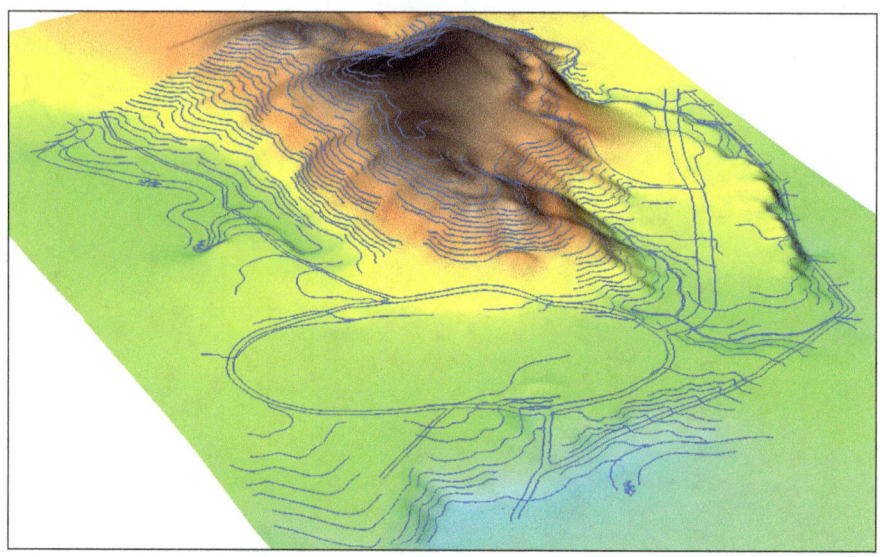

Digital elevation model of Bukit Gombak
Source: Manfred Tonch, Berlin.

FIGURE 3.4

Aerial view (from north to south) over the central plateau of Bukit Gombak and the southern slope of Bukit Kincir: in the foreground are the excavation trenches

Trench B

This east–west oriented trench lay at the northeastern edge of the Bukit Gombak settlement plateau on a gentle slope down to the east. It encompassed two squares with a total excavated area of 182 m^2 (see Figure 3.5). The western sections of both squares followed the sequence of layers typical of the entire settlement plateau. A thin surface layer 10–15 cm deep was followed by a humus layer, known as the cultural layer. In the eastern square this cultural layer reached a maximum depth of 70 cm before the next layer started. In the eastern square of the trial excavation C-0011, this unusually deep layer was closely investigated but no archaeological material was found.

In Trench B, the frequency of sherds and small finds in the surface layer was higher than in the cultural layer beneath it. Due to erosion, the material near the surface may have been transported down from the summit to this area on the slope and have been deposited here. Consequently,

FIGURE 3.5

Bukit Gombak: excavation of Trench C, in the background is Mount Merapi

when interpreting the find-distribution, post-depositional processes must be taken into account, and negatively affect the information on the settlement pattern. The ceramic assemblages contained considerable quantities of local earthenware, totalling 16.59 kg (see Figure 4.2: A, C, K; Figure 4.3: A, D, E, G; Figure 4.4: D, K–P; Figure 4.5: C; Figure 4.10: D, G–I; and Table 1.1), and sherds of Chinese blue-and-white ware from the late fifteenth or early sixteenth century, the middle Ming dynasty. A considerable number of small finds were also present, including iron nails, one bullet of a modern handgun, a clay tuyère from the surface layer (see Figure 4.7: B), a bronze or copper fragment, a perforated metal object from the surface layer, and other metal fragments (see Figure 4.20: B), a whetstone(?), a stone tool, five obsidian pieces including tools (see Figure 4.14: E), and a red glass bead (see Colour Plate 3: F). Two accumulations of pieces of iron slag in the eastern square, which may have been connected to iron smelting activities in the settlement area of Bukit Gombak (see Chapter 4.4), were of particular note. The clay tool was probably connected to ironworking as well (see Figure 4.7: B).

With regard to archaeological features and installations in this trench, the following observations were made: a large deposit around 2 m long and 1 m wide in the west half of the western square contained numerous brick fragments, which appear to have been from burnt mud bricks from an earlier date. The first cultural layer in the eastern square had two fire pits around 9 m apart that contained charcoal remains and burnt clay fragments (C-0005, C-0007). Three postholes of similar size (15 × 15 cm) were found in the southwest corner of the eastern square and in the southern part of the western square (C-0006, C-0010, C-0016), but their architectural relation if any could not be determined. ^{14}C-dating of a piece of charcoal (BG-0512) from the C-0006 posthole yielded a calibrated age of CE 1451–1608 (Sigma 1) or CE 1446–1617 (Sigma 2) (see Table 3.1). Thermoluminescence dating of a pottery sherd tempered with quartz and feldspar from context C-0004 yielded an age of 930±110/350 BP; thus the date of the sherd has a theoretically wide chronological range from the eighth to the fifteenth centuries.

Trench C

This north–south oriented trench lay in the middle of the northeastern spur of the plateau, south of Trench E and encompassed two squares covering 191 m² (see Figure 3.6). The 1 m wide strip ground between

FIGURE 3.6

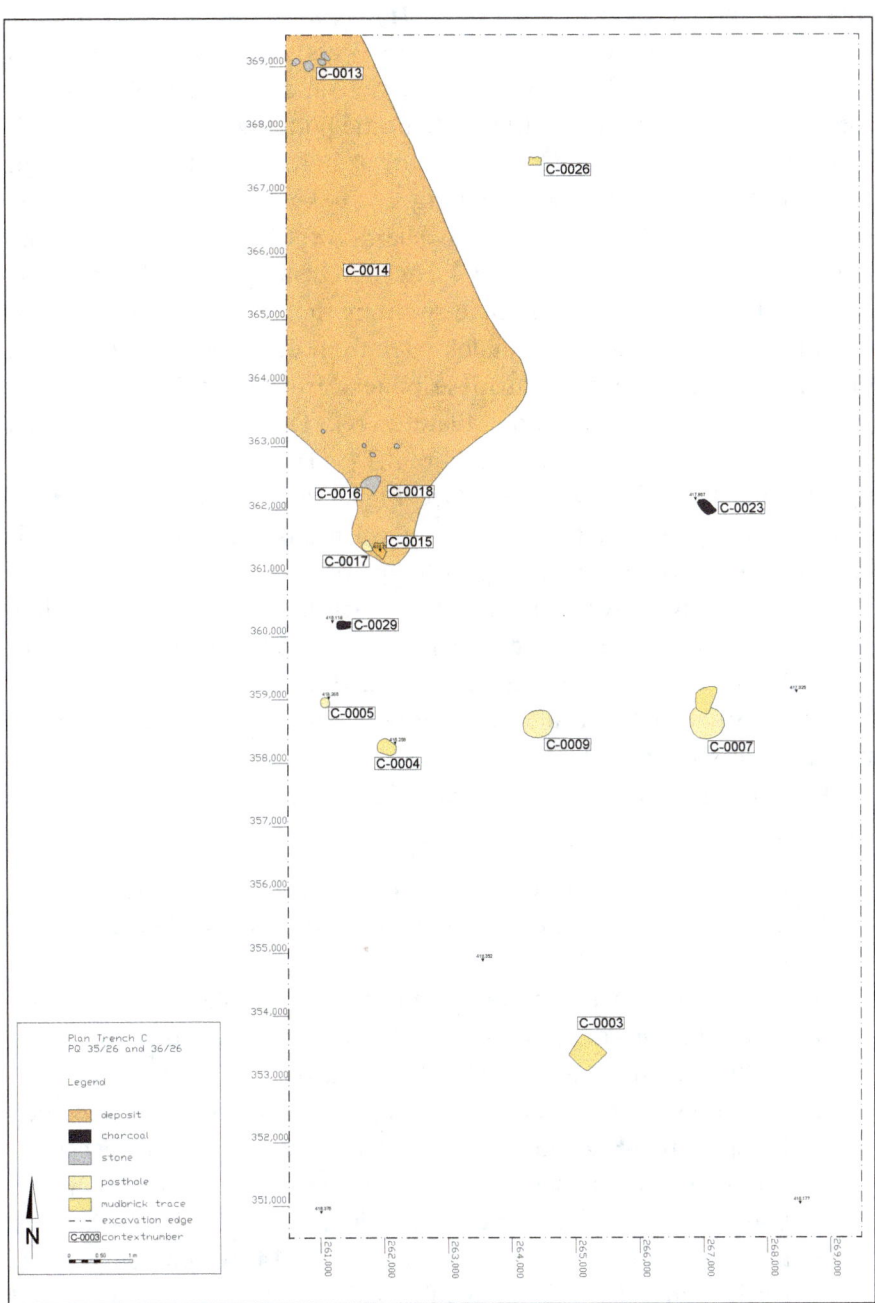

Bukit Gombak: excavation plan of Trench C

the two squares was removed during the excavation. Beneath the grass cover and surface layer of earth (C-0001) lay a continuous layer of dark humus up to 15 cm deep, cut through by roots and scattered with loam inclusions (C-0003). Both layers were rich in finds. The assemblages contained numerous sherds of local domestic pottery (e.g. see Figure 4.2: B, F, H–J; Figure 4.4: B–C, H–I; Figure 4.5: A, E, G, I–J; Figure 4.6: E, G–H; Figure 4.10: F, J) weighing 26.76 kg (see Table 1.1). They also contained middle Ming-period sherds of Chinese blue-and-white ware from the fifteenth or early sixteenth century (see Figure 4.11: B–C), a fragment of a celadon dish from the fourteenth or fifteenth centuries, incised Thai/Sawankhalok ware from the fifteenth century (see Colour Plate 1: C), and Vietnamese pottery from the fifteenth century (see Figure 4.13: F and Colour Plate 2: N). The small finds included seven obsidian flakes (see e.g., Figure 4.14: G), five stone objects (see e.g., Figure 4.16: C), two adzes (see Figure 4.15: D–E), a few metal objects (see Colour Plate 3: A, D), glass beads (see Colour Plate 3: E, G–I), modern coins, bullets, and lumps of iron slag.

The upper layers were excavated to reach the natural ground below C-0003 to check for possible installations buried deeper in the earth (C-0010, C-0024). This investigation yielded no results and both layers turned out to be without any debris (see west-section Trench C on the stratigraphic sequence, see Figure 3.7).

All notable archaeological features in this trench were observed in the C-0003 layer (see Figure 3.6):

1) a large circular posthole 0.55 m in diameter (C-0007) in the eastern part of the trench, and two small postholes in the western part (C-0005, C-0017);
2) a pit (C-0009) 1.5 m west of the large posthole;
3) concentrations of strongly eroded brick material in different areas of the trench (C-0003, C-0004, C-0026);
4) numerous scattered andesite river cobbles, which must have been brought up to Bukit Gombak from the valley and a large concentration of cobble stones was excavated in the northwest of trench C-0013; their function as tools or in construction is not known;
5) a deposit in the northwest of trench C-0014, which consisted of earth with a large amount of remains of both, burnt loam and carbonized wood.

3. Excavations

FIGURE 3.7

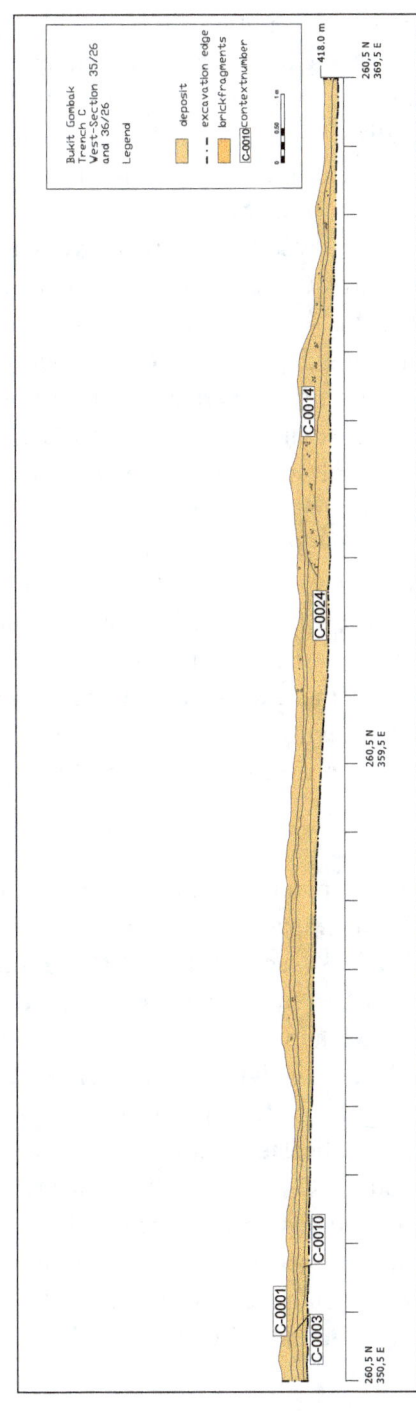

Bukit Gombak: excavation plan of the west-section of Trench C

Burnt loam remains were initially interpreted as tiny fragments of brick. However, observations in other areas of Bukit Gombak later revealed that these clay elements are embedded in the earth and had been baked to a grainy, light-reddish, brick-like material due to high temperatures caused by fire on the surface (large-scale firing is characteristic of this area). This fire was probably from ancient times, as ^{14}C-dating of a carbonized piece of wood (BG-1023) from the deposit C-0014 yielded a calibrated age of CE 1413–1429 (Sigma 1) or CE 1405–1438 (Sigma 2) (see Table 3.1). A collection of cobble stones associated with trench C-0013 cut into this deposit and could either be remains from the destruction caused by the fire or part of the firing process.

Before the trench was extended to the north, geomagnetic investigation detected a zone with a high number of anomalies (MF3, see pp. 18–20, Figures 1.4–1.5) that largely corresponded to the fire layer C-0014. This layer continued to the northwest into an area that was not excavated. The anomalies were created by the high magnetic resistance of andesite stones, eroded brick, and burnt clay material as well as concentrations of ferrous clastic material embedded in the ground through the area. The results of the excavation in the adjacent layer and the geomagnetic survey suggest that these concentrations of ferrous clastic material are anthropogenic iron prills and vitrified concretions.

Trench D

This east–west oriented trench lay in the centre of the ridge of the settlement plateau. It encompasses two excavation squares with a total excavated area of 182 m^2 (see Figure 3.8). The surface layer, which has been severely disturbed by ploughing, can be distinguished from a humus layer with a maximum depth of 30–40 cm. Most archaeological features in this trench cut through both layers. There were many postholes with diameters varying from 12–28 cm. The largest concentration of postholes was in the southeastern half of the eastern square (C-0004, C-0006, C-0008, C-0010, C-0012, C-0022, C-0025, C-0027, C-0029, C-0031, C-0042), with two postholes in the northwestern corner (C-0017, C-0019). A striking feature was a series of postholes that ran across the square diagonally from southwest to northeast. In the western square only two postholes were found (C-0036, C-0038).

3. Excavations
105

FIGURE 3.8

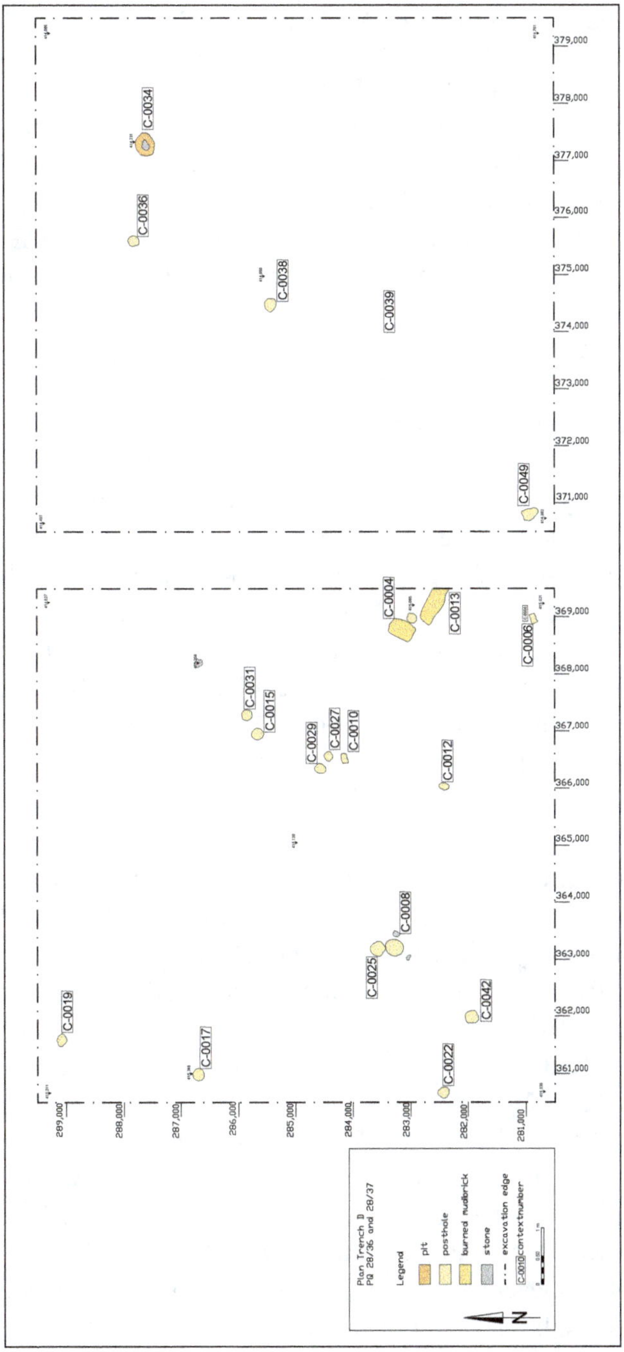

Bukit Gombak: excavation plan of Trench D

^{14}C-dating yielded the following ages for charcoal taken from four of the postholes: D-10, BG-0069: CE 1643–1661 (Sigma 1) or 1529–1795 (Sigma 2); D-19, BG-0078: CE 1643–1661 (Sigma 1) or 1529–1796 (Sigma 2); D-22, BG-0067: CE 1407–1425 (Sigma 1) or 1330–1436 (Sigma 2); D-25, BG-0093: CE 1665–1950 (Sigma 1) or CE 1662–1951 (Sigma 2) (see Table 3.1). Postholes D-10, D-19, and D-25 were only observed in the surface layer, which explains their more recent dates. Only D-22 corresponds to the earlier dating of the postholes in Trenches A and B.

The ceramic assemblages from contexts excavated over a wide area encompassed a broad spectrum of local earthenware and import wares from China, mainland Southeast Asia, and West Asia (see Figure 4.2: D; Figure 4.4: C; Figure 4.5: F; Figure 4.10: E; Colour Plate 1: D, I–J; Colour Plate 2: B, G, I–J). This group included monochromes and sherds of blue-and-white bowls and dishes from the Yuan and Ming period—particularly from the fifteenth and early sixteenth centuries (see Figure 4.12: B; Figure 4.13: B). The small finds included pieces of obsidian, fragments of unidentified iron tools, a metal chisel (see Figure 4.20: A), bronze tweezers (see Figure 4.20: C), an eighteenth-century coin from the Dutch colonial period, and three possible stone tools that may have been grindstones or whetstones.

Trench A

Trench A lay at the highest point in the centre of the settlement plateau and consisted of a single excavation square with an area of 81 m^2 (see Figure 3.9). The layers excavated contained relatively few archaeological finds. Apart from sherds of local domestic pottery, the ceramic assemblages included imported ware such as monochromes from the Yuan period and blue-and-white dishes from the Ming period (see Figure 4.11: A, D, E and Colour Plate 2: K), and a few small finds, including two grindstones and an obsidian tool (e.g., see Figure 4.14: C).

Two larger pits in the southern (C-0013) and northwestern (C-0023) parts of the square were filled with brownish and clayey, silty soil, pieces of charcoal, and a few potsherds. The pits may have been used for household activities. The numerous postholes in the area, which can only be detected in the lowest excavation layer through thin

3. Excavations 107

FIGURE 3.9

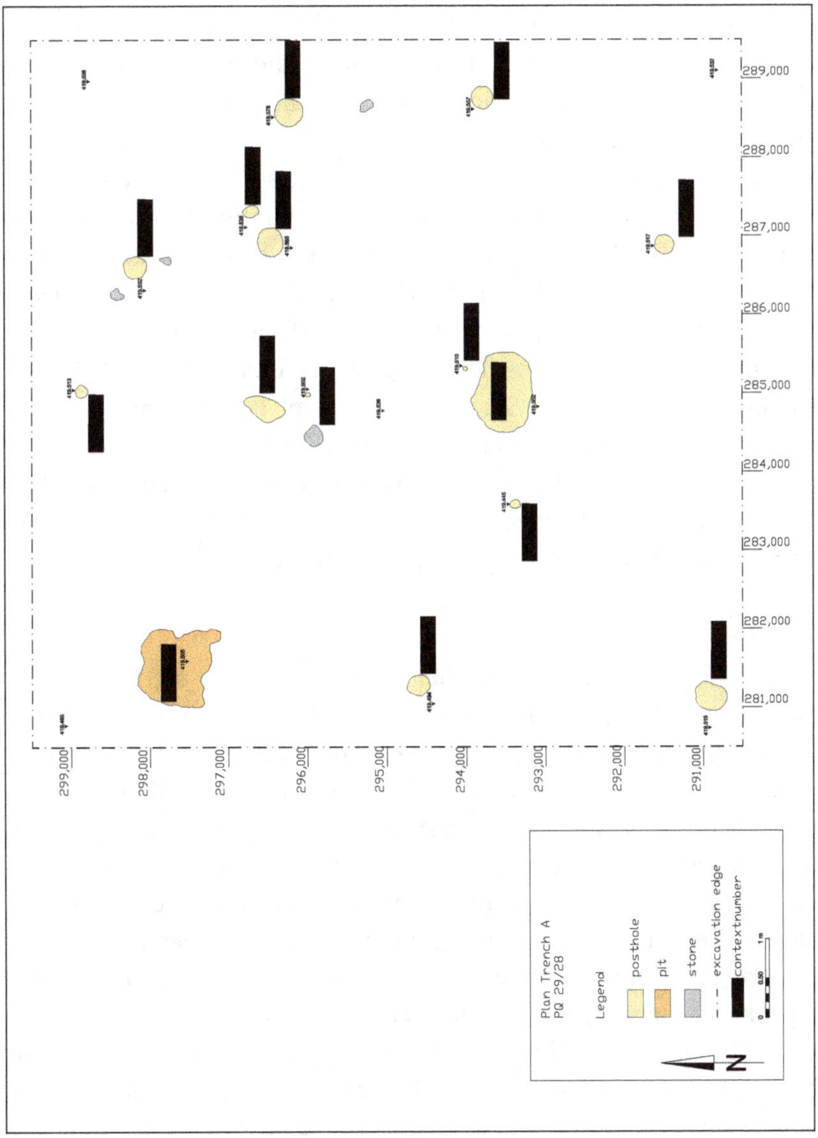

Bukit Gombak: excavation plan of Trench A

impressions in the ground, suggest that the houses were raised on stilts. The larger postholes had an average diameter of 30 cm (C-0007, C-0009, C-0011, C-0015, C-0019, C-0021) while the smaller ones measured between 12 and 20 cm (C-0017, C-0021, C-0026, C-0030, C-0031). Their distribution in the excavation square did not permit unambiguous inferences about building units, although the group of postholes in the northwest of the square (C-0007, C-0009, C-0011, C-0017, C-0021, C-0026) along with the posthole in the southwest (C-0017) could possibly trace the position of a single stilted house. ^{14}C-dating of a piece of charcoal (BG-0010) from C-0026 yielded a calibrated age of CE 1418–1434 (Sigma 1) or 1410–1440 (Sigma 2) (see Table 3.1). However, ^{14}C-dating a piece of charcoal (BG-0013) from C-0031 in the southern half of the squares gave the unexpectedly early age of BCE 748–428 (Sigma 1) or 753–415 (Sigma 2). It cannot be ruled out that charcoal remains from postholes could be intrusive, which means that they were not necessarily derived from burnt and carbonized wooden posts. However, if the charcoal was indeed derived from a post then it could indicate very early, albeit isolated, settlement activity at this spot.

Trench E

Trench E lay near the northeastern tip of the settlement plateau, encompassing two squares with an area of 162 m². In the eastern square on the right, however, only the surface layer was excavated. In the western square below the grass cover, a homogeneous context of humus earth with loam inclusions was unearthed in which only two anthropogenic traces could be documented (C-0002): a nearly right-angled posthole in the west of the square (C-0003) and a round, fired site with remains of charcoal and burnt loam in the southwest of the trench (C-0005). This meagre result matched the small number of objects found: some local domestic pottery from the surface context C-0001 and the humus context C-0002 beneath it, a bronze ring (see Figure 4.20: E), a bullet from a handgun, a copper weight (see Figure 4.20: F), a modern Indonesian coin from C-0001, a nail, and some obsidian fragments from contexts C-0001 and C-0002. The excavations reached a depth of 25 cm below the surface where the natural ground started.

Trench K

Trench K lay northeast of Trench D at the foot of the northern slope down Bukit Gombak. The 10 × 5 m trench, with a total excavated area of 36 m², was intended to investigate the archaeological find-situation at the northern edge of the settlement plateau. Except for two meagre collections of pottery (see Figure 4.4: B; Figure 4.5: I–K) and scattered modern finds (bullets, pieces of iron) from the surface layer and the humus layer beneath it, the excavation yielded no significant results for older periods and was therefore not continued.

Trench N

The excavation of Trench N was pursued under the direction and careful documentation of Lucas Partanda Koestro from the Balai Arkeologi Medan. This east–west oriented trench lay on the narrow eastern spur of the settlement plateau (see Figures 3.10–3.11). It consisted of two squares each measuring 10 × 5 m with a total excavated area of 72 m².

FIGURE 3.10

Bukit Gombak: excavation of Trench N at a paved street

FIGURE 3.11

Bukit Gombak: excavation plan of Trench N at a paved street

The archaeological material found in this trench was clearly influenced by modern construction immediately below the present-day surface. An artificially created track runs at a slight diagonal through the entire length of the trench. The bedding (C-0002) of the track consisted of small, thickly packed quarried river stones mixed with a large quantity of potsherds from local earthenware (see Figure 4.5: A, D). The edges of the track are bordered by a straight line of quarried stones. In the western square, two large andesite cobble stones cut into the northern edge of the track. Beneath the track the natural ground begins. Two lumps of iron slag were unearthed from under the track and in the area to the north of it.

According to local information, the track is 30 to 40 years old. It was built in the course of the agricultural reclamation of Bukit Gombak and led from the horse racecourse at the eastern foot of the hill up to the plateau. Some finds from the track bed were from this later period, such as glass of unknown date and batteries. However, older archaeological material, such as the large number of potsherds and tiny obsidian flakes, might have been introduced for the construction of the track.

Trench S (The Spring)

The site at the spring was rediscovered at the start of the 2011 excavation campaign (see p. 50). One of the local workers directed us to the location, which was hidden by trees and covered with thick bushes and foliage, on the steep southern slope roughly 200 m below Trench D on the settlement plateau. The area was defined as Trench S. Excavations were conducted in an area 11 × 6 m under the direction and careful documentation of Andri Restiyadi from the Balai Arkeologi Medan.

Due to the steep slope, it was necessary to remove the thick bushes and the erosion layers (C-0001, C-0004, C-0005), which reached a maximum of 1 m high, to reach bedrock and thus gain a clear picture of the spring's natural state along with any anthropogenic alterations (see Figures 3.12–3.14). Relatively few archaeological finds were retrieved from the earth deposited above the spring. Aside from a few sherds of local earthenware (see Figure 4.3: F, G), there were only four stone objects (see Figure 4.15: B; Figure 4.16: A; Figure 4.17: B). Among these objects, however, a particularly noteworthy find was a fully preserved,

FIGURE 3.12

Bukit Gombak: the water spring, Trench S

FIGURE 3.13

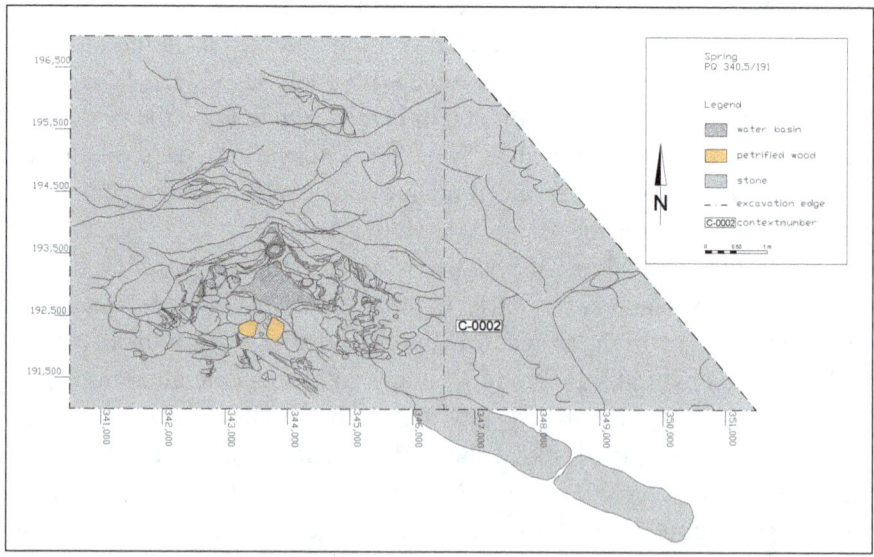

Bukit Gombak: excavation plan of the water spring, Trench S

FIGURE 3.14

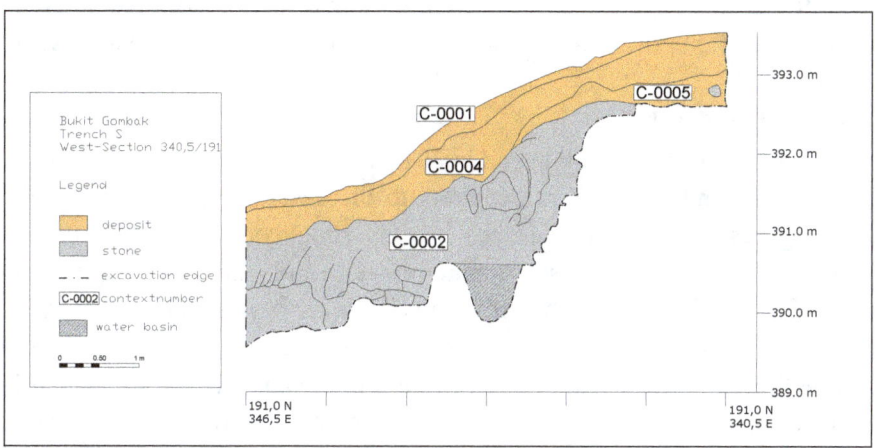

Bukit Gombak: excavation of the west-section of the water spring, Trench S

polished adze (see Figure 4.15: B). Its presence may indicate that ritual practices or a ritual deposition took place in the area around the spring (see p. 50).

The spring rises from a porous, sandstone-like, reddish rock. It is vertically stepped in several layers of stone and forms a concave depression 2.5 m deep (see Figure 3.14). The opening of the spring lies between the stone layers at the deepest point of the depression and water runs into a pool 1.10 × 0.90 m in size with a maximum depth of 0.70 m, from there over a barrage into a broad, shallow pool more than 1 m deep, and finally into a small stream that passes the southern foot of Bukit Gombak, 300 m away. The barrage after the first pool was manmade and consisted of three blocks of petrified wood. It acted as a dam to hold water in the spring-pool. Similar blocks of petrified wood were scattered around the lowest area of the spring and similar, smaller blocks were also found in the excavation area on the settlement plateau (e.g., in Trench D). Other anthropogenic features included small furrows at the edge of the pool, and the stone terraces at the eastern edge of the spring had been smoothed and deepened. If the spring was used as a bathing and washing site, these terraces would have been ideal for resting and sitting, and the furrows could have held washing utensils or offerings. The spring was the nearest and most convenient source of water for the settlement plateau.

The water flow today is limited and, assuming this was the case in the past, the spring may have had difficulty supporting a larger settlement. If so, restrictions on access to and use of the spring may have existed.

Trenches F, M, and T

The excavation of Trench F began in 2011 and was continued in 2012, with Trenches M and T added immediately to the east and north respectively (see Figures 3.15–3.16). The trenches lay roughly in the centre of the long eastern half of the settlement plateau, and encompassed a total area of 243 m². The find-bearing cultural layer was severely disturbed by agricultural activities and preserved to only 20 cm thick as a result. Below this layer, 20 postholes were found in the eastern half of Trench F (C-0005, C-0007) (see Figure 3.15). These postholes are probably related to two postholes found in Trench T (C-0007, C-0008), which adjoins to the north (see Figure 3.17). The postholes cut into the natural, clayey ground, which was otherwise devoid of finds. The diameter of the posts varied between 19 and 34 cm. The positions of the 20 postholes map out a rectangular ground plan for a building measuring 7.72 × 2.62 m, with two spans from west to east and seven to eight from north to south. On the shorter southern and northern sides of the building, a double pair of small postholes along the central, long axis of the building seemed unconnected to the other posts. Such stilt houses were a common type of dwelling in the nineteenth century (Tjoa-Bonatz 2013*a*, p. 150, figure 4; Tjoa-Bonatz 2013*b*, pp. 75–76, figure 12) but it is rare to find archaeological evidence of house plans of stilted architecture. The postholes found on Bukit Gombak may be the earliest traces of these houses to have been discovered. Another significant example found in the highlands was a 15.50 × 9.90 m stilted house reconstructed from 22 postholes discovered in Pondok in the Kerinci region. This house has been dated from the eleventh to the thirteenth centuries (Bonatz 2012, p. 60, figure 12; Tjoa-Bonatz 2013*b*, pp. 70–72, figures 6–7).

The stilted house on Bukit Gombak is bordered to the west by a wide area (C-0002, C-0004) filled with tufa, reddish sandstone, and occasionally andesite cobble stones. The ground is especially close to the natural rock, but the cobble stones must have been brought up from the valley to this spot. They may have been used as a platform for sitting or

FIGURE 3.15

Bukit Gombak: excavation of Trench F in 2011, groundplan of a house on stilts

FIGURE 3.16

Bukit Gombak: excavation of outdoor-hearths in Trench M

FIGURE 3.17

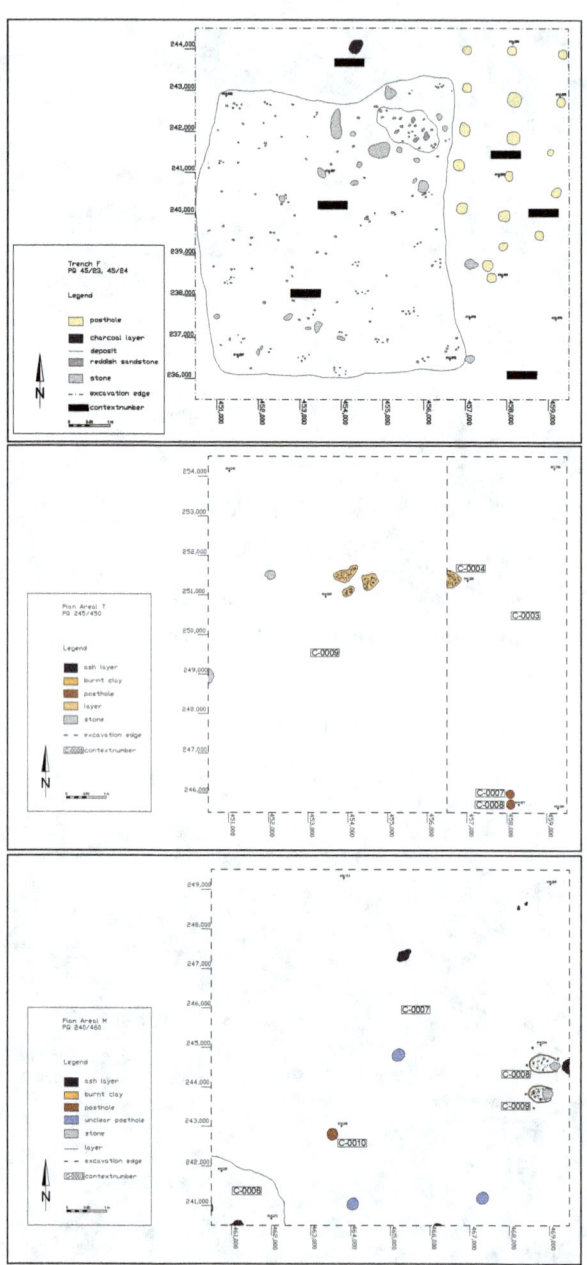

Bukit Gombak: excavation plan of Trenches F, M, and T in 2012, around the house on stilts

working, but it is unclear whether they were associated with the house. The same was true of the context C-0006 in the southwestern corner of Trench M, which consists of rocky-sandy material with ash remains and inclusions of volcanic material. It can be assumed that domestic activities such as cooking took place near the house because a high concentration of charcoal (C-0002) was documented 2.5 m west of the stilted house in Trench F. Two structures (C-0008, C-0009) at the eastern edge of Trench M may have been external stoves that were part of a domestic area (see Figure 3.16). The two structures included single, large stone, which would have served as a hob or stand of the stove. In front, an oval area with remains of burnt loam and brick was found. Behind the hob-stone of C-0008 a layer of ash might have originated from the stove. To the west beyond the stove, small holes in the soil were most likely intended for some form of structure serving as a shield against the prevailing western winds. Alternatively, they may have been left by a rack on which wood was dried to be used as fuel. This type of rack, locally called *selayan*, is common today.

Among the small finds in the three trenches were several pieces of obsidian tools and debris (see Figure 4.14: A–B, D), stone tools and other objects (see Figure 4.15: C; Figure 4.16: D), and a single metal lid (see Figure 4.20: D). The collections of local earthenware (see Figure 4.6: B) mainly included vessels for storage and cooking. A few noteworthy pieces among the Chinese imported pottery was a sherd of a moulded celadon dish (Longquan celadon) with a fish motif (see Colour Plate 1: A) from the thirteenth or fourteenth century and two sherds of Jingdezhen bowls with cobalt blue painting (see Colour Plate 2: C–D) from the mid-Ming period of the late fifteenth or early sixteenth century. A charcoal sample (BG-0305) from the deposit C-0005 near the stove installation yielded a calibrated ^{14}C-age of CE 1416–1433 (Sigma 1) or 1408–1440 (Sigma 2) (see Table 3.1).

Conclusion

The excavations on Bukit Gombak show that the area on the plateau, estimated at 1.7 ha, was intensively settled in the past. The spectrum of datable Chinese ceramics indicates a period from the fourteenth to the sixteenth centuries while radiocarbon dating of objects from Trenches

A–D and M indicates the fifteenth to seventeenth centuries. The main period of the settlement must fall within those dates, confirming the working hypothesis that the old settlement on Bukit Gombak is connected to the highland kingdom of Adityavarman. The settling of the site likely coincided with the beginning of his reign in the middle of the fourteenth century. The inscription on the Bukit Gombak I inscription indicates a date around 1356, although a small number of datable individual finds, such as a sherd from Trench B that was dated by thermoluminescence to the tenth or twelfth century, point to the possibility of earlier settlement activity at this location. A single charcoal sample from Trench A that was dated to around the sixth century BCE stands in sharp contrast to the bulk of datable finds and hence cannot be taken as proof of continuous settlement at Bukit Gombak.

The settlement process that began in the period of Adityavarman was very dynamic, affecting all areas off the settlement plateau including the neighbouring Bukit Kincir. Only in the extreme northwest (Trench E) and at the edge of the eastern slope (Trench K) was a notable decrease in the frequency of finds observed. Because the contexts cannot be related stratigraphically, the widely scattered finds and ground features, such as postholes, cannot be placed in a relative chronology. However, the distribution of the finds still allows some aspects of a functional-spatial division and social differentiation within the settlement to be identified.

Residential architecture, namely stilted constructions, is attested through the postholes found in the settlement areas of Trenches A, D, F, and T, although only the findings in Trench F/T permit the reconstruction of a nearly complete, 9 × 3 m house plan. Based on this, the houses on Bukit Gombak were not especially large. However, it is possible that a palace-like stilted building was located in one of the areas of the settlement that was not excavated, or archaeological traces of such a structure have not been preserved. The smaller stilted buildings indicated in various parts of the excavation area argue, nonetheless, for a large settlement area of unique dimensions for the precolonial history of the highlands.

Specialized craft skills in smelting and working iron were indicated by smelting residues, tools, and fired sites in Trenches B and N at the edge of the settlement. This confirms the presence of the iron craftsmanship typical of this highland region (see Chapter 4.4).

Imported ceramics and beads from China, Southeast Asia, and even western Asia indicate exchange with the lowlands and connection with maritime trade (Tjoa-Bonatz forthcoming; see also pp. 159–72). The concentration of these luxury items in Trenches D, F, M, and T in the central and eastern part of the settlement could indicate the presence of inhabitants with higher socio-economic status. The increase in cobalt-blue painted porcelain from the mid-Ming period and contemporary imported wares from mainland Southeast Asia during the late fifteenth century supports the argument that trade intensified at this time and raises the possibility that regionally-specific exchange relations supported the special economic status of the highland region of Tanah Datar in the century after Adityavarman (see pp. 51–53).

Despite the unquestionable relevance which the old settlement on Bukit Gombak must have had in the realm of Adityavarman's highland kingdom, it is not possible to decide purely on the base of the excavation results whether it held the position of the capital. No indications of monumental architecture were found, but questions about the seat of government and centre of early state organization in the highlands of West Sumatra should not necessarily be focused on large buildings and long-lasting construction materials. For example, the palace of later Minangkabau kings in Pagaruyung was an imposing building constructed entirely from wood and raised on stilts. Over the last two centuries the palace was destroyed by fire multiple times, in 1803, 1966, and most recently in 2007. Today, it has been rebuilt on concrete foundation posts and is a museum featuring heritage objects of the Minangkabau.

In conclusion, the settlement on Bukit Gombak represents a significant hill settlement from during and after the time of Adityavarman. When compared to other potential settlement locations in Tanah Datar outlined in Chapter 2, this site is clearly the largest. Its special geostrategic position makes it one of the principal sites, if not the major site, in the early history of the Minangkabau. The dynamic development of the settlement and its rich material culture result from the political ambitions and economic networks of the era of Adityavarman. However, the settlement also fills a gap in the history of the Minangkabau for which few sources exist. Thus,

Bukit Gombak takes precedence over all the other results of the Tanah Datar research project as archaeological evidence of a well-established, socially and economically complex society where the capital for the first, independent phase of state identity formation was set in motion.

3.3. The Burial Site on Bukit Kincir (*Johannes Greger*)

Trenches G and H

Anthropogenic stone formations were uncovered on the slope of the Bukit Kincir. Some remained upright while others were tilted or had collapsed (see Figures 3.18–3.23). These stone formations were on the east slope of the plateau and parts of the northern slope of the hill. Often two stones, one larger and one smaller, were grouped in opposing pairs. The stones making up Structure 1 were mostly knee-high and directed to Mount Merapi to the northwest (see Figure 3.18). During the last week of excavation in 2011, an area

FIGURE 3.18

Burial place on Bukit Kincir: erected stones (Structure 1)

FIGURE 3.19

Burial place on Bukit Kincir: grave pits in Trench L

FIGURE 3.20

Burial place on Bukit Kincir: aligned stones in Trench G (Structure 2)

FIGURE 3.21

Burial place on Bukit Kincir: aligned stones in Trench L3 (Structure 2)

FIGURE 3.22

Burial place on Bukit Kincir: aligned stones in Trench L3 (Structure 2)

3. Excavations

FIGURE 3.23

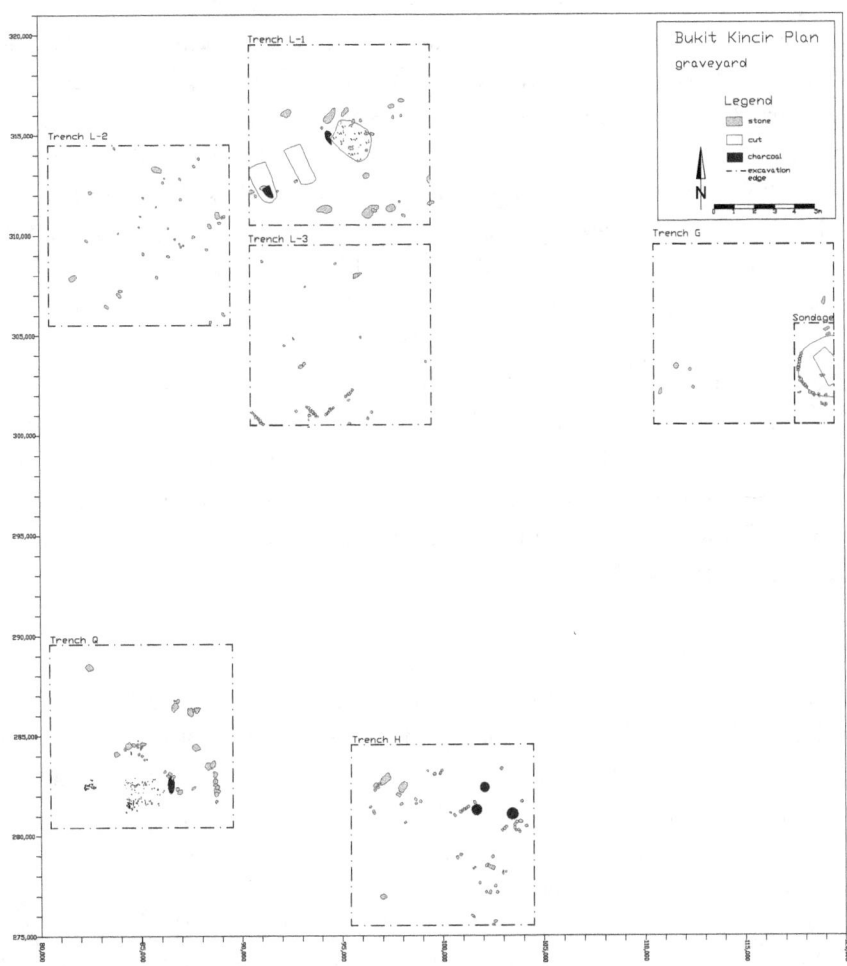

Burial place on Bukit Kincir: excavation plan of Trenches G, H, L1–L3, and Q

of the plateau was cleared and two 9 × 9 m trenches were created: Trench G in the northeast and the higher situated Trench H in the south (see Figure 3.23).

Stones found below the surface layer were tightly packed together and aligned geometrically. In Structure 2 they formed a semicircle (see

Figure 3.22), a straight line, or an angular shape (see the foreground of Figure 3.19). Two pits were found in Trench G, one associated with Structure 1 in the northwestern part of the site (Locus G-5) and the other, which was surrounded by a semicircle of stones, associated with Structure 2 in the southeast part of the excavation area (see Figure 3.20, Locus G-3). Both pits were orientated to the northwest, in the direction of the volcano, Mount Merapi. The dimensions (2 × 1 m) and depth (1.5 m) of the excavated pits correspond to pits dug as graves for full body burials. Traces of charcoal mixed with burnt clay were discovered in both pits, suggesting the practice of fire rituals. Near a sandstone rock in the lowest layer of the pit of Structure 1, a fragment of a stone adze was found (see Figure 4.15: F). An obsidian flake was discovered un-stratified under the surface layer of Trench G and a copper alloyed tray was found in Trench H. Only a few ceramics were collected throughout the area. Most were local pottery but some imported Chinese wares were found in Trench G (see Figure 4.9). No human remains were preserved due to the acidity of the soil.

Trenches L1–L3, and Q

The aim of the 2012 excavation of the stone field at Bukit Kincir was to gain an overview of the positioning of stones throughout the entire area and additional information about the burial culture and the proximity in time with the settlement at Bukit Gombak. By excavating at least some of the grave pits, we sought to find whether human skeletons were preserved on exposed parts of the site.

During a single year, 2012, the landscape of Bukit Kincir changed. In the course of the clearing work we had to step carefully around recently planted fruit trees on the once strictly shunned hill. The 9 × 9 m^2 in Trenches L1–3 and Q were arranged on the area with the highest concentration of visible stone formation, which was located westward above Trench H (see Figure 3.18). From this area a path was cleared to the top of Bukit Kincir, where indications of a settlement had been found (see Chapter 3.4).

During the excavations in 2012, a concentration of stones (Structure 1) was found in the northern part of the plateau. In Trench L2, 36 stones were identified as part of Structure 1, apparently including a headstone

3. Excavations

and a smaller footstone, insofar as any conclusion could be drawn from the stones, which were tilted and overthrown. The stones of Structure 1 had diameters of 40 cm and 80 cm. Most of these natural river stones were oval, flat, and slightly curved. The southern and flatter part of the plateau was dominated by another arrangement of stones (Structure 2) in Trenches G, H, Q, and the southern part of L3, which was made up of significantly smaller natural river stones. Most were circular or oval with a maximum size of *c.* 10 × 15 cm. They formed semicircles, parallel or angled lines. Many stones of the same sizes were found in this area, suggesting that they also may have belonged to anthropogenic structures. In L1 a posthole of 20 cm in diameter was found in the southern part of the section.

Fire deposits in ritual contexts, with charcoal mixed with pottery, were unearthed in all trenches and in combination with both stone structures. A deposit in the southwestern profile of Trench L1 contained a vessel of burnt clay 25 cm wide and 15 cm high, which contained fire utensils (Locus L1-16). Trench L3 contained just three pieces of imported ware: a Khmer sherd (see Colour Plate 1: L), two fragments of a Ming dynasty blue-and-white, and a Chinese bowl with a green glaze. The fire deposits in Trench Q suggested extensive fire-related activities.

The burial ground only had a few small finds: a copper alloyed tray of Trench H, a silex under the surface of Trench Q and four isolated flakes of obsidian under the surface of the L-Trenches. In Trench L1 two test trenches comprised pits of 7 m^2 and 5 m^2. As in Trench G, pits measuring 220 × 100–180 cm with a depth of 150 cm were interpreted as graves and were oriented towards the volcano Mount Merapi to the northwest. It was not possible to match the two pits precisely to an erected stone, but at least one of the pits in Trench L1 belonged to Structure 1. That pit is correlated to a stone structure, and directly in front of this headstone there was a deposit of charcoal and burnt clay (see Figure 3.21).

Dating

The imported ceramics, which included Vietnamese ceramics, greenware, and Chinese blue-and-white ceramics from the fourteenth to the sixteenth centuries, provide an indication of the period of use for the burial site. One TL-measured local pottery sample (BG-0265) came from the deposit L3-24 dated to 200±65 BP, and another (BG-0269) from the deposit L3-C-0029 to 470±200 BP/460±70 BP. Analysis of a coarse-grained sample of quartz from the deposit L3-C-0029 by Optically Stimulated Luminescence (OSL) dated the sample to 460±70 BP, thus it is almost in line with the pottery sample. For the charcoal sample (BG-0222) from the deposit L2-30, ^{14}C-radiocarbon dating provided a calibrated date of CE 1190–1252 (Sigma 1) or 1170–1258 (Sigma 2) (see Table 3.1). The period of use goes back to a time between the early twelfth and eighteenth centuries and thus coincides with the settlement on Bukit Gombak.

Conclusion

The presence of graves indicates that full body burials took place in the settlement, and their orientation is related to the veneration of Mount Merapi. The orientation of the graves is indicated by the presence of a headstone and a footstone, and the location of the cemetery was chosen to face the volcano. No graves were found on the west side of Bukit Kincir, only on the east side which directly faces Mount Merapi. The dimensions of the graves suggest that the bodies were buried in a stretched out position. It is possible that the burial site also includes the remains from Hindu-Buddhist cremations, following the practice of Adityavarman's religion. It is difficult to estimate the total number of burials because the graves do not necessarily correspond with the gravestones, and there were numerous stone structures that were not accompanied by graves. Considering the length of time that the cemetery seems to have been active, burial traditions may have changed during its use. For example, the 20 cm diameter posthole in Trench L1 (L1-8) may have been part of a roof installation that covered one or more graves for long-term rituals or a canopy for a cremation. The extensive fire deposits in Trench Q, the largest measuring 6 m², supports the hypothesis that cremations took place alongside full body burials.

The gravestones were taken from the River Silaki on the western side of Bukit Kincir at the foot of the mountain and carried uphill. During the excavation of the burial site, more than 200 anthropogenically-placed stones were in the 54 m² excavated area. Possibly the stones of Structure 1 served some unknown practices for the deceased. The placing of a headstone and a footstone on a grave as well as the use of fire are part of a ritual tradition that is still extant, although it has been integrated with the local Islamic burial custom of orienting graves towards Mecca (see Figure 2.15). Nine geometric stone settings could be assigned to Structure 2. The outline of the stones and the numerous scattered stones around them gave the impression that they were originally a part of rectangular and ovular boundaries of graves. The greater number of ceramic goods found around Structure 2 compared to Structure 1 argues for burials of different social classes. Accordingly, Structure 2 denotes elite burials. The stone adze fragment found by Structure 1 could not have been a working tool because it shows no marks of use, and can therefore be interpreted as burial good, probably associated with an elite burial. It is difficult to draw conclusions concerning the other eight small finds—five obsidian flakes.

3.4. The Settlement Site on Bukit Kincir
(*Annika Hotzan-Tchabashvili*)

Topography of the Excavated Area

The decision to start an excavation on the summit of Bukit Kincir was guided by its topography. Local residents said that megaliths were supposedly found at the site, which was planted with bamboo and, we assumed, fortified by a rampart. In 2011, the forest was cleared to open three trenches, and the investigation hoped to determine whether settlement structures existed there and, if so, how they could be dated and related to settlement on the adjacent Bukit Gombak.

A total area of 304.25 m² was excavated on top of Bukit Kincir between three trenches, O, P, and R. On the northwestern part of the summit, Trenches O and P were installed next to bamboo vegetation and a slope, first interpreted as a rampart. No surface finds were made owing to a thick layer of vegetation. Trench O lay 5 m southeast of Trench P at 435.7 m. This area had a sharp drop-off to the west and south, where Bukit Kincir slopes steeply with the Silaki River at the bottom. This river flows into the Selo River a few kilometres further east. Trench P was the northernmost trench and was located on a flat and slightly sloping area at 433.8 m. A very shallow stratigraphy and a small number of finds guided the excavator's decision to extend this trench to the south and east. Trench R lay 40 m southeast of Trench O, separated from the latter and Trench P by a shallow ditch (see Figure 3.24). It was located on the highest point of Bukit Kincir at around 437.3 m. South of Trench R was a steep downhill slope. Northeast of the excavation area, the ground declined to the plateau on which the graveyard is located.

Structures and Finds

Underneath a surface layer of approximately 10 cm, a deposit layer was found that seemed to cover the entire area. The latter was interspersed with pottery finds and a few obsidian and stone fragments.

In Trench O, the 10 cm vegetation layer was followed by a deposit layer of approximately 10 cm where a relatively large number of lithic objects was discovered (see Chapter 4.2.1). Out of 44 pieces, five tools with very fine retouches were identified (see e.g., Figure 4.18). One flake of quartz was found. Some pottery finds were made and samples from charcoal remains (BG-0738) were taken for ^{14}C analysis, which yielded a date of CE 1662–1950 (Sigma 1) or 1653–1951 (Sigma 2) (see Table 3.1). However, there was evidence that this occupation layer might be even older based on the presence of imported finds such as five sherds of a storage jar made of Fujian brittle ware and a nearly complete celadon jarlet (see Figure 4.12: A). These Chinese imports can be dated to the Song or Yuan dynasty of the thirteenth or fourteenth century. The discrepancy in date between the ^{14}C date and the stylistic evaluation of the ceramics might be caused by fires that occurred in more recent times and left traces suggesting a younger date than the actual settlement phase. The pottery assemblage mostly consisted of local earthenware, including two nearly complete jars (see Figure 4.8: D–E).

The excavated parts of the rampart, which borders Trenches O and P, showed no traces of artificial construction. Thus, it can be regarded

3. Excavations

FIGURE 3.24

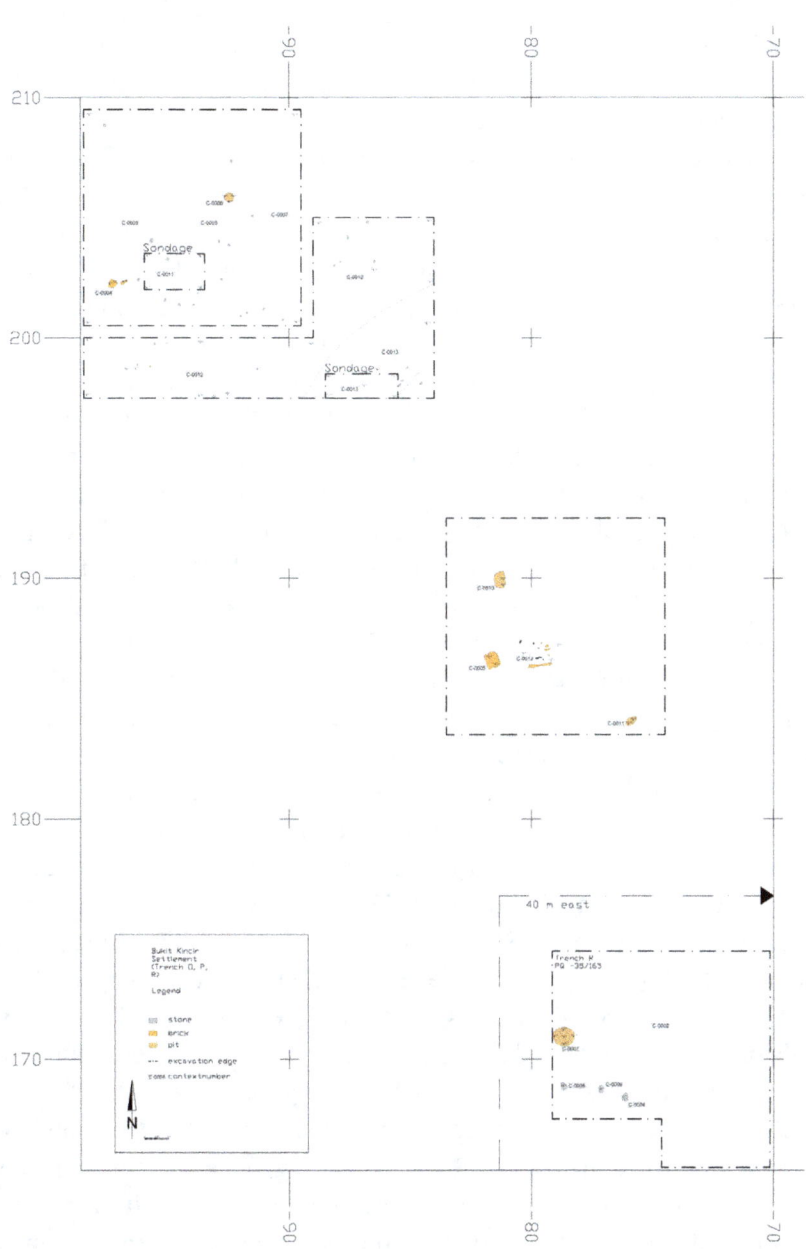

Bukit Kincir: excavation plan of Trenches O, P, and R at the settlement site

as a natural slope that might have been used for protection and defence along with the adjacent bamboo vegetation. No architectural remains or postholes were discovered. A few pieces of iron slag were retrieved from Trench O resulting in a similar find assemblage to Trench P. Both suggest small-scale iron smelting processes.

In Trench P four pieces of obsidian tools were found (see Figure 4.18: A, J). Flakes and a core point to lithic production. Clay objects and an egg-shaped andesite that was interpreted as a hammerstone might have been used for metal working (see Figure 4.7: D–F; Figure 4.19: A, D). This assumption is based on similar find contexts of metal working and lithics, for example, in Sulawesi between the sixteenth and eighteenth centuries (Bulbeck and Caldwell 2000, pp. 25, 32). Altogether 13 pebble tools were found (see Figure 4.19). A piece of iron ore seems to support the assumption of metal working in the area. Fired clay fragments also show the impact of fire or heat in this area, and a charcoal sample (BG-0658) in context area P-4 taken for ^{14}C dating yielded a date of CE 1452–1613 (Sigma 1) or 1446–1620 (Sigma 2) (see Table 3.1). The pottery density in Trench P was much higher than in Trenches O and R and mainly consisted of local earthenware except for one potsherd of Chinese blue-and-white ware from the Ming dynasty of the fifteenth and sixteenth centuries. As in Trench O, no postholes, pits, ovens or other settlement structures were recognized.

In Trench R, a deposit of dark brown colour and silty soil was encountered under the 10–12 cm vegetation layer. This trench contained local pottery interspersed with a greater amount of obsidian than was found in the other layers. In total 75 pieces were counted including 67 flakes and eight tools. Six of them were flakes with retouches (see Figure 4.18: B–D, F–G). One piece was used as a chopping tool (see Figure 4.18: H) and another as a scraper (see Figure 4.18: E). Two grindstones, two grinding slabs, and six other stone tools were found, one of which was a faceted whetstone. Three aligned flat stones of around 30 × 20 cm in size were unearthed that might have been used as foundation stones for a stilted house. One pit measuring 60 × 70 cm and about 20 cm deep was excavated north of the stone alignment. It contained a few potsherds of local production. Two fired clay traces were recognized

FIGURE 3.25

Settlement site of Bukit Kincir: excavation of Trench P with remains of burnt clay of a metal working site

in the western part of the trench, presumably the remains of fireplaces (see Figure 3.25). A charcoal sample (BG-1360) for ^{14}C analysis taken from a small pit in the southwest corner of the trench yielded a date of CE 1650–1793 (Sigma 1) or 1644–1950 (Sigma 2) (see Table 3.1). The sample was taken from pit fill R-11 where no imported ceramic finds were retrieved.

Conclusion

The summit of Bukit Kincir overlooks the valley of Tanah Datar with a direct line of sight to Gunung Merapi, and offers space for a small, well-defended settlement site. Compared to the excavation results from Bukit Gombak, the remains at Bukit Kincir have more production traces. The numerous obsidian fragments in Trench O suggest a lithic production area, while most of the finds in Trench P can be linked to metalworking, including casting moulds, iron slag, stone tools, and burnt clay fragments.

Trench R, like Trench O, contained large amounts of obsidian, consisting of very tiny flakes and some tools. The total amount is even higher than in Trench O. Although the obsidian flakes were spread widely in the excavated area, there was a remarkable concentration of finds in the southwestern corner, suggesting a working area in that place where obsidian tools were produced and used.

Although no architectural structures or organic materials were located, some pieces of burnt clay were identified (indicating fireplaces) and Trench R contained three flat aligned stones that could have been foundation stones for a house. The stone and pottery assemblage resembles that at Bukit Gombak and clearly indicates contemporaneous settlement activities. The dates might extend from the thirteenth or fourteenth to the eighteenth centuries. The latter date mainly relies on a ^{14}C sample in Trench R (see Table 3.1).

The stone tools and iron slag in this area also point to a metal workshop. The association of small-scale lithic industries with ironworking is also recorded at other archaeological locations in island Southeast Asia, such as Sulawesi. The use of obsidian tools apparently overlapped with the production of metal tools, especially iron implements, which increased from the fourteenth century onwards. Iron tools might have been prestigious, and possibly reserved for special circumstances and elite use, while obsidian provided an alternative resource for less valuable but therefore more commonly used working tools. The presence of both materials at the same spot provides an interesting insight into the specialization and division of work close to the large Bukit Gombak settlement. As a precaution, this specialist production area was some distance from the main settlement to avoid the spread of fire used in processing iron. The summit of Bukit Kincir was an ideal place to minimize these dangers, and because it was easily defended, gold processing might also have taken place at this location. In the Minangkabau language, *kincir* denotes a water-powered mill wheel that could be used to grind grains, but at least in the nineteenth century such equipment was used to pulverize gold ores. The toponym Bukit Kincir could thus allude to a former place of gold production, but apart from the name there is no evidence for such a conjecture. The excavations provided no evidence of gold processing in the area.

NOTE

1. Johannes Moser, personal communication, 20 July 2011.

4

MATERIAL CULTURE STUDIES

Mai Lin Tjoa-Bonatz

Three categories of finds were distinguished during the excavation: samples (soil or charcoal), bulkfinds, and small finds. The bulkfinds include pottery, collections of stones, fired clay, or iron slag; within the bulkfinds, only the pottery sherds received individual inventory numbers. Small finds are artefacts with a distinct value due to their material, dating, or function, and therefore received an individual inventory number. If required, their exact location was mapped to facilitate three-dimensional documentation.

4.1. Ceramics

The largest group of finds comprised the ceramic material. The total quantity of ceramics from Bukit Gombak and Bukit Kincir amounted to 18,767 sherds with a weight of 84.5 kg (see Table 1.1).[1] Within this collection, 1,767 sherds were categorized as diagnostic, consisting of 1,244 earthenware and 523 foreign ceramics sherds. The largest number selected for analysis came from Bukit Gombak (1,017 sherds), while 203 sherds came from Bukit Kincir, and 24 from the burial site.

Diagnostic sherds included imported sherds, tools, parts of a rim, spout, base, handle, knob, decorated body sherds, and carnations—inflected fragments that formed part of the neck or ring foot and show a significant change in curvature. All sherds were counted and weighed, and the diagnostic sherds were numbered consecutively. Joints of the same vessel were counted once. There is a bias between the count of the earthenware and imported ware. Whereas all foreign sherds were counted, among the earthenware only decorated body fragments and sherds bigger than 2 cm were regarded as diagnostic and therefore documented. Each diagnostic sherd was measured and catalogued according to standardized references to provide accuracy and consistency: the type of sherd, rim form, fabric, surface finish, decoration, and colour. The quantity of temper, its grain size and type was applied to earthenware alone in order to define the fabric. The description of the pottery colour appeared to be an unreliable feature owing to the irregular colouring from the firing process and postfiring conditions, which also changed the original colour.

Agricultural activities have greatly affected the archaeological material. The sherds are generally small and rarely exceed 10 cm. Because the edges of the earthenware sherds were soft and badly weathered, crossmending vessels was a difficult task. No complete vessel was found among the excavated earthenware assemblage, making it difficult to reconstruct vessels and determine the proportions between body diameter and height. We thus have to be cautious about attributing specific vessel forms and functions to certain rim types.

4.1.1. Earthenware

Earthenware was the most abundant type of artefact found at our excavations and represents 97 per cent of the diagnostic sherds (see Table 1.1; Map 4.1). Locally produced earthenware in Southeast Asia has received less attention than foreign imports of porcelain or stoneware. This neglect is mainly due to the difficulty of dating the local earthenware and an incomplete knowledge of chrono-typological markers. Many pottery types and decoration patterns were persistent for centuries, and earthenware vessels continued to be produced using traditional techniques today. In island Southeast Asia, chrono-typological

TABLE 4.1
Chemical Analyses of Earthenware Sherds from Bukit Gombak (BG-1100-3, Lab. No. MD5128) and Bukit Kincir (BG-919-70, Lab. No. MD5129), per cent by weight, in ppm

	SiO_2	TiO_2	Al_2O_3	Fe_2O_3	MnO	MgO	CaO	Na_2O	K_2O	P_2O_5	V	Cr	Ni	Total
Bukit Gombak	56.97	0.89	21.65	11.88	0.101	1.69	4.94	1.17	0.67	0.03	297	39	21	99.86
Bukit Kincir	68.60	0.92	18.36	6.74	0.050	0.87	1.64	1.62	1.15	0.05	161	25	12	100.14

	(Cu)	Zn	Rb	Sr	Y	Zr	(Nb)	Ba	(La	Ce	Pb	Th)	l.o.i.	Total
Bukit Gombak	129	93	21	311	12	122	—	379	<5	33	9	14	5.69	99.86
Bukit Kincir	29	52	45	147	11	218	5	331	13	n.d.	17	17	6.77	100.14

4. Material Culture Studies

MAP 4.1

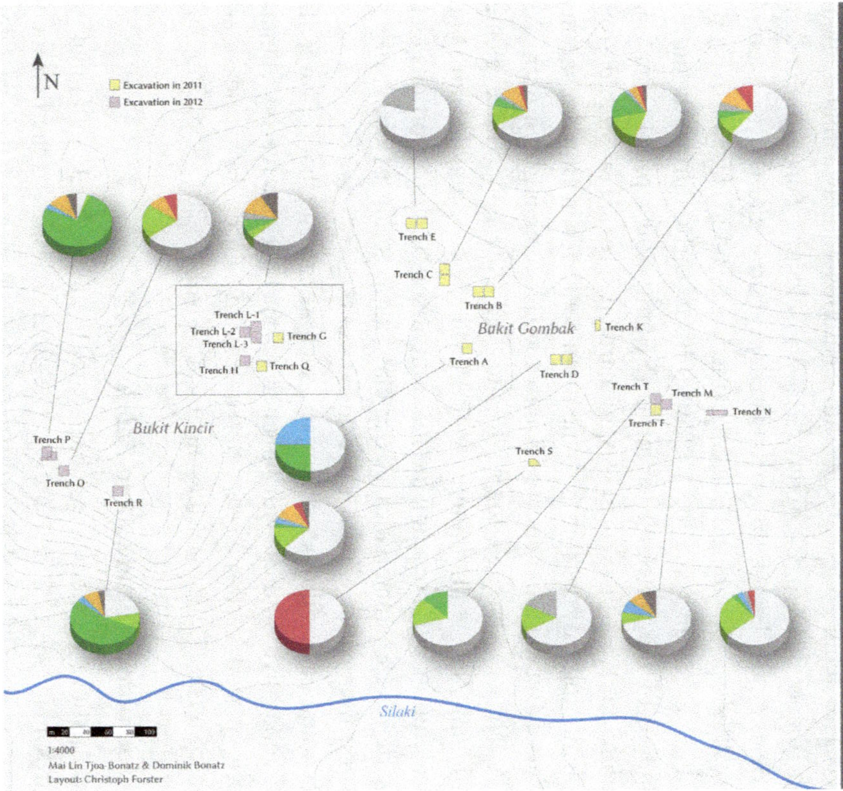

Distribution of earthenware sherd types in the excavated areas of Bukit Gombak and Bukit Kincir

Source: Mai Lin Tjoa-Bonatz, Dominik Bonatz; lay-out: Christoph Förster.

studies of earthenware are still scarce, as are comparative studies within historic times. Statistical analysis of the excavated earthenware assemblages that would allow better intra-site comparisons are also rare.

More chemical and thin-section analyses are needed to show the geographical extent of regionally distinct clay compositions. The chemical composition of two sherds from Bukit Gombak and Bukit Kerinci displayed in Table 4.1 can be added to the few available analyses of pottery in Sumatra dating from prehistory to the sixteenth century: four samples from Bukit Arat in Serampas between 1400–900 BCE (Bonatz 2006, figure 29.9), one sample from Lolo Gedang in Kerinci of the late tenth to early eleventh centuries in the Jambi highlands (Tjoa-Bonatz 2012, p. 20, figures 2.3–2.4), Padang Sepan in the district Air Besi, North Bengkulu, an undated jar burial site (Ni Komang Ayu Astiti 2004, p. 5, tab. 1.1), local pottery of Bukit Hasang, Northwest Sumatra, a trading site of the twelfth or early thirteenth until the beginning of the sixteenth centuries (Schmitt 2009, p. 304, tab. 1). In addition, in West Java analyses of earthenware are available from a temple complex of the fourth to the ninth centuries in Blondongan in the district of Batujaya, regency of Karawang (Ni Komang Ayu Astiti 2007, p. 19, tab. 2). Although for some sites only the major trace elements of silicium (SiO_2), aluminium (Al_2O_3), iron (Fe_2O_3), magnesium (MgO), and calcium (CaO) are available for comparison, their proportions clearly show distinct characteristics of the clay composition of each site. This allows a fingerprint for each site to be defined.

Typological catalogues of pottery, such as the one that follows, allow for comparative studies with an interregional perspective on Sumatra's historic period earthenware what has been started by at least some archaeologists (Edwards McKinnon 2003; Miksic 2013, pp. 265–80).

Archaeometric Analyses and Fabric

Three distinct earthenware fabrics are found on Bukit Gombak and Bukit Kincir (see Colour Plate 4). The characteristics of the first include a fine texture, light red to brownish colour, and a small-sized temper. A few grains of temper of up to 0.5 mm can be seen macroscopically (see Colour Plate 4: BG-1100-3/BG-0412-1). The clay that was the raw material of the second ware is red to dark brown colour and consists of a moderate content of poorly sorted temper with grains of up to 1 mm in diameter (see Colour Plate 4: BG-0005-1). The sherds often show a darker core due to an inconsistent firing temperature and an unfinished oxidation process. The third ware fabric is brown with a brittle texture and a lot of coarse temper (see Colour Plate 4: BG-0514-47/BG-0919), with grains up to 3 mm in diameter. The first two ware types are characteristic of Bukit Gombak, whereas the brittle ware of type three are typical for Bukit Kincir. The first ware type is absent on Bukit Kincir but the moderately tempered ware of the second type is found on both sites. The burial site had all three ware types.

Archaeometric analysis was carried out on four pottery fragments from Bukit Gombak and three from Bukit Kincir to compare their thermal behaviour and chemical composition.[2] Thin slices were fired in an electric laboratory chamber furnace in air static with a heating rate of 200°C/h and a soaking time of one hour at the peak temperature. By comparing the change of colour and documenting the density of the matrix type group under a high-temperature microscope, the analysis distinguished two matrix types. Three of the sherds from Bukit Gombak (see Colour Plate 4: BG-1100-3/BG-0005-1/-0412-1) displayed almost identical thermal behaviour after refiring at 1.100°C, 1.150°C, and at 1.200°C, turning to a red-brown colour. This outcome is solid evidence that they were high-fired and all made of the same clay raw material. Two ceramic sherds from Bukit Kincir (see Colour Plate 4: BG-0919-70/ BG-0701) with a lot of coarse temper are of the sintered type and turn a beige-brownish colour when fired at 1.200°C. The sample from Bukit Kincir (see Colour Plate 4: BG-0919-70) and one from Bukit Gombak (see Colour Plate 4: BG-0514-47) were made of the same clay using the same technology, both in terms of firing as well as in the type and quantity of temper used.

Two samples deemed representative for each site were selected for chemical analysis by WD-XRF (wavelength-dispersive x-ray fluorescence) to determine the presence of major elements.[3] Differences in thermal behaviour are also clearly marked in their chemical composition (see Table 4.1), which attests to the fact that clays of distinctly different phase and chemical composition were used at both sites. The colour of pottery from Bukit Gombak is attributable to a very high content of iron

(Fe_2O_3)—11.88 per cent compared to 6.74 per cent in the sherd from Bukit Kincir. Silicium (SiO_2), titanium (TiO_2), and potassium (K_2O) are more prevalent in the sherd from Bukit Kincir than in one from Bukit Gombak.

The analyses of the thermal and chemical composition reveal that different fabrics of earthenware were used on the two sites. The pottery sherds made from a clay raw material typical of a given site generally indicate on-site production, or at least a preference for a certain ware type at each site. However, some vessels made at these workshops were present at both sites, suggesting that their proximity led to exchanges. Both ware types also occur at the burial site, indicating that both communities used the graveyard.

Vessel Types

The earthenware at the prehistoric site of Tanah Dua consists of restricted or closed and unrestricted or open vessel of coarse ware. Jars with everted rims (see Figure 4.1: A–B) are more frequent than large restricted vessel with straight rim (see Figure 4.1: C). Some vessels might have been lidded or footed (see Figure 4.1: E). The Bukit Gombak and Bukit Kincir sites have eight main types of earthenware vessel forms used for daily consumption: restricted and unrestricted vessels, lids, footed vessels, drinking containers (*kendi*), vessels with handles, cooking stands, and clay tools (see Table 4.2).

The sherds of restricted vessels make up the majority of the diagnostic sherds. On Bukit Gombak restricted vessels (62 per cent) greatly outnumber the unrestricted ones (15 per cent), suggesting that there was a high demand for cooking and storage jars. A clear predominance of closed vessels is a common feature for settlements sites.[4] For Bukit Kincir, the weighting is less marked: 24 per cent closed vessel versus 9 per cent open, a difference that can be explained by the smaller settlement on Bukit Kincir, representing mainly a manufacturing site with a different household structure. On Bukit Gombak the estimated diameter of restricted vessels falls between 8 and 48 cm with wall thicknesses of 0.5–1.2 cm. The figures for Bukit Kincir are slightly smaller, a diameter of 8–34 cm and a wall thickness of 0.5–1 cm.[5]

FIGURE 4.1

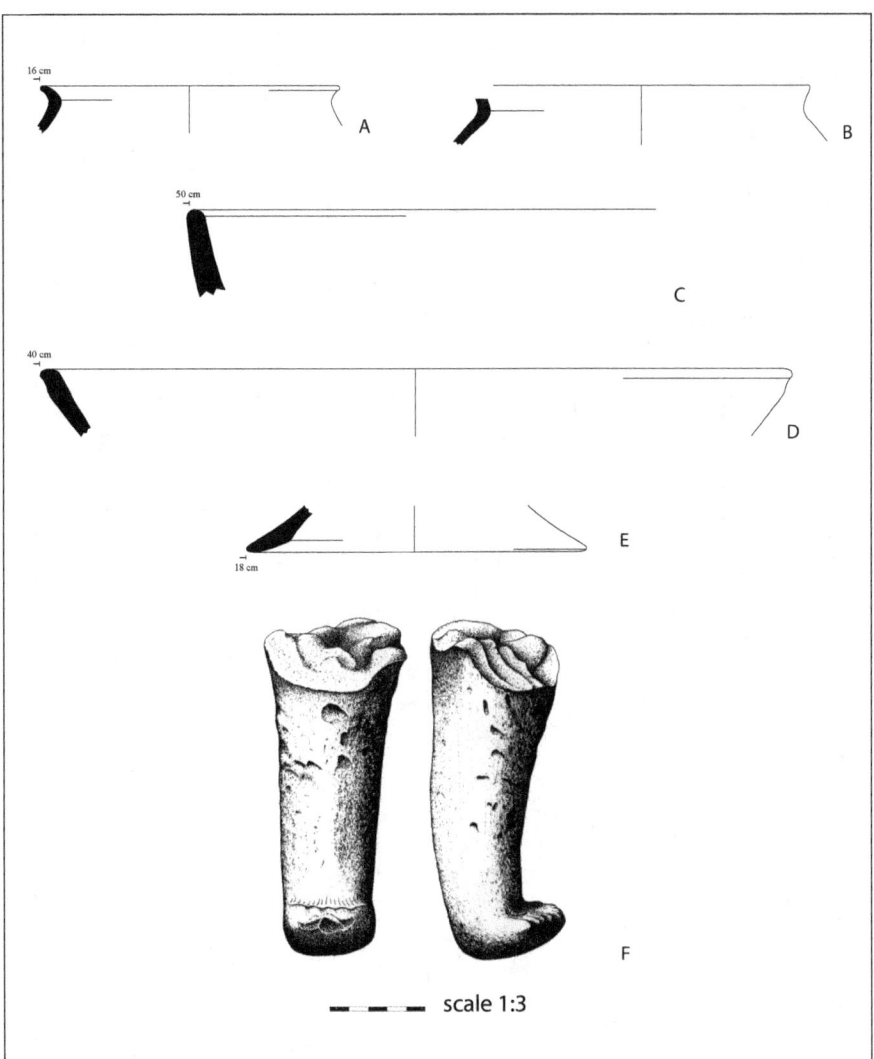

Earthenware of Tanah Lua

Jars with everted rim (A–B; BG-0756-015, BG-0756-018), large unrestricted vessel with straight rim (C; BG-0761-001), large oblique rimmed unrestricted vessel (D; BG-0756-006), cover or stand of a footed vessel (E; BG-0756-004), probably a cooking stand (F; BG-0756-002)

Source: Dayat Hidayat.

TABLE 4.2
Distribution of Earthenware Shard Types in the Excavated Areas of Bukit Gombak, Bukit Kincir, and Tanah Lua

Bukit Gombak	Trench	Closed vessel	Open vessel	Body	Carnation	Knop	Foot	*Kendi*	Others*	Total
Core area	B	129	37	42	2	3	10	5	5	233
	C	250	48	21	2	7	35	7	8	378
	D	89	19	4	4	2	14	6	5	143
Extended settlement area	A	2	–	1	1	–	–	–	–	4
	E	4	–	–	–	1	–	–	–	5
	K	23	4	2	–	2	4	3	–	38
	N	97	37	4	5	3	–	5	–	151
	S (spring)	2	–	–	–	–	–	2	–	4
	Z (survey)	7	1	3	–	1	–	–	5	17
House site	F	4	1	–	–	1	–	–	–	6
	M	10	1	–	1	–	1	–	1	14
	T	17	4	3	–	–	–	–	–	24
Total		634	152	80	15	20	64	28	24	1,017
		62%	15%	8%	2%	2%	6%	3%	2%	100%

4. Material Culture Studies

Bukit Kincir	Trench	Closed vessel	Open vessel	Body	Carnation	Knop	Foot	Kendi	Others*	Total
Settlement site	O	22	7	–	–	–	3	2	–	34
	P	3	1	47	2	–	6	–	3	62
	R	24	10	58	4	–	8	–	3	107
Total		49	18	105	6	–	17	2	6	203
		24%	9%	52%	3%	–	8%	1%	3%	100%
Burial site total	G, H, L, Q	15	1	2	–	1	3	–	2	24
		63%	4%	8%	–	4%	13%	–	8%	100%

Tanah Lua	Trench	Closed vessel	Open vessel	Body	Carnation	Knop	Foot	Kendi	Others*	Total
Total	A–F, Z survey	12	7	50	15	1	–	–	4	89
		14%	8%	56%	17%	1%	–	–	5%	100%

Note: * Others include not defined ones, handles, tools, cooking stands.

A few specimens have an opening wider than 35 cm, e.g., a wide-mouth jar with a large diameter of 46 cm (see Figure 4.3: A). Everted rim jars with a diameter between 18 and 26 cm are the most commonly retrieved, suggesting that a certain size of the opening was standardized what is enabled by a characteristic tool in the production process documented in the ethnographic context and explained on pp. 152–53.

Generally, the excavated jars are neckless and have rounded shoulders, and were probably bulbous or conical with round bottoms. Their everted rims describe various shapes (see Figure 4.2): from more straight to almost horizontally inclined, internally recessed or pinched rims with a thickened lip. Combinations of these features are also possible; for example, pinched and internally recessed rims (see Figure 4.2: J). The internal ridge may have allowed the vessel to support a lid (see Figure 4.2: I). Jars and jarlets with straight or inverted rims are restricted to the core area of Bukit Gombak (see Figure 4.3: B–E) and the burial site.

Black remains of soot on the external and internal rim of jars indicate the use as cooking pots over open fires (see Figure 4.2: B). The openings are 18–22 cm in diameter, which would provide accessibility and defines them as medium-sized pots.[6] Knobs and sherds of unrestricted vessels with burnt food remains indicate cooking pot lids. The diameter of 17–24 cm fits the rim size of the cooking pots. Lid handles are appliqué knobs with a flat, convex, or concave surface (see Figure 4.5: C–E). The lid's interior is smoothed much as exterior bowls are and often polished, which makes distinguishing the sherds of cover from those of open vessels difficult (see Figure 4.5: D). A steeper wall may indicate a lid rather than a bowl, but as all the sherds were small such distinctions were difficult to see (see Figure 4.5: A–B).

Most of the vessels are round-bottomed. If jars are elevated on a ring base, their rim base is generally rather flat and everted, with a diameter between 7 and 18 cm.[7] A few exceptional pieces among the base sherds are high and straight feet found only on Bukit Kincir (see Figure 4.8: C, E, H). One ring foot was perforated to hang the vessel up (see Figure 4.5: F).

Cooking pots in Southeast Asia are generally round-bottomed vessel with everted rims and are wider than they are tall. There are regional variations. In Malaysia, Singapore, the Philippines, and Northwest

FIGURE 4.2

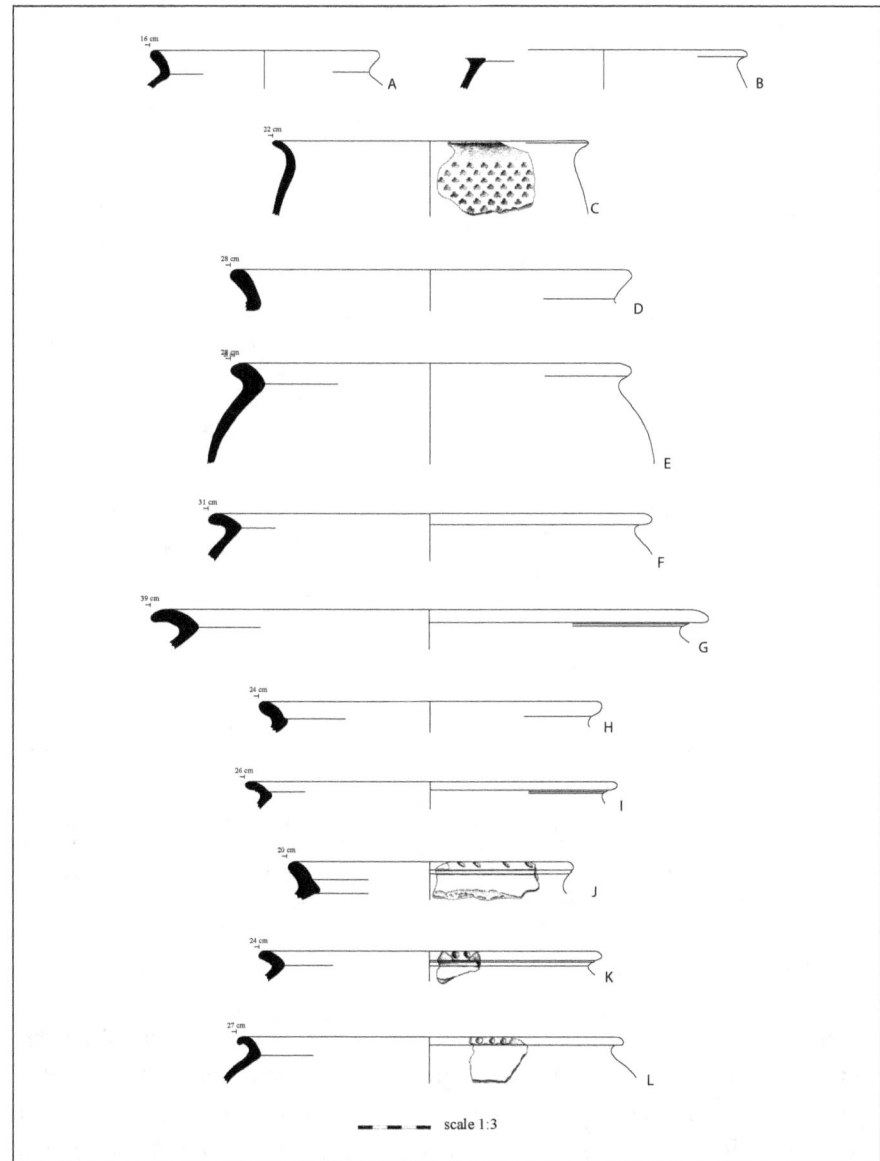

Restricted vessel of Bukit Gombak

Jar with everted rim (A–G; BG-0501-132, BG-1006-041, BG-0514-088, BG-0063-084, BG-2008-014, BG-1000-116, BG-1006-036), cooking pot due to soot remains (B; BG-1006-041), jar with everted and internally recessed rim (H–I; BG-1000-058, BG-1021-010), jar with pinched everted rim (J–L; BG-1000-031/-008, BG-0501-067, BG-1006-072)

Source: Dayat Hidayat.

FIGURE 4.3

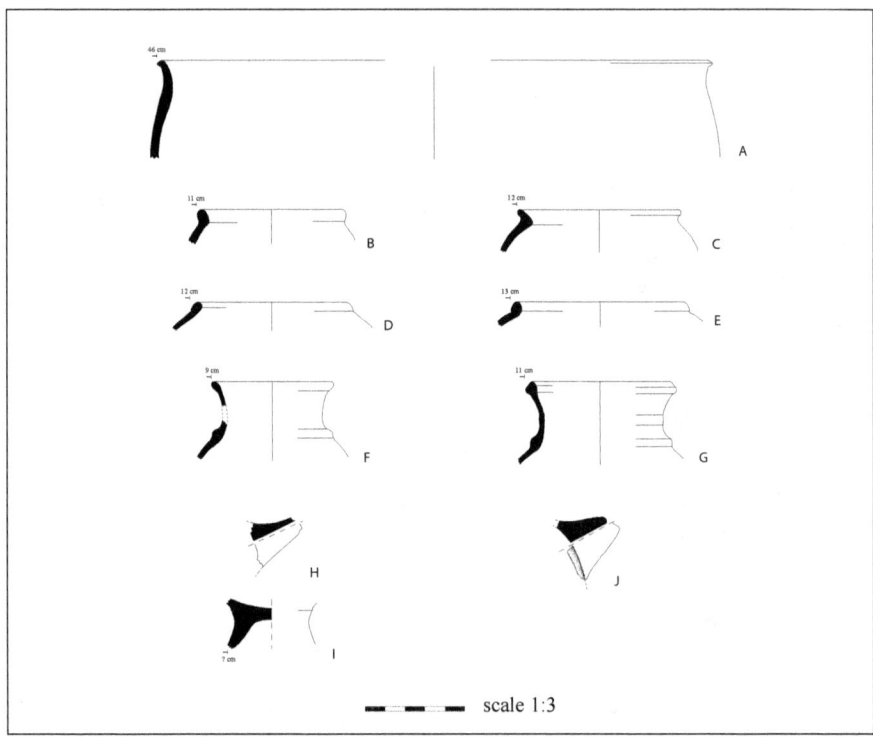

Restricted vessel of Bukit Gombak

Wide-mouth jar (A; BG-0526-012), jarlet with everted rim (B–C; BG-1006-078, BG-1000-013), jarlet with straight rim (D–E; BG-0501-201, BG-0501-130), drinking vessel/*kendi* (F–J; BG-1503-002/-004, BG-0511-001/-004, BG-1006-014, BG-1505-002, BG-1006-001), due to their fabric and finding spot the fragments (H–I; BG-1006-014, BG-1006-001) may come from the same vessel

Source: Dayat Hidayat.

Sumatra cooking pots tend to be carinated, and incised on the shoulder (Perret and Heddy Surachman 2009, pp. 162–70; Tanaka and Dizon 2011, figure 2; Miksic 2013, p. 269). Ethnographic comparisons from West Sumatra indicate that the standard repertoire of cooking pots produced today consists of short-necked, round-bottomed containers that are ovoid or bulbous and have paddle marks on the exterior wall. The form and size of the pots differ according to the food being prepared: pots for steaming vegetables or for soup, locally called *belanga* or *tarenang*, have larger diameters and are taller than those used for boiling rice, known as *periuk* (Erman Makmur 1983–84, pp. 10–12).

In the fourteenth century, in Kerinci storage vessels used for both liquids and cultivation products are called *tapayan* (Kozok and Waruno Mahdi 2015, pp. 78, 127). This implies that probably their form was also not distinct. In later times water containers, locally called *menggu*, are generally higher than they are wide. They are represented by long-necked, carinated jars with everted rims. Such vessels, which were documented in the late nineteenth and early twentieth centuries, remained in production in Tanah Datar in the 1980s.[8] Similar rim shapes were found on Bukit Kincir (see Figure 4.8: A).

Loop handles of different shapes attached horizontally or vertically to the body are rare in the excavated material (see Figure 4.5: J–K). Ethnographic comparisons suggest that they may belong to jars or pots (Erman Makmur 1983–84, pp. 17–18; Wiyoso Yudhoseputro 1995–96, pp. 34, 39).

Kendi are vessels with up-turning spouts of up to 4.5 cm that are attached to a bulbous body (see Figure 4.3: F–J). On Bukit Kincir a short necked *kendi* with everted rim had a rather wide opening of 20 cm in diameter but a relatively small spout.[9] It is likely that it had ring feet to improve stability (see Figure 4.3: H–I). A few examples from the first, finer textured ware type, have ribbed necks of 8–11 cm in diameter, which probably reflects a design feature of non-local fine-paste *kendi* which are known during the fourteenth to the sixteenth centuries (see p. 170). Such vessels were only found in the core area of Bukit Gombak and at the water source. The rarity of spouted vessels suggests that other drinking vessels were in use. Spouted jars were probably used on specific occasions or by small groups. Following the interpretation of Sumarah Adhyatman (2004), the *kendi* also had special ceremonial significance.

The standard repertoire of vessels with everted or straight rims consists of shallow and globular bowls (see Figure 4.4). The variations among open vessels at Bukit Kincir are less marked than at Bukit Gombak, where exceptionally large straight-walled containers with a diameter of up to 33 cm, pinched rim bowls, or carinated bowls with inverted or everted rims are part of the standard repertoire. Outstanding

FIGURE 4.4

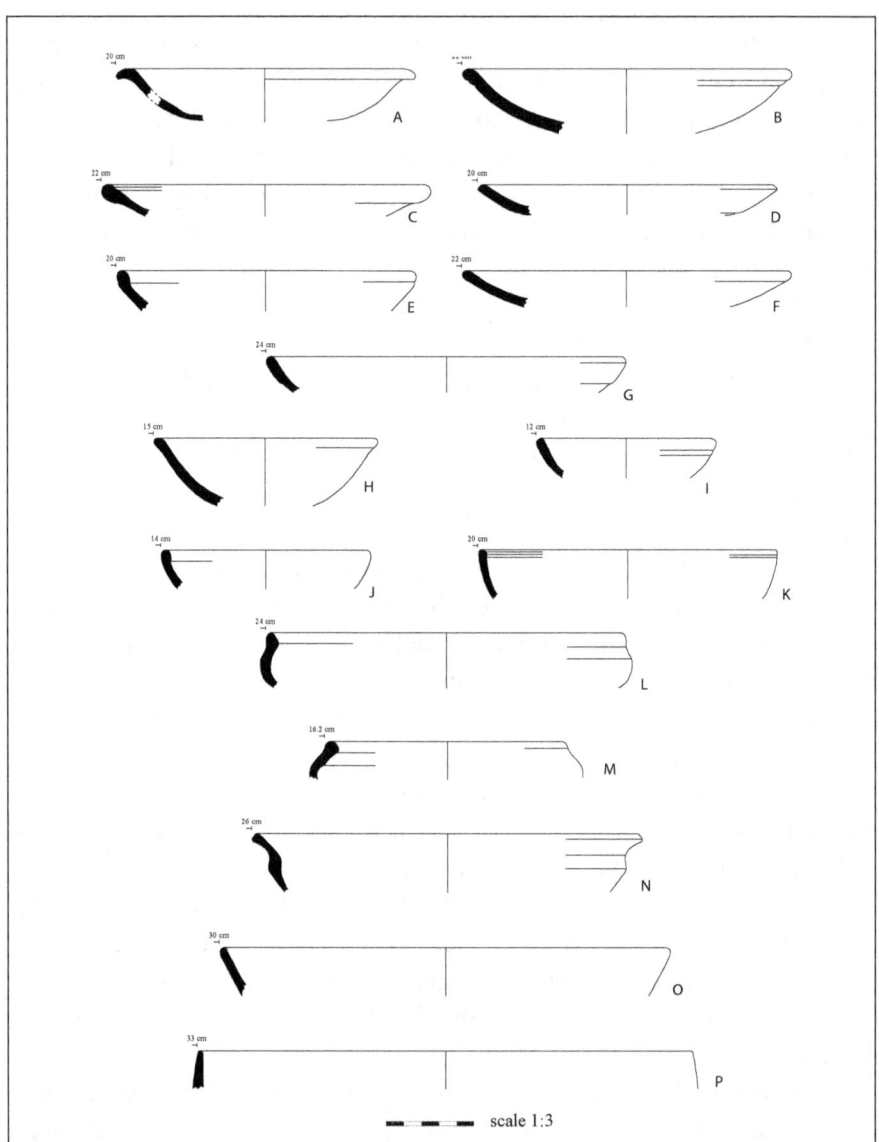

Unrestricted vessel of Bukit Gombak

Shallow bowls or cover with everted or straight rim (A–G; BG-1006-076/-079, BG-0154-001, BG-0050-029, BG-0514-050, BG-1021-003, BG-1000-656, BG-1006-060), globular bowls or cover with everted or straight rim (H–K; BG-0501-011, BG-1006-060, BG-1021-001, BG-0501-092), carinated bowls (L–N; BG-0509-010, BG-0509-009, BG-0501-113), oblique rimmed conical vessel (0; BG-0526-004), straight-walled vessel (P; BG-0509-007)

Source: Dayat Hidayat.

FIGURE 4.5

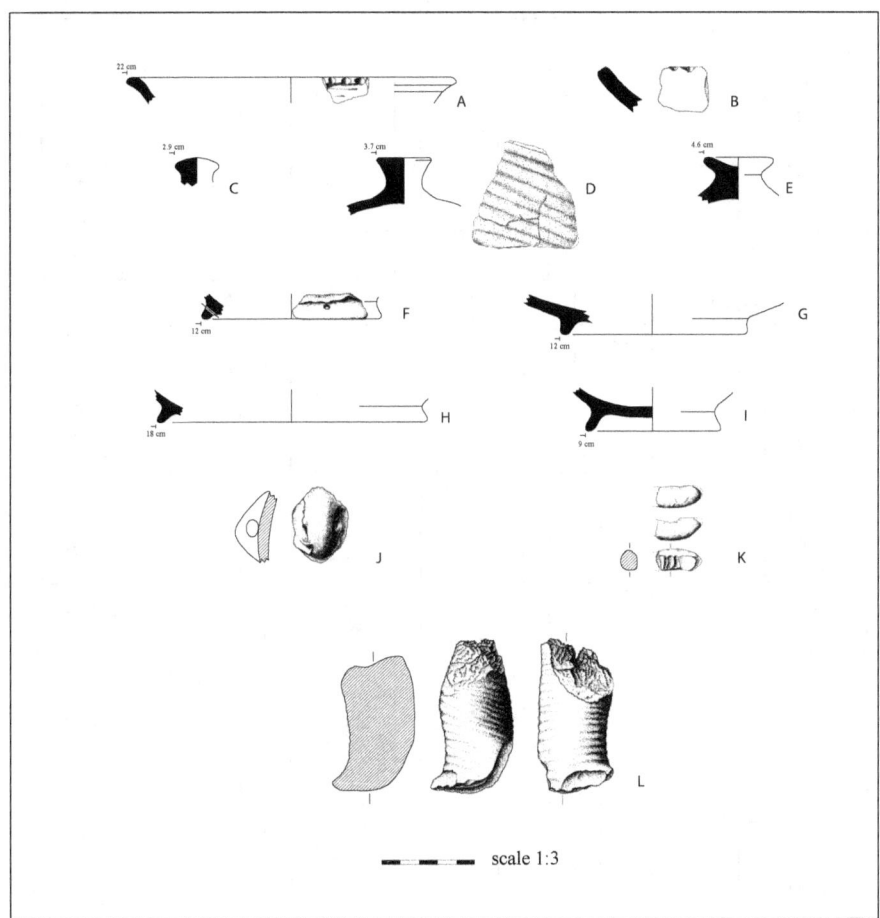

Other earthenware finds of Bukit Gombak

Bowls or cover with pinched rim (A–B; BG-0412-042, BG-0958-006), knob of cover (C–E; BG-0526-005, BG-0412-002, BG-1000-147), footed vessel (F–I; BG-0097-068, BG-1006-010, BG-1000-011, BG-0154-007), handle (J–K; BG-0154-002, BG-0150-031), cooking stand (L; BG-2008-005)

Source: Dayat Hidayat.

pieces in the earthenware assemblage of Bukit Gombak include vessels with an s-shaped wall profile (see Table 4.3). The diameter of open vessels from Bukit Gombak tends to be slightly larger (15–33 cm) than at Bukit Kincir (14–30 cm), though with a similar wall thickness of 0.6–1 cm.

TABLE 4.3
Detailed Distribution of Earthenware Shard Types in the Excavated Areas of Bukit Gombak, Bukit Kincir, and Tanah Lua

Bukit Gombak	Trench	Everted Rim Jar	Everted/ Flattened Rim Jar	Pinched Rim Jar	Straight Rim Jar	Inverted Rim Jar	Everted Rim Bowl	Straight/ Oblique Rimmed Bowl	Pinched Rim Bowl	Inverted Rim Bowl	Carinated Bowl	Body	Carnation	Knop	Foot	Kendi	Handle	Cooking Stand	Tool	*	Total
Core area	B	85	7	32	4	1	30	3	–	2	2	42	2	3	10	5	1	1	1	2	233
	C	165	32	44	7	2	44	1	1	–	2	21	2	7	35	7	2	–	–	6	378
	D	61	–	19	8	1	19	–	–	–	–	4	4	2	14	6	1	–	–	4	143
Extended settlement area	A	2	–	–	–	–	–	–	–	–	–	1	1	–	–	–	–	–	–	–	4
	E	4	–	–	–	–	–	–	–	–	–	–	–	1	–	–	–	–	–	–	5
	K	16	2	5	–	–	2	–	–	1	1	2	–	2	4	–	2	–	–	1	38
	S	1	–	1	–	–	–	–	–	–	–	–	–	–	–	2	–	–	–	–	4
	N	72	8	17	–	–	36	–	1	–	–	4	5	3	–	5	–	–	–	–	151
	Z	6	–	1	–	–	1	–	–	–	–	3	–	1	–	–	–	2	1	2	17
House site	F	4	–	–	–	–	1	–	–	–	–	–	–	1	–	–	–	–	–	–	6
	M	10	–	–	–	–	1	–	–	–	–	–	1	–	1	–	–	1	–	1	14
	T	13	2	2	–	–	3	–	1	–	–	3	–	–	–	–	–	–	–	–	24
Total		439	51	121	19	4	137	4	3	3	5	80	15	20	64	25	6	3	2	16	1020

Bukit Kincir	Trench	Everted Rim Jar	Everted/ Flattened Rim Jar	Pinched Rim Jar	Straight Rim Jar	Inverted Rim Jar	Everted Rim Bowl	Straight/ Oblique Rimmed Bowl	Pinched Rim Bowl	Inverted Rim Bowl	Carinated Bowl	Body	Carnation	Knop	Foot	Kendi	Handle	Cooking Stand	Tool	*	Total
Settlement	O	6	5	11	–	–	2	5	–	–	–	47	–	–	3	2	–	–	–	–	34
	P	3	–	–	–	–	–	–	–	–	1	–	2	–	6	–	–	–	3	–	62
	R	22	–	2	–	–	1	9	–	–	–	58	4	–	8	–	–	–	–	3	107
Total		31	5	13	–	–	3	14	–	–	1	105	6	–	17	2	–	–	–	3	203
Burial site total	G, H, L, Q	12	1	–	2	–	1	–	–	–	–	2	–	1	3	–	1	–	–	1	24

Tanah Lua	Trench	Everted Rim Jar	Everted/ Flattened Rim Jar	Pinched Rim Jar	Straight Rim Jar	Inverted Rim Jar	Everted Rim Bowl	Straight/ Oblique Rimmed Bowl	Pinched Rim Bowl	Inverted Rim Bowl	Carinated Bowl	Body	Carnation	Knop	Foot	Kendi	Handle	Cooking Stand	Tool	*	Total
Total	A–F, Z	12	–	–	–	–	3	4	–	–	–	50	15	1	–	–	–	4	–	–	89

Note: * undefined; S (spring), Z (survey)

The decorations are rather basic. They include impressions and incised lines, applied decoration, surface wiping, and a red slip. The most common are shallow paddle and anvil patterns that cover the whole body of the vessel, including the shoulder (see Figure 4.10: A–B, D–E, L–M). The widths and depth vary, creating different design patterns: parallel impressions, irregular patterns, and hatches creating a grid or net design.[10] They result from the use of an incised or wrapped wooden paddle. Today the paddles used in Tanah Datar are plain, but in the nineteenth century a grid-pattern incised on a broad paddle with short handle was in use, for example, in the region of Sungai Pagu, South Solok (Hasselt 1881, pp. 406–7, pl. CVII: 1). Round impressions of the anvil are well marked on the interior of some vessels. The pinched rim was produced by pressing a finger or a stick e.g., made of bamboo on the wet clay to produce a simple but eye-catching embellishment. Pinched rim jars represent 19 per cent of the restricted vessels found at Bukit Gombak, and 26.5 per cent of those at Bukit Kincir (see Table 4.3). The surface of open vessels is often polished. Today this effect is obtained by rubbing a pebble, called *panggisa*, onto the surface when the vessel is leather-hard. Other documented forms of decoration include a relief of incised triple or double bands of wavy lines which were made by a pointed instrument on the wet clay.[11] Vessels from Bukit Kincir are covered by a fine red-brown slip on which parallel horizontal bands are applied (see Figure 4.10: N; Figure 4.8: G). When the clay fires to a reddish colour, the wiped or smoothed surfaces appear as though a slip has been intentionally applied, but it is possible that weathering has caused the outer surface to deteriorate. It seems safe to assume that some vessels were decorated by a slip that has dissolved in the post-depositional times.[12] The use of a slip is documented at the prehistoric site at Tanah Lua, but in other highland regions—prehistoric Jambi, for example—this treatment of surfaces is absent (Tjoa-Bonatz 2009, p. 221, ft. 17).

There was strong demand for cooking and storage vessels on both sites of the twin-mound. Certain site characteristics of the earthenware assemblage suggest the presence of larger households in the core area of Bukit Gombak. Larger diameters indicate a need to prepare or store food for large groups. Moreover, a broader range of variations among vessel forms and specific types such as the earthenware *kendi* found only at Bukit Gombak may suggest the presence of elite households. Both communities appreciated decorated earthenware but Bukit Kincir has a higher concentration of pinched vessels. This might lead to the assumption that the lack of imported and more elaborated ware directed preferences to locally produced pottery with rim decoration.

Ethnoarchaeological Comparison: Pottery Making Technique

Today, in the pottery making process of Galo Gandang in Tanah Datar the use of twisted bamboo loops called *bingkai* in forming vessels ensures an even diameter and normative size of its neck (see Figure 4.6).

FIGURE 4.6

At the pottery workshop in Galo Gandang, bamboo loops ensure an even diameter and normative size; paddle and anvil are used to form the vessel

They are part of the initial steps and therefore crucial for differentiating specific pottery technologies according to ethnoarchaeological studies in Southeast Asia (Cort et al. 1997). The potter had prepared several of these loops of various diameters. A lump of clay is slightly flattened and joined to the bamboo loop of suitable diameter by expanding it so that it forms a disc within the loop. The potter then begins to raise the walls of the vessel by pinching and squeezing the clay between the thumb and the fingers or by the potter's fist. This work continues gradually around the loop. When the vessel is round-bottomed and has obtained a certain height the beating with a paddle and anvil begins. To grow it into a basic vessel, the potter uses the right hand to beat a wooden paddle against the outer wall and uses the left hand to hold an anvil against the inner wall while turning the piece. The loop is removed when the bottom assumes a hemispherical shape and the walls are thin enough. Then the paddle and anvil make the wall of the finished vessel even thinner and round off the shoulder.

These loops are characteristic of the Minangkabau area and can be traced back to the nineteenth century in ethnographic literature (Hasselt 1881, pp. 406–7, pl. CVII: 10). Apart from Tanah Datar this instrument is also used in other areas with residents of Minangkabau descent but is extremely rare in other parts of Southeast Asia.[13]

Clay Objects Tools

A clay fragment shaped like an elephant's trunk was retrieved as surface find on Bukit Gombak (see Figure 4.5: L). It is 10 cm long with a maximum diameter of 5 cm. A similar but more elongated object was discovered at the prehistoric site of Tanah Lua, firm evidence that this kind of clay artefact has long been present in the region (see Figure 4.1: F). The Tanah Lua specimen is 23 cm long with a maximum diameter of 7.6 cm. Both examples are broken off at the larger end, and bent and flattened at the other end. Eleven objects with a similar shape have been found in the Jambi highlands, one of which reaches a maximum length of 13 cm. They were found in burial and settlement sites dating from 1400 BCE to the thirteenth century CE, and they probably belong to matching sets.[14] Sometimes their surfaces are embellished with incisions, comb-impressions, or paddle-marks like those in West Sumatra. They have been tentatively identified as cooking stands, the same interpretation given to similarly shaped fragments at a prehistoric site in Vietnam, where they are described as clay stoves (Prior 1998, figure 8). However, none of the Sumatran examples show soot blackening, which raises doubts about whether they could have been hearth stands. Other interpretations, that they represent fragments of elephant sculptures, stands, or anvils, have been rejected (Tjoa-Bonatz 2012, p. 23).

Two clay tools of unknown function are found on Bukit Gombak and four on Bukit Kincir. A small cone with a maximum diameter of 2.6 cm and of only 3.3 cm in height may have served as a ceramic blow-pipe associated with metallurgy on Bukit Gombak found in Trench B (see Figure 4.7: B).[15] This tuyère could have blown air into a smelting furnace or a crucible similar to those found in Banten Girang (Lukman Nurhakim 1994, p. 184, figure III.116). Although Vincent Pigott[16] critically remarks that the lack of obvious slagging at the tip calls this suggestion into question, the bulkfinds of iron slag on the site leave no doubts about the association of metal working. Four clay objects with a brittle texture were made locally as tools for some kind of industrial activity. A conical tool, a surface find from Bukit Gombak, is 10 cm in height (see Figure 4.7: C). The smoothed but slightly inward slanting larger end is 8 cm in diameter and attached to a thick handle. Scholars have proposed that it could have been used as an anvil or as a pestle for grinding food, but it was not possible to check starch residues to test this idea.[17] Throughout Southeast Asia in the pottery making, clay anvils are relatively rare compared to stone anvils, which were used widely. In Indonesia they take different forms such as mushroom-shapes[18] or hollow cones, as in Kota Rentang.[19] Three clay fragments from Trench P also indicate that Bukit Kincir was a manufacturing site connected to metal working: a fragment of a container with a rectangular section (4.7 × 3.9 × 4.7 cm) may have served as casting mould, whereas the function of two slabs is unknown (see Figure 4.7: D). One has a square section (5.2 × 4.5 × 1.4 cm) and the other one forms a cuboid with well smoothed sides (7.4 × 2.6 in × 7.4 cm) (see Figure 4.7: E–F).

FIGURE 4.7

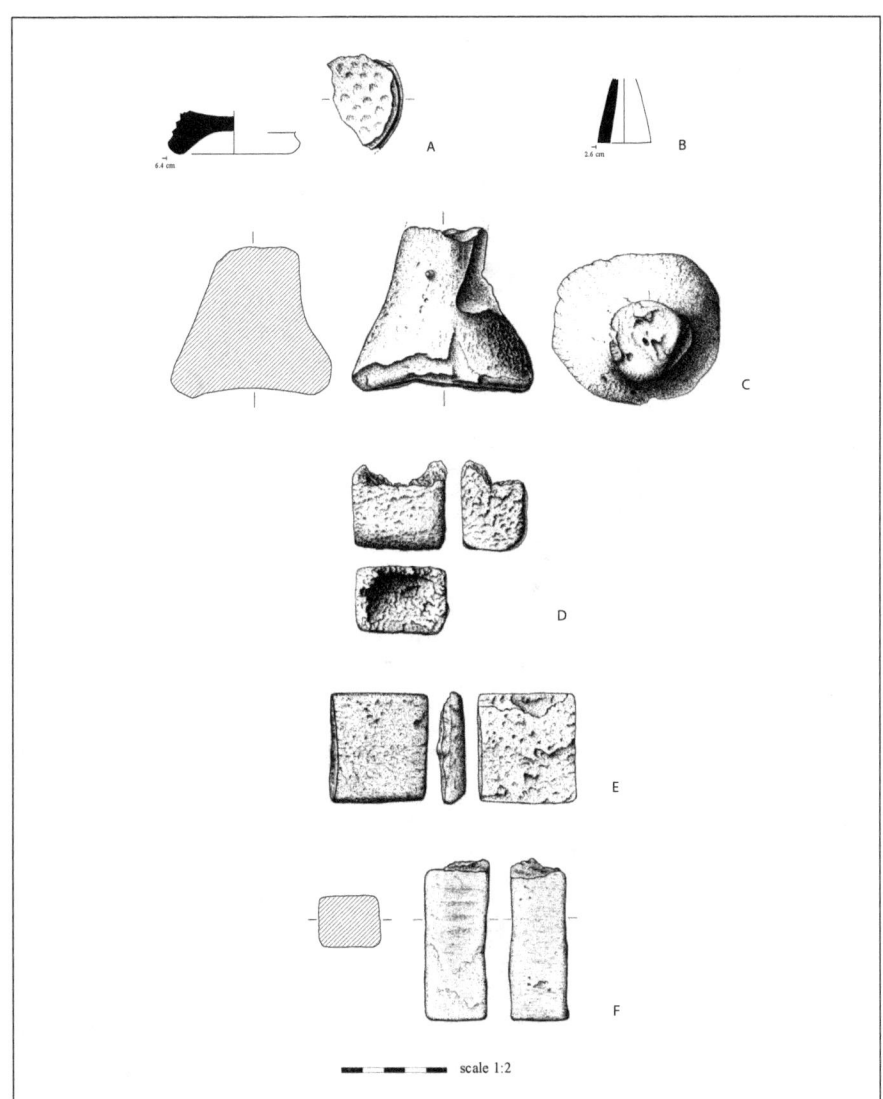

Ceramic tools of Ponggongan (A), Bukit Gombak (B–C), and Bukit Kincir (D–F)

Crucible (A; no. inv. no.), cone or tuyère (B; BG-0504), unknown tools for metal working(?) (C–F; BG-2008-006, BG-0660, BG-0661, BG-0689)

Source: Dayat Hidayat.

FIGURE 4.8

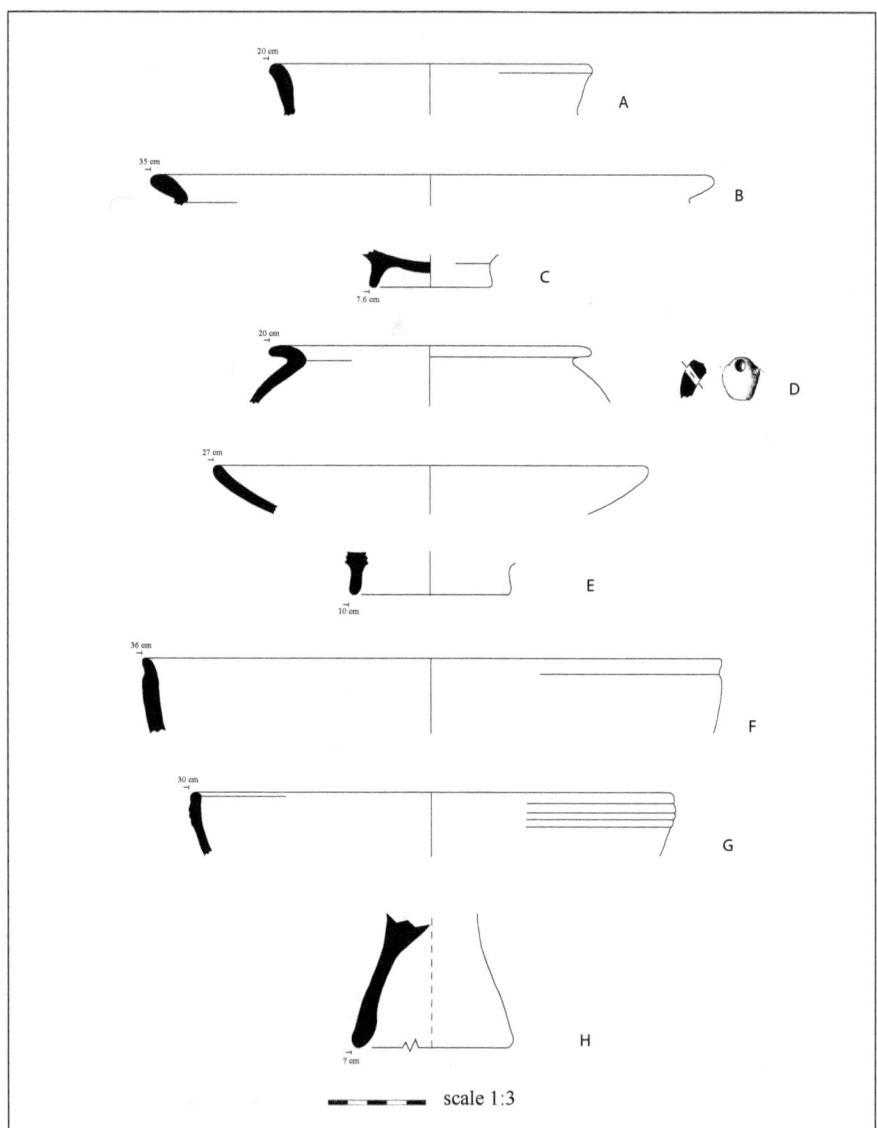

Earthenware of Bukit Kincir

Jar with long everted rim (A; BG-0910-002), everted rim of a large jar (B; BG-0701-032), ringfoot (C; BG-0701-033), large open vessel (F–G; BG-0919-081, BG-0942-001), high stand (H; BG-0919-046), spouted everted rim jar—due to their fabric and finding spot a rim sherd and a spout may come from the same vessel (D; BG-0701-004), footed shallow bowl with straight rim—due to their fabric and finding spot these two sherds may come from the same vessel (E; BG-0701-031)

Source: Dayat Hidayat.

FIGURE 4.9

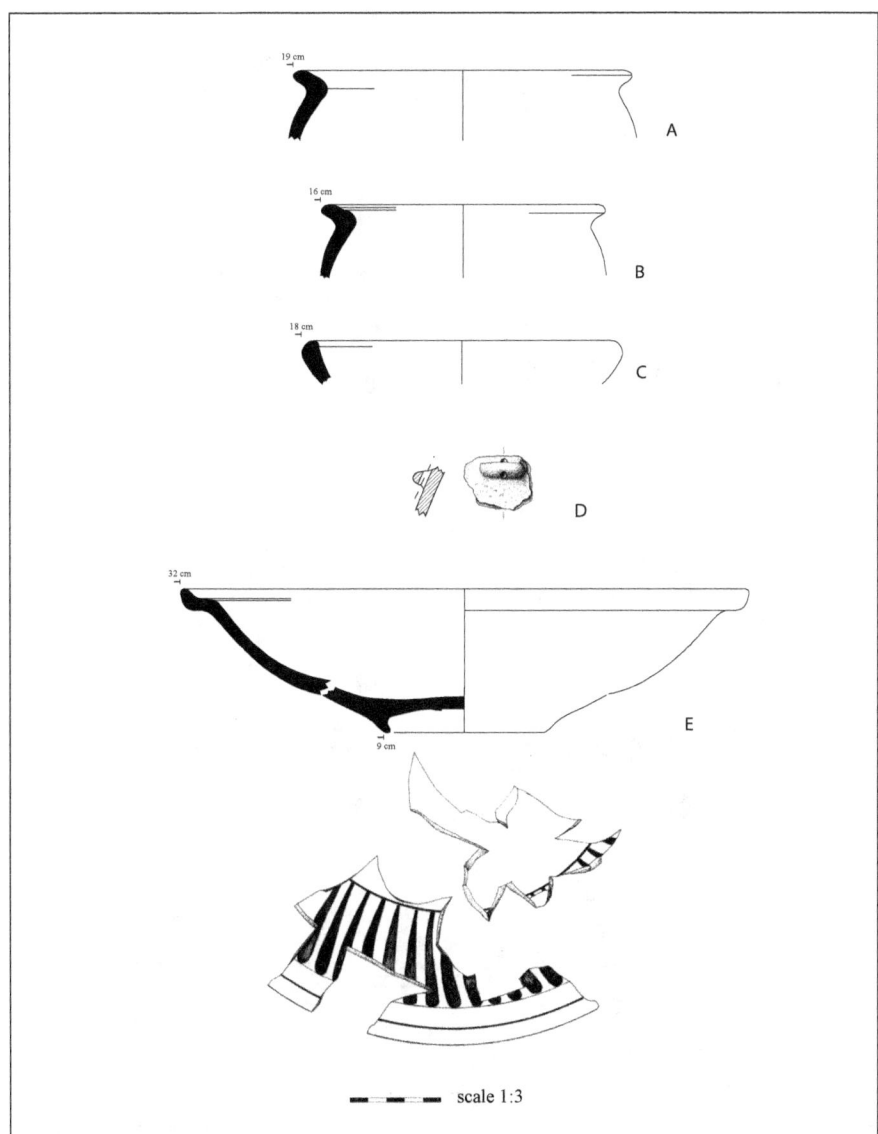

Vessel of the burial site

Jar with everted rim (A; BG-1605-001), jar with everted and internally grooved rim (B; BG-0802-007), shallow bowl with straight rim (C; BG-0802-003), handle (D; BG-0802-006), large Longquan greenware dish of the late fourteenth or fifteenth century (E; BG-1602-001)

Source: Dayat Hidayat.

FIGURE 4.10

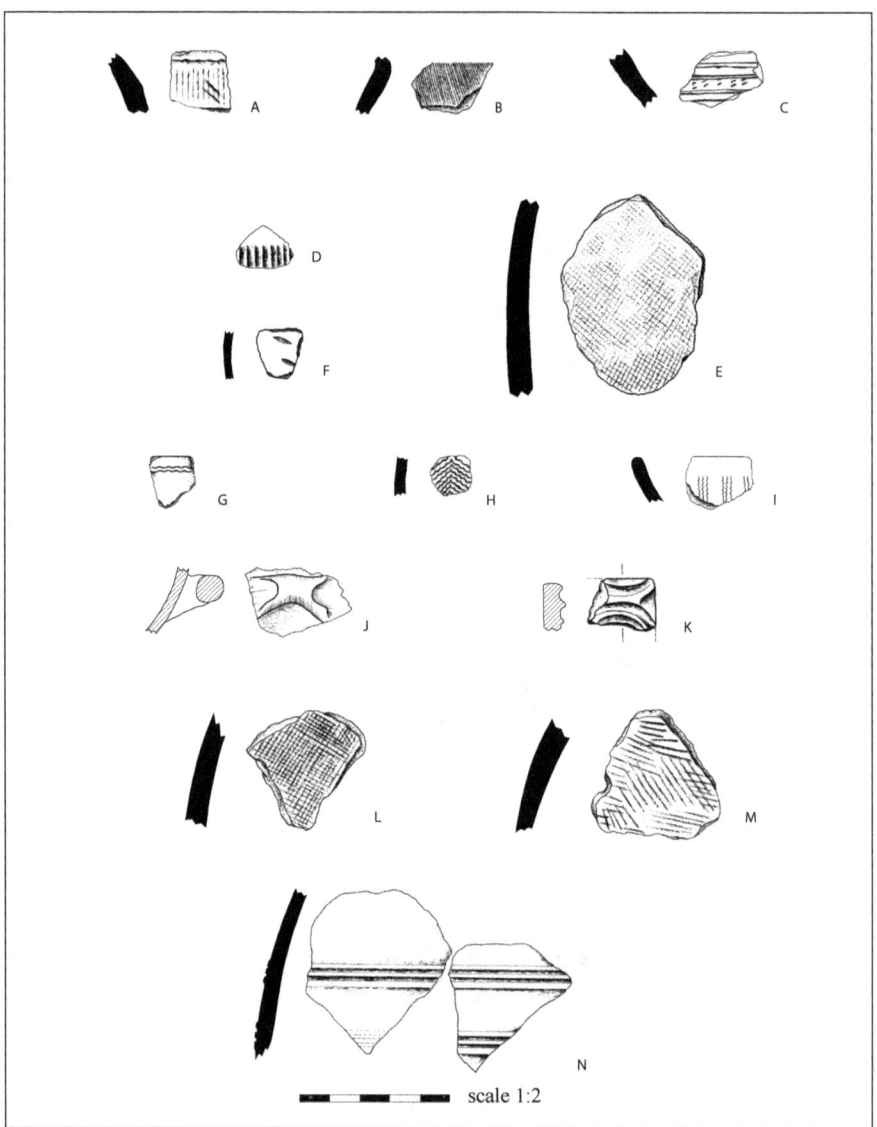

Decoration of Tanah Lua (A–C), Bukit Gombak (D–K), and Bukit Kincir (L–N)

Paddle and anvil impressed (A–B, BG-0751-007, BG-0779-006; D–E; BG-0501-080, BG-0084-021; L–M; BG-0910-005, BG-0686-001), incised (C; BG-0779-005), impressed lenticular shapes (F; BG-1021-020), incised (G–I; BG-0514-064, BG-0509-023, BG-0501-008), appliqué (J–K; BG-1000-021, BG-0503), applied horizontal bands (N; BG-0919-003/-080)

Source: Dayat Hidayat.

4.1.2. Imported Ceramics

Imported ceramics constitute 33.5 per cent of the diagnostic material, 526 sherds in all (see Table 4.4, Map 4.2). The assemblage of foreign ceramics is distinguished by their decoration, paste, colour, or glaze, which often makes it possible to identify their place of origin and time of manufacture.

Chinese Monochromes

In the inventory of imported ware, Chinese ceramics greatly outnumber those from Southeast Asia. Chinese monochromes of the thirteenth to seventeenth centuries are the second largest class of wares in the excavated foreign material. Greenwares from China account for 22 per cent of the imported ceramics. Out of 315 datable Chinese sherds, 60 sherds are from the thirteenth or fourteenth century, 57 from the Yuan or early Ming period and 198 from the middle or late Ming dynasty. On Bukit Gombak the category of greenware consists exclusively of medium-sized bowls of 18–20 cm in diameter with ring feet. They are plain with straight rims, decorated either with shallow ribs parallel to the rim (see Colour Plate 1: H) or with lotus-petals on the exterior wall (see Colour Plate 1: G). Lotus-petal bowls dating from the Song and Yuan dynasties of the thirteenth to the fourteenth centuries are widespread in island Southeast Asia (e.g., Dupoizat 2009, pl. 7, 9–10; Miksic 2013, figure 7.02). The varying colour of the clay and the quality of the glaze, ranging from an opaque thick bright green glaze to more translucent bluish-green or brownish-green glazes, suggest that the greenwares originate from different kiln sites in China. Most of the green-glazed wares exported to Southeast Asia are assigned to the Longquan area in the Zhejian province, but other regions in southern China, such as Fujian and Guangdong, have produced similar wares.

A sherd with a fish application of thick green glaze was found near the southeastern section of the house in the eastern area of Bukit Gombak (see Colour Plate 1: A). The fish, mostly applied in pairs, are placed in the central medallion of dishes and plates of different shapes and displaying additional decorations such as lotus petals or impressed floral scrolls. A few examples have up to five fish applications. There are wide variations in their modelling, workmanship, and depiction. Although it was proposed that the lotus-petalled relief and the moulded fish may have been made over a long period prior to the

TABLE 4.4
Distribution of Imported Ware Types in the Excavated Areas of Bukit Gombak and Bukit Kincir

Bukit Gombak	Trench	Whiteware	Chinese Greenware	Thai Greenware	Blue-and-White Ware	Chinese Stoneware Jar	Southeast Asian Ceramics	Persian Earthenware	Others*	Total
Core area	B	2	10	26	50	4	–	–	–	92
	C	4	17	3	57	40	–	–	–	121
	D	9	55	2	45	30	3	6	–	150
Extended settlement area	A	–	1	–	20	6	–	–	–	27
	E	–	5	–	–	–	–	–	–	5
	K	1	6	2	6	8	–	2	–	25
	N	1	5	–	8	–	–	–	5	19
	S (spring)	–	–	–	1	–	3	–	–	4
	Z (survey)	–	2	–	9	–	–	–	–	11
House site	F	–	5	–	12	–	–	–	–	17
	M	–	4	–	25	1	–	–	–	30
	T	–	–	–	7	–	–	–	1	8
Total		17	110	33	240	89	6	8	6	509

4. Material Culture Studies

Bukit Kincir	Trench	Whiteware	Chinese Greenware	Thai Greenware	Blue-and-White Ware	Chinese Stoneware Jar	Southeast Asian Ceramics	Persian Earthenware	Others*	Total
Settlement site	O	–	1	–	–	5	–	–	–	6
	P	–	–	–	1	–	–	–	–	1
	R	–	–	–	–	–	–	–	–	–
Total		–	1	–	1	5	–	–	–	7
Burial site total	G, H, L, Q	–	5	–	1	–	1	–	–	7

	Whiteware	Chinese Greenware	Thai Greenware	Blue-and-White Ware	Chinese Stoneware Jar	Earthenware	Persian Earthenware	Others*	Total
Total	27	114	33	242	90	14	8	6	534

Note: * modern, Chinese over-glazed ware

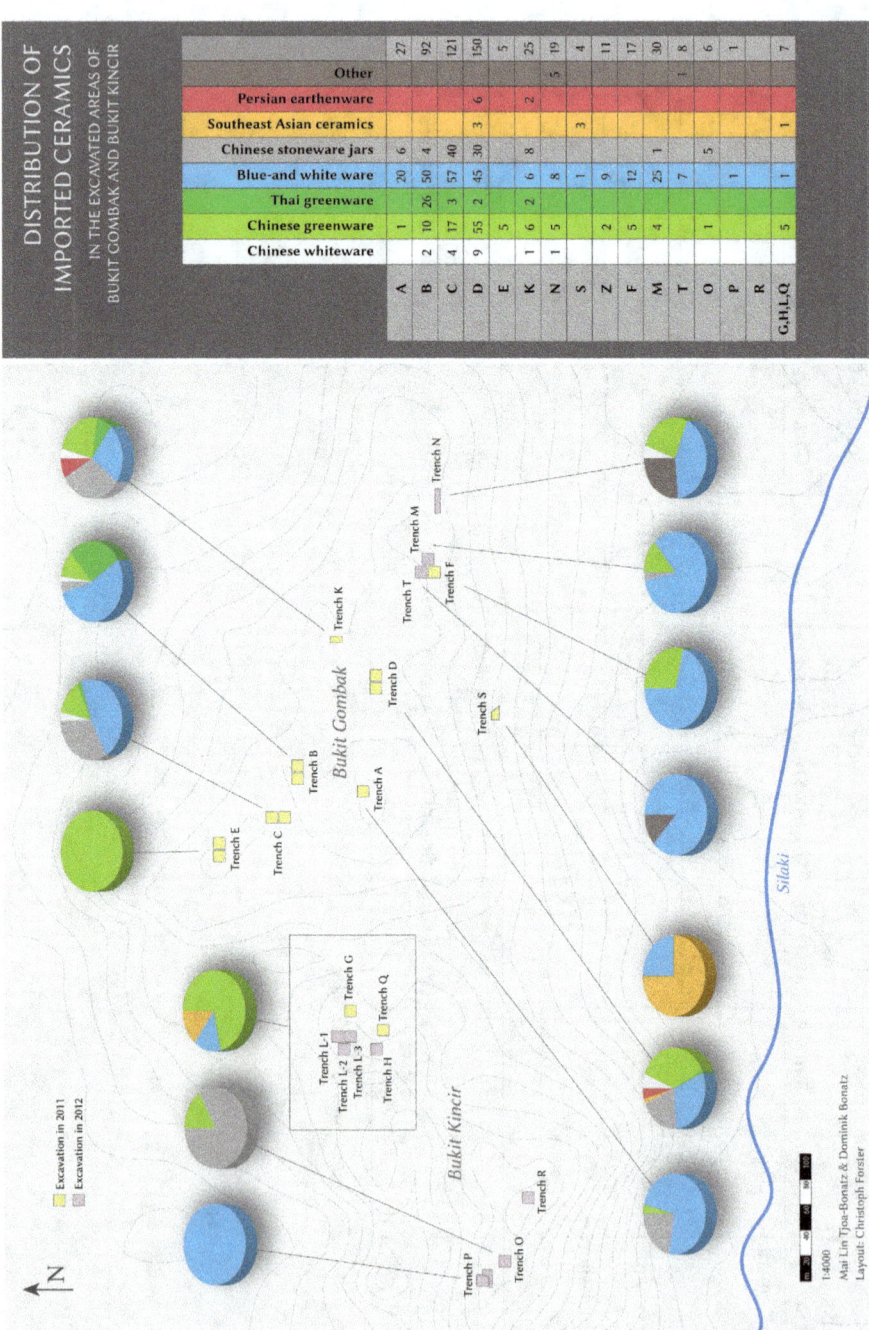

Distribution of imported ceramics in the excavated areas of Bukit Gombak and Bukit Kincir

Source: Mai Lin Tjoa-Bonatz, Dominik Bonatz; lay-out: Christoph Förster.

fifteenth century (Lam 1985, p. 142, no. 375), their origins are generally placed at Longquan and they are usually dated to the late thirteenth to fourteenth centuries. These wares are common in the Indonesian archipelago and have been found in Istanbul, Turkey, and Africa (Dupoizat and Naniek Harkantiningsih 2007, p. 36, figure 4). The fish relief has not been recorded previously in a controlled excavation in the upland regions.

A comparatively large dish of 26 cm in diameter shows a ridged lip on which thin incisions made by a four-pronged tool emphasize the undulating rim (see Colour Plate 1: D). Broader floral scrolls are incised on the cavetto. The reverse side is fluted and the glaze ends before the foot. The dish is potted from cream-coloured stoneware. The glaze is shiny and bright green in colour. It is tentatively dated as 1490–1510,[20] based on similar dishes from the Longquan kilns found at the Lena shoal in Philippine waters (Goddio and Casal 2002, nos. 267–68). Several base fragments of green-glazed dishes raised on heavy ring-feet attest to the persistent popularity of greenware during the Yuan and Ming dynasties from the fourteenth to the mid of the seventeenth centuries (see Colour Plate 1: B; Figure 4.13: C). One example has spiral design incised on the cavetto (see Figure 4.12: G) and another has a moulded floral relief (see Colour Plate 1: E). The latter exposes an unglazed base which has turned rust colour. Other sherds, which might be Swatow greenware of the late sixteenth to the mid of the seventeenth centuries, have a heavy and sandy base with uneven glaze.

Whitewares are extremely rare at the excavation site (3 per cent), represented by dishes up to 24 cm in diameter with everted or straight rims and fluted sides. Probably due to misfiring or post-depositional reasons their colour has turned to buff and light brown. The few sherds originate from an undetermined kiln in China of the Song and Yuan dynasties.

Brown and black stoneware jars constitute a distinct group representing 17.5 per cent of the imports. In Indonesia, the most common examples of this type of ware are ovoid with a short neck above high shoulders, lugs, and are partly covered by a black, golden-brown, or dark brown glaze. Used as freight containers for maritime shipping, they stored household supplies of food and liquids, and also fulfilled ritual functions.[21] Among

Chinese stoneware jars from the Song and Yuan periods, two main types are distinguished (Miksic 1985*c*, pp. 67–71; Miksic 2013, p. 322). One type, potted from a cream-coloured paste with little or no temper, is associated with the southern Chinese province of Guangdong. The other, called "brittle ware", is from Fujian or northern Vietnam. These jars are high fired, with sand or other highly visible material added as temper. On Bukit Gombak, Fujian brittle ware is represented by sherds with an uneven dark brown colour, for example, a rolled rim and a loop (see Colour Plate 1: K), or a golden-brown glaze that easily flakes off (see Colour Plate 1: J).[22] Light brown jars from the thirteenth to fifteenth centuries are commonly found in Indonesia, for example, at Trowulan on Java (Dupoizat and Naniek Harkantiningsih 2007, p. 70). The origins of two sherds from stoneware jars are unknown. One has a diameter of 31 cm and is made of coarse-grained grey clay. The other, which is 11 cm in diameter, is made of fine-grained clay of dark reddish-brown colour. It is partly glazed and the interior shows striations from the potter's wheel.

Among the very few sherds of Chinese origin which were obtained at the settlement site on Bukit Kincir (see Table 4.3) were brown and green glazed sherds of the thirteenth or fourteenth century retrieved in the eastern part of the settlement. The excavation produced a nearly complete celadon jarlet (see Figure 4.12: A), which was a unique find. The bulbous and plain body, which is 6.5 cm at its maximum extension, rests on a straight foot of 2 cm in diameter. Four loops are attached vertically on the shoulder. This kind of two-lug jarlets of the Song or Yuan dynasties were specially "linked to Southeast Asian needs" and were therefore produced for a long time (Dupoizet and Naniek Harkantiningsih 2007, p. 37). The absence of this vessel type on Bukit Gombak is in marked contrast to contemporaneous sites in island Southeast Asia, where jarlets are common.

Blue-and-White Ware

The imported ceramics are mainly blue-and-white ware, which constitutes 46 per cent of the total of the late fifteenth and early sixteenth centuries finds. A majority of the underglazed blue dishes are middle Ming period bowls and dishes 9–23 cm in diameter and embellished by floral and geometric pattern.

A nearly complete bowl, crudely potted with a straight foot and an unglazed base (see Colour Plate 2: K; Figure 4.11: E) is decorated with a band of fuzzy clouds or alternatively described as floral motif, roughly painted in dark blue on the outer wall. This is done with minimal care, and resembles the sketchy strokes of what appears to be a mutilated Chinese character set in a concentric circle on the central medallion. Bowls of this style, assigned to the reigns of Hongwu (1368–98) and Yongle (1402–24), were still exported from Jingdezhen to Southeast Asia in the late fifteenth century (Gotuaco et al. 1997, p. 111; Goddio and Casal 2002, no. 231).

Floral decoration in cobalt blue ranges from stylized but recognizable chrysanthemum blossoms (see Colour Plate 2: H) and delicate featherlike plantain leaves (see Colour Plate 2: I) to hastily sketched but densely filled flower scrolls with pointed leaves (see Colour Plate 2: G; Figure 4.11: B). Lotus panel are found on the lower part of the wall (see Colour Plate 2: B). Flower scrolls and spiral-centred flowers at the centre of the fond might point to the early Ming period, the fourteenth to the early fifteenth centuries (see Colour Plate 2: F).[23] The motif of carefully drawn flower sprays allows comparisons to finds from Singapore and the Royal Nanhai wreck, found in Malaysia and radiocarbon dated to 1320–1460, therefore to the Chenghua-era (1465–87) seen on Colour Plate 2: J.[24] On bowls of the Chenghua-era and Hongzhi-period (1488–1505) made in Jingdezhen a double *vajra* surrounded by floating ribbons occurs as a principal motif in the central medallion, exemplified by two base sherds from middle-sized bowls with a diameter of 6–8 cm (see Colour Plate 2: E).[25] For comparison, this motif as well as the following are documented at shipwreck sites at the Lena shoal, Brunei Junk, or the Santa Cruz found in the Philippines: a band of mutilated Sanskrit characters[26] at the inner mouth-rim (see Figure 4.11: C); featherlike leaves[27] which are carefully outlined and positioned at the edge of the bottom of the outer wall (see Colour Plate 2: D).

The range of geometric patterns is less diversified than the floral patterns. The most eye-catching design is a honeycomb pattern of hexagons with several dots at the centre (see Figure 4.11: A; Colour Plate 2: C, L). On bowls, this pattern is bordered by lotus panels towards the bottom but fully covers the outer wall up to the everted rim. Such bowls also originate from Jingdezhen and were found from 1490–1510 in the archipelago.[28] On Bukit Gombak the honeycomb pattern is combined either with a beaded design[29] on the inner cavetto (see Colour Plate 2: L) or a trellis pattern painted on the inner rim (see Colour Plate 2: C). Both motifs, the honeycomb and the trellis pattern, are particularly characteristic of the Hongzhi period. The trellis border reoccurs at the inside rim of another dish together with a classic scroll spreading across the outer wall (see Figure 4.11: D). An exceptionally large blue-and-white plate dated to the fifteenth or early sixteenth century has a heavy, fully glazed base of 22 cm in diameter (see Figure 4.12: C). The fragmented central motif is set against a background of waves surrounded by a ring of trefoils, with a classic scroll on the outside wall. Dishes with roughly sketched lines (see Figure 4.12: B; Figure 4.13: A) might be assigned to Swatow ware from the end of the sixteenth or beginning of the seventeenth century, one of which has a sandy base.

The underglaze blue fragments from China can almost exclusively be assigned to the second half of the fifteenth or the very beginning of the sixteenth century. Most are trade ware from Jingdezhen in Jiangxi province.

Imports from Southeast Asia and Persia

Southeast Asian ceramics on Bukit Gombak, though very small in number, come mainly from what is now Thailand. Sawankhalok green-glazed ceramics account for 6.5 per cent of the imported ware (see Table 4.4). Apart from fine-paste-ware from an unknown site in Southeast Asia, glazed pottery from Vietnam, Burma, and Persia support the idea that wares from various Asian regions reached the highlands of Sumatra.

The glazed sherds from Persia are ridged at the exterior and expose a pinkish-coloured clay (see Colour Plate 1: N). The Sawankhalok celadon vessels of the fourteenth to sixteenth centuries include medium to large dishes with a diameter of 21–32 cm, a flat recessed rim, and unglazed ring bases 8–13 cm in diameter (see Figure 4.13: D–E). They are made from grey clay, and the glaze is a shiny vitreous, light green. Their plain exterior walls seem more characteristic of the earlier period (Brown 2009, p. 56). Incised concentric circles or undulating foliage on the upper cavetto are the only decoration on some of the Thai pieces

FIGURE 4.11

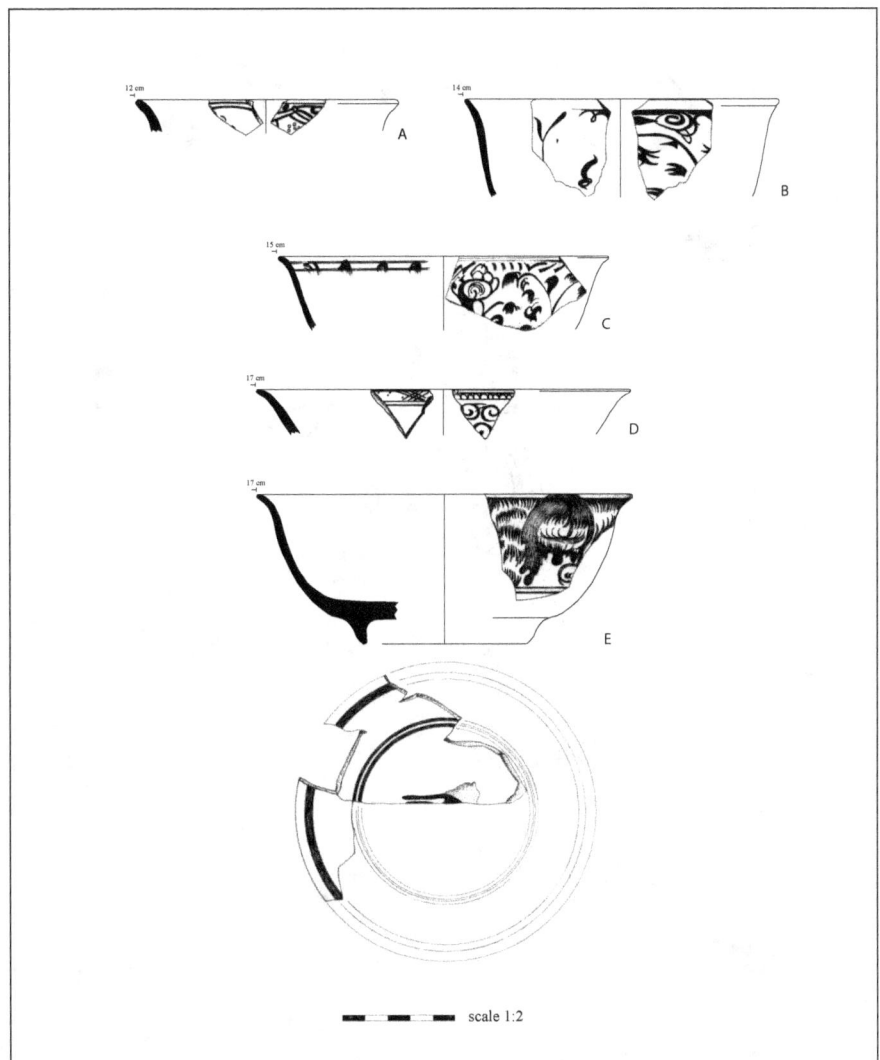

Chinese ceramics of Bukit Gombak

Blue-and-white dishes from Jingdezhen, second half of the fifteenth or early sixteenth century (A–E; BG-0003-005, BG-1000-104, BG-1000-179, BG-0003-007, BG-0001-003/-007/BG-0003-019)

Source: Dayat Hidayat.

FIGURE 4.12

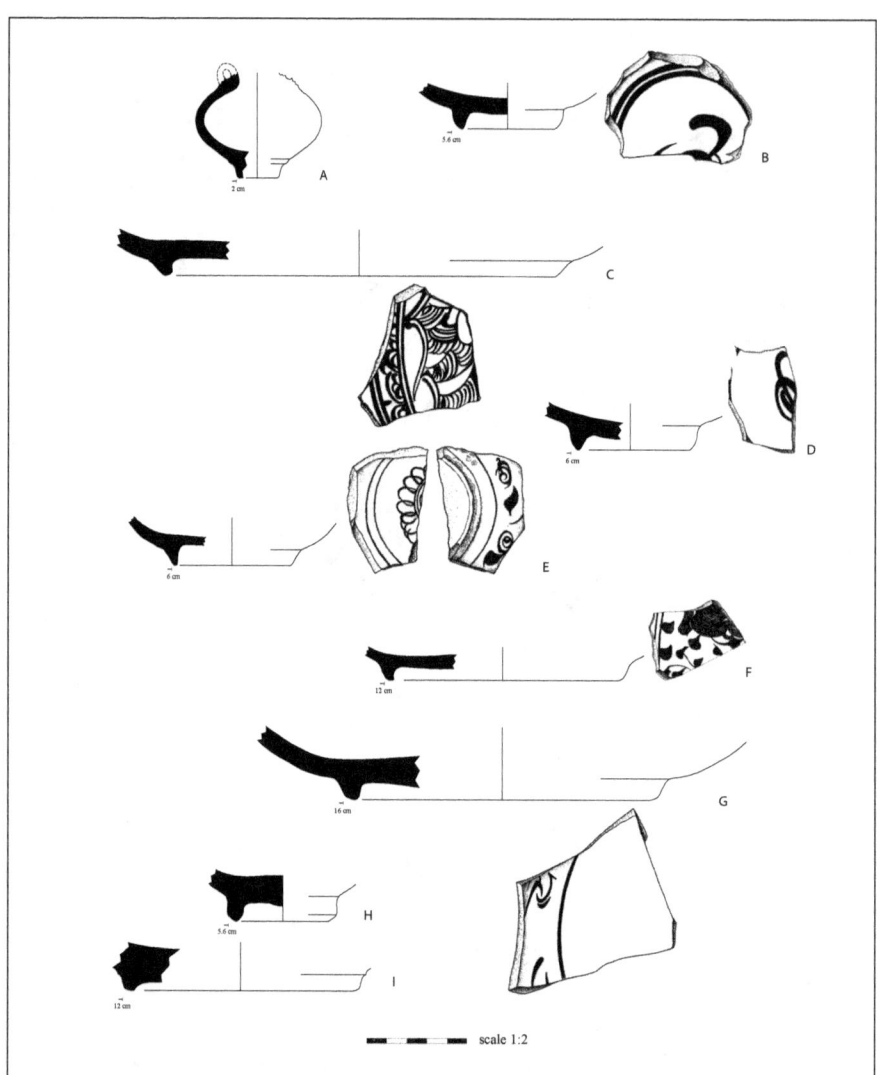

Chinese ceramics of Bukit Kincir (A) and Bukit Gombak (B–I)

Celadon jarlet, thirteenth to fourteenth centuries (A; BG-0701-011), blue-and-white Swatow ware of the end of the sixteenth or early seventeenth century (B; BG-0063-001), blue-and-white dishes, fifteenth to sixteenth centuries (C; BG-0050-066 with a base of 20 cm; D–F; BG-1505-001, BG-1006-157, BG-0600-010), celadon dish of the fourteenth to sixteenth centuries (G–I; BG-2008-008, BG-2008-017, BG-1006-083)

Source: Dayat Hidayat.

FIGURE 4.13

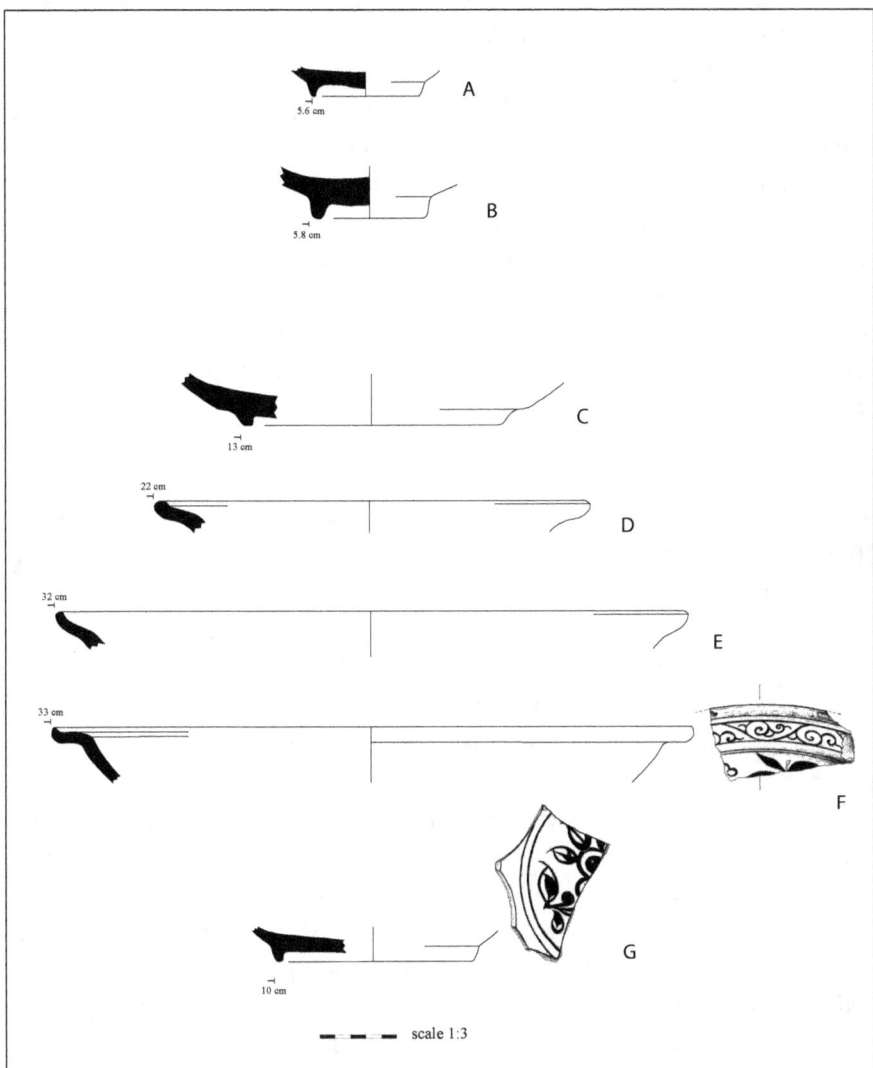

Chinese ceramics of Bukit Gombak

Celadon dish, survey find (A; BG-0600-001), celadon dishes of Bukit Gombak, fourteenth to sixteenth centuries (B–C; BG-0063-070; BG-0514-103); imported ware from mainland Southeast Asia: Sawankhalok celadon vessel of the fifteenth to sixteenth centuries (D–E; BG-0501-153, BG-1022-033), Vietnamese blue-and-white dishes of the mid fifteenth to early sixteenth centuries (F–G; BG-1006-160, BG-1022-001)

Source: Dayat Hidayat.

found at Bukit Gombak. A floral band is indicative for the second half of the fifteenth century (see Colour Plate 1: C).[30] The same timeframe is assumed for a large dish tentatively ascribed to Vietnam. The blue-and-white saucer of 33 cm in diameter has a flat recessed rim on which a finely drawn scroll expands. Flowers at the inner wall and petals at the outer one are drawn in light blue colour (see Colour Plate 2: N).[31] An unglazed ring base of another Vietnamese dish measures 8 cm in diameter and has typically turned violet-red (see Colour Plate 2: M; Figure 4.13: G). The central medallion shows a flower in bloom encircled by leaves and raised on a leafy branch, the back towards the base is decorated by jewelled lappets. This simplified floral motif and the staining of the glaze is similar to a saucer from the Hoi An shoal, which suggests a date of the late fifteenth or early sixteenth century (Butterfields 2000, no. 1640; Miksic 2013, p. 203).

Investigations of shipwrecks in Southeast Asian waters only show items from Burma for a short period between 1470 and 1505 (Brown 2009, pp. 7–8). A single light-brown sherd is a rare piece of evidence that this trade was also connected to Bukit Gombak.[32]

Fine-paste wares were found at the water source and at one place in the core area of Bukit Gombak (see Colour Plate 1: M). The thin sherds are ribbed in a way that is characteristic of *kendi* which often have many flanges. The pieces are 11 cm in diameter, and the clay is buff-coloured and has no discernible temper. This type of ware has been termed as fine-paste ware to distinguish it from local earthenware at Kota Cina (Edwards McKinnon 2009). On the basis of content analyses, several production centres have been identified in Southeast Asia. Wares from Kota Cina came from East Java, while those from Singapore matched examples from Southern Thailand.[33] Dated fine-paste artefacts from the eighth to the fifteenth centuries have been retrieved from Song/Yuan-period shipwrecks, at numerous Majapahit sites in East Java, and from Muara Jambi, Singapore, the Philippines, and Malaysia (Miksic 2013, pp. 358–59).[34] Some of the drinking vessels were found in ceremonial contexts in Java and used in the "context of Hindu symbolism and aesthetics" (Miksic and Yap 1990, pp. 49–50). Their rarity and the places sherds were found at Bukit Gombak, for example, at the spring, does not rule out the possibility that they served as fine ceremonial ceramics.

Conclusion

The ceramic material collected provides evidence that the site may have been occupied as early as the thirteenth century and remained occupied until the early seventeenth century. A limited range of forms reached the highlands: mainly jars, bowls, and plates. The quality ranges from a few fine examples (see Colour Plate 2: A) and large dishes to rather sketchy painted small to medium size pieces with modest decoration and poorly fired discoloured glazes. Among the blue-and-white wares of Bukit Gombak a thin teacup with shiny glaze is a rare, high quality ware from Jingdezhen in the Jiangxi province. The decoration, which depicts a dragonfly, is also recorded in Banten Lama[35] (see Colour Plate 2: A). The preference for small and medium sized vessels is explained by the fact that they could more readily be transported hundreds of kilometre to upland regions. Large vessels only appear in the later periods of the find assemblage.

Sustained long-distance trade relations during this period allowed the population on Bukit Gombak to acquire ceramic luxury goods that were a sign of wealth and prestige. I, therefore, assume that a sophisticated society lived at this site, one whose economic surplus was invested in trade and the conspicuous consumption of foreign luxury goods. For supplies, the highlanders depended on trade, which passed through the harbour sites, but we do not know if they may have demanded specific ware types and shapes. Cobalt-blue Chinese bowls and dishes with geometric and floral designs were relatively numerous in the retrieved assemblage. Foreign goods may have been brought directly to the highlands by Chinese traders visiting the Minangkabau region or indirectly through an integrated market system. A letter of 1636 found in colonial records attests to the existence of an already well-established direct trade, saying that the Minangkabau did not come down to Jambi because they were "now so spoiled having Chinese bring the goods to them" (Reid 1993, p. 312).

The distribution pattern of the imported ceramic groups in the excavation trenches reveals obvious spatial differences (see Table 4.3). The foreign material is concentrated in the settlement cores on Bukit Gombak (Trenches B–D), but it is also spread across the hill, so that I assume that ceramics were available to various groups living there.

The ceramic imports were used along with earthenware and household items in a domestic context. On Bukit Gombak storage jars were not found in every trench but were concentrated in the northern and central part of the hill, where most of the early white- and greenware were also retrieved. The rare pieces from Persia, Burma, and of fine-paste *kendi*, are concentrated in Trench D. The *kendi* was also retrieved near the water source, obviously in connection with its use as a drinking vessel.

The amount of imported ware on Bukit Gombak is in marked contrast to the very few sherds of Chinese origin retrieved on the settlement site of Bukit Kincir, where they are concentrated in the eastern part of the settlement and represented by ceramics of the thirteenth or fourteenth century.

4.2. Stone Artefacts

The second largest assemblage, after ceramics, were the lithic finds. This material consists of obsidian and non-siliceous rock, along with a single artefact of quartz and another of chert. Obsidian is locally available in the volcanic highland of Sumatra. Different kinds of fine- and coarse-grained, sedimentary, and magmatic rocks were retrieved from the riverbeds nearby. The geological source for the quartz and chert is not known but chert is unavailable in the highlands, indicating that there was intraregional exchange of stone raw material (Bonatz 2012, p. 54).

Certain use-wear patterns and design differences discussed by pre-historian and lithic technologists help to distinguish morphological variations of the stone assemblage. By recognizing morphological attributes, technical drawings by Dayat Hidayat provide a basis for the following surface description.[36] Ethnographic records add more information about lithic traditions, but existing lithological studies are based on external observations only. Thus, the distinction between retouched and utilized flakes as well as knapped stones—described as artefacts—and naturally crushed stones remains ambiguous. Macroscopic use wear and petrographic analyses would help resolve these ambiguities. If the collected stones were not tools, excavators have assumed that they were deposited intentionally and collected them as artefacts.

Archaeologists have debated whether descriptive patterns of prehistory are applicable to later times, when percussion instruments made from metal were available.[37] The scarcity of archaeological records of ground stone tools and flaked lithic at settlement sites from the historic period draws attention to the urgent need for thorough documentation of stone material at later period sites. The extremely small amount of lithic is in marked contrast to much larger find assemblages from other sites that are contemporaneous or from later periods, such as Bukit Hasang, Banten Girang, or Bengkulu.[38] Their stone assemblages include decorative art and imported stone objects, items not found in West Sumatra. This leads to the conclusion that stone tools were either not recognized as such or did not exist to the same degree. The broad range of stone tools and the different materials used seem particularly characteristic of the highland region, where the manufacture and use of stone implements persisted in historic times despite the availability of metal instruments.

A total of 258 stone artefacts were recovered: 89 from Bukit Gombak and 151 from the settlement of Bukit Kincir (see Table 4.5). The assemblage can be distinguished into flaked lithics and ground stone tools. The lithics made from obsidian encompass unretouched flakes, angular debris, and retouched artefacts. Flakes are fragments with a length smaller than their width. The latter include potentially utilized core tools, micro- or macro-sized flakes such as scrapers and borers. Regularly retouched edges generally define flakes as items that have been used, but these traces can also result from accidental damage caused during the depositional period. The ground stones comprise choppers, grinding tools including a grinding slab, pestles, and striking tools such as adzes, hammerstones, and assumed pottery anvil. This range of stone artefacts is seen as demonstrating their use in food processing, cultivation, and craft production.

4.2.1. Flaked Lithic

Flaked lithic are mainly obsidians apart from flakes of quartz at Bukit Kincir and chert at the burial ground (see also on p. 198). At the prehistoric site of Tanah Lua, a bilateral retouched obsidian flake with proximal-medial use retouches and edge damages was found. The obsidian assemblage of Bukit Gombak comprises 47 waste flakes and

TABLE 4.5
Stone Artefacts from Bukit Gombak, Bukit Kincir, and Tanah Lua

Bukit Gombak	Trench	Obsidian			Chert	Quartz	Non-siliceous Rock	Total	Stone Finds/ Excavated Vol.
		Debris	Retouched						
Core area	B	6	2	–	–	–	3	11	–
	C	5	1	–	–	–	7	13	–
	D	3	1	–	–	–	4	8	–
Extended settlement area	A	–	1	–	–	–	2	3	–
	E	–	4	–	–	–	–	4	–
	K	–	–	–	–	–	–	–	–
	N	6	–	–	–	–	–	6	–
	S (spring)	–	1	–	–	–	3	4	–
	Z (survey)	3	–	–	–	–	2	5	–
House site	F	1	–	–	–	–	1	2	–
	M	1	3	–	–	–	2	6	–
	T	22	3	–	–	–	2	27	–
Total		47 (52%)	16 (18%)	–	–	–	26 (30%)	89 (100%)	0.26

4. Material Culture Studies

Bukit Kincir	Trench	Obsidian		Chert	Quartz	Non-siliceous Rock	Total	Stone Finds/ Excavated Vol.
		Debris	Retouched					
Settlement	O	40	4	–	1	3	48	–
	P	1	3	–	–	13	17	–
	R	69	8	–	–	9	86	–
Total		110 (72%)	15 (10%)	–	1 (1%)	25 (18%)	151	1.1
Burial site	G	1	–	–	–	1	2	–
	H	–	–	–	–	–	–	–
	L	–	–	–	–	–	–	–
	Q	5	–	1	–	–	5	–
Total		6 (75%)	–	1 (12.5%)	–	1 (12.5%)	8 (100%)	0.04

Tanah Lua	Trench	Obsidian		Chert	Quartz	Non-siliceous Rock	Total	Stone Finds/ Excavated Vol.
		Debris	Retouched					
	A	2	–	–	–	–	2	–
	B	–	1	–	–	–	1	–
	C	6	1	–	–	1	8	–
	D	8	3	–	–	–	11	–
	E, F	–	–	–	–	–	–	–
	Z (survey)	1	1	–	–	–	5	–
Total		17 (63%)	6 (22%)	–	–	4 (15%)	27	1.6

TABLE 4.6
Other Small Finds in the Excavated Areas of Bukit Gombak and Bukit Kincir

Bukit Gombak	Trench	Bone	Glass	Metal	Iron Slag	Modern	Total
Core area	B	1	1	8	–	2	12
	C	–	4	8	3 (40 g)	4	32
	D	–	–	9	1 (10 g)	5	23
Extended settlement area	A	–	–	–	–	–	–
	E	–	–	3	–	1	4
	K	–	–	3	–	2	5
	N	–	35	–	12 (510 g)	1	54
	S (spring)	–	–	–	–	–	–
	Z (survey)	–	–	1	–	–	1
House site	F	–	–	2	–	3	5
	M	–	–	–	–	–	–
	T	1	–	–	–	–	1
Total		2	40	34	16 (560 g)	18	199

Bukit Kincir settlement	Trench	Bone	Glass	Metal	Iron Slag	Modern	Total
	O	–	–	–	1 (20 g)	–	49
	P	–	1	–	1 (10 g)	–	18
	R	–	–	1	19 (210 g)	–	106
Total		–	1	1	21 (240 g)	–	173
Burial site	G	–	–	2	–	1	3
	H	–	–	1	–	–	1
	L	–	–	–	–	4	4
	Q	–	–	–	–	–	–
Total		–	–	3	–	5	8

15 retouched flakes retrieved in the settlement core and its northeastern extension (Trenches A–D, E). In the northeastern part of the hill, obsidian was recovered close to the postholes of the house in the northeast and northwest, which suggests use in a domestic context, possibly small-scale industrial activities at the outdoor hearth in the northeastern section of Trench M (see Figure 3.16). The flakes show possible use retouches at the lateral side of the distal end (see Figure 4.14: A–B). The flake from the northwestern side of the house site (Trench T) is retouched on the lateral side with a notched retouch on the distal side (see Figure 4.14: D).

The working instruments from the core area of Bukit Gombak include a composite tool with endscraper-like, oblique edge retouches and on the left-lateral side notches on the ventral face (see Figure 4.14: C), a fragment with borer-like modifications at its distal end on the ventral side (see Figure 4.14: E), and an end-scraper with straight edges at its distal end (see Figure 4.14: F). Two elongated negatives indicate the removal of two bladelets. Similar traces are seen on the lateral and distal sides of another retouched flake (see Figure 4.14: G). A surface find shows damage to the distal end and edge that suggests a composite tool, probably with a double function as a borer and a perforator for woodworking or a notched piece (see Figure 4.14: H).

On Bukit Kincir, the obsidian finds comprise 15 retouched flakes, 110 waste flakes (including pieces with cortex) and one quartz flake. The debris are more than double the amount at Bukit Gombak, where debris constitutes 52 per cent of the lithic assemblage compared with 72 per cent on Bukit Kincir. The number of retouched flakes at Bukit Kincir relative to the excavated volume is also much higher than at Bukit Gombak, a factor of 0.26 stands in sharp contrast to 1.1 at Bukit Kincir. The highest concentration of debris and flaked obsidian is in the western settlement zone in Trench R. This distribution pattern and the finding of an obsidian core strongly suggest that obsidian tools were not only used but also produced on site. Most of the flakes from this trench exhibit multiple retouched edges, which may represent retouches or edge damages (see Figure 4.18: A–B). The following examples are representative: a core tablet with a scraping edge and retouches on the ventral and dorsal sides at the proximal end and on the dorsal side at the distal end (see Figure 4.18: C), flakes with lateral

FIGURE 4.14

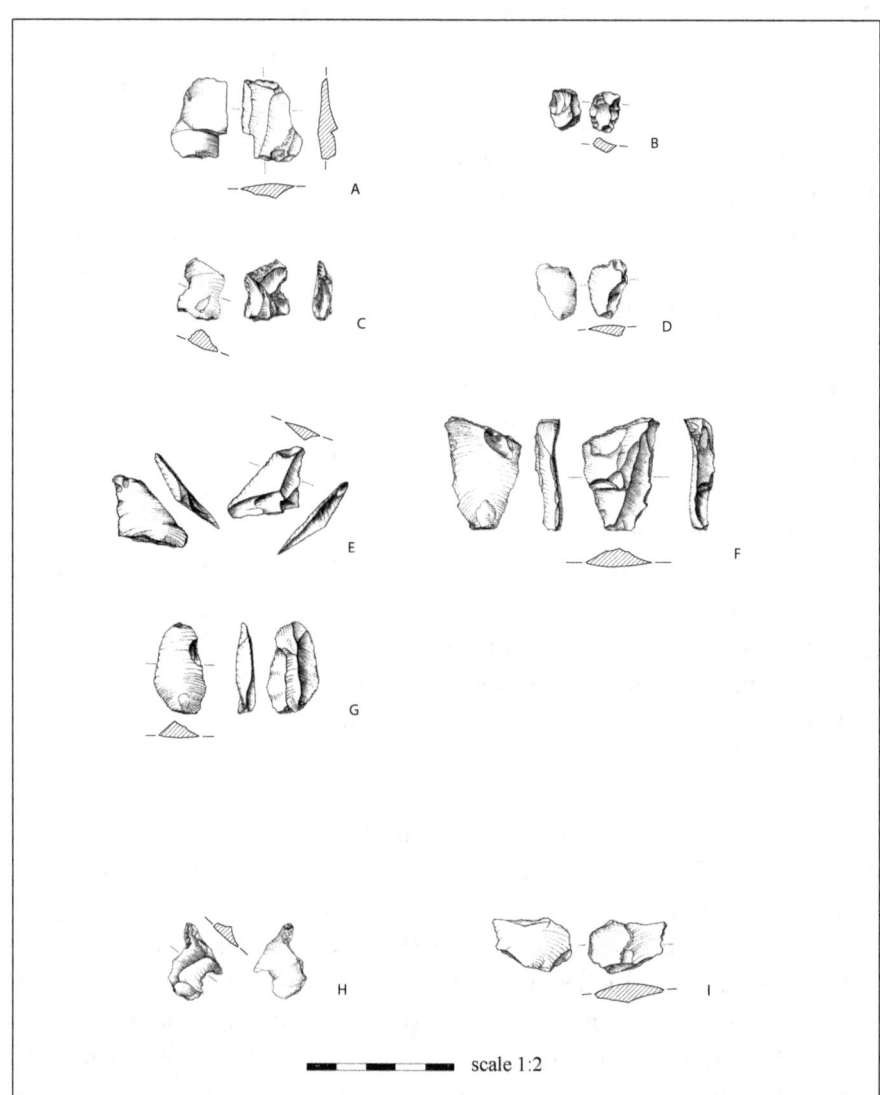

Flaked lithics of Bukit Gombak and Tanah Lua

Flakes of Bukit Gombak (A–E; BG-0307, BG-0303, BG-0004, BG-0968, BG-0525), end-scraper (F–G; BG-0072, BG-1050), perforator or borer of Tanah Lua (H; BG-2001), flake of Tanah Lua (I; BG-0762)

Source: Dayat Hidayat.

edge retouches on the ventral side (see Figure 4.18: D), lateral dorso-ventral use retouches with a notch in the basal part (see Figure 4.18: E), with edge retouches on the dorsal side and in the proximal part with two notch-like retouches (see Figure 4.18: F), and with two flake scars on the ventral side (see Figure 4.18: G). Use retouches on a core tool used for chopping (see Figure 4.18: H) are oblique what indicates an unidirectional percussion technique. In adjacent excavation trenches on Bukit Kincir obsidian tools are less frequently documented, although some of them show traces of utilization such as finely worked edge retouches (see Figure 4.18: I) or serrated retouches.

The single find of a quartz flake in Trench O on Bukit Kincir can be associated with a strike-a-light tool. Burnt areas are found in this excavation area. Fire-making equipment recorded ethnographically on Sumatra and elsewhere in island Southeast Asia includes a steel blade, prepared tinder, and a chalcedony or quartz flake carried in a bamboo container as part of personal possessions.[39] In addition to percussion stones and lighting tools, clay tools, baked clay, charcoal, and iron slag provide firm evidence for small-scale iron smelting at Bukit Kincir. Similar iron smelting deposits, for example, on Sulawesi also contain obsidian tools and flaked chert artefacts (Bulbeck and Caldwell 2000, pp. 25, 32).

Moser emphasizes the need for further investigation of a blade industry on Sumatra.[40] Blade making is known in Sabah on Borneo, Java, Sulawesi, and the lesser Sunda Islands, but not in the Malay Peninsula or Southern Thailand.

4.2.2. Ground Stone Tools

The ground stone tools were crafted from two kinds of non-siliceous materials. One group was made of fine-grained sedimentary rock of two different colours. A light brown-greyish colour may represent sandstone or crystalline limestone and red-brown colour with a banded surface, possibly denoting quartzite or chalcopyrite. The second group is represented by coarse-grained magmatic rock such as andesite or riolite, with a porous surface and light brown-greyish colour showing a large amount of glimmer, with black and white inclusions. The percussion and grinding tools take a variety of forms. Most of the 26 tools were found in the core area of Bukit Gombak.

Fragments of six tanged adzes made from fine-grained sandstone form a distinct group of hafted percussion tools. When hafted, the blades of these adzes are set at right angles to the handle. Three were recovered in the central area on Bukit Gombak, at the northwestern part of the house site in the eastern area and at the water source (Trenches C, S, T). A fully preserved adze was retrieved at the burial ground (see Figure 4.15: F). Two of them have a plano-convex section and the planes at the front, back, and sides intersect at sharp angles with a tapered cutting edge (see Figure 4.15: B, E). The find seen in Figure 4.15: B from the water source is the most widespread adze-type in Southeast Asia.[41] A similar specimen with a plano-convex section and a tapered cutting edge was recovered at Tanah Lua (see Figure 4.15: A), indicating continuous use of this type of shafted percussion tool since prehistory. Variations of shape within this tool group include an edge-ground tool (see Figure 4.15: D)[42] and a pick adze (see Figure 4.15: C) with a pointed-convex section and a remarkable multi-faceted ridge at the convex part of the cutting edge,[43] although this ridge might simply indicate an unfinished adze. All these artefacts are characterized by high quality workmanship and finish. They lack obvious traces of use, suggesting a possible symbolic dimension.

In an ethnographic context, small polished adzes are used to sharpen a cock's spurs prior to a cockfight.[44] In an archaeological context, polished stone adzes from the metal-using period that were made from semi-precious stones were found close to jar burials in Lintang, Pasemah, and are thought to have had a ceremonial or status-enhancing purpose (Guillaud 2006, pp. 42–43, figures 30–32; Bonatz 2009, figure 3-5). The dating of stone adzes is problematic because most of them come from an unsafe archaeological context. Various examples of polished black adzes and unpolished adzes made from grey or brown non-siliceous material are in the Padang Museum but the context of the finds is lacking. Esteemed as *pusaka*, they are kept by the local population for generations, while others were sold by antique dealers. Fragments of six polished stone adzes from Tanah Datar, including common ones with a plano-convex section, were obtained by duke Johann Albrecht during

4. Material Culture Studies

FIGURE 4.15

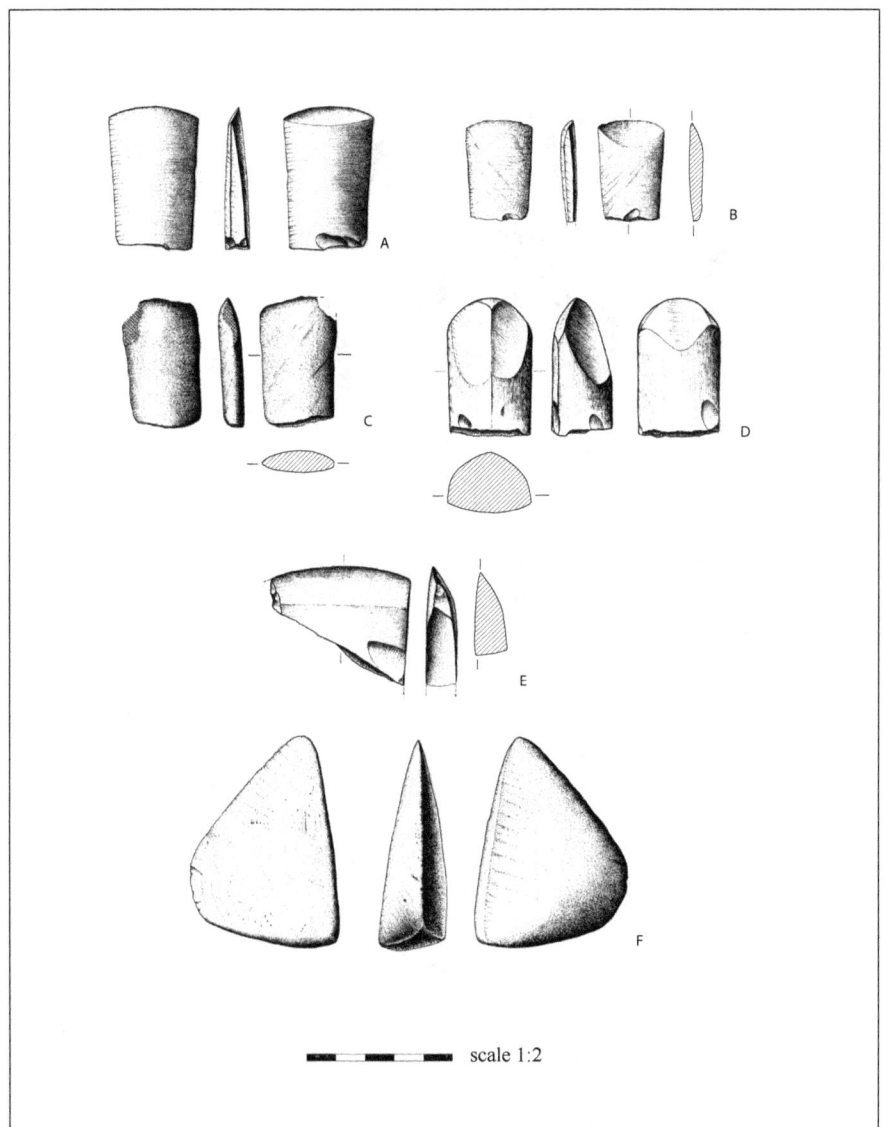

Adzes of Tanah Lua, Bukit Gombak, and Bukit Kincir

Adzes of Tanah Lua (A; BG-2003), Bukit Gombak (C–E; BG-0963, BG-1005, BG-1020), from the water source (B; BG-1500), and the burial site of Bukit Kincir (F; BG-1212)

Source: Dayat Hidayat.

FIGURE 4.16

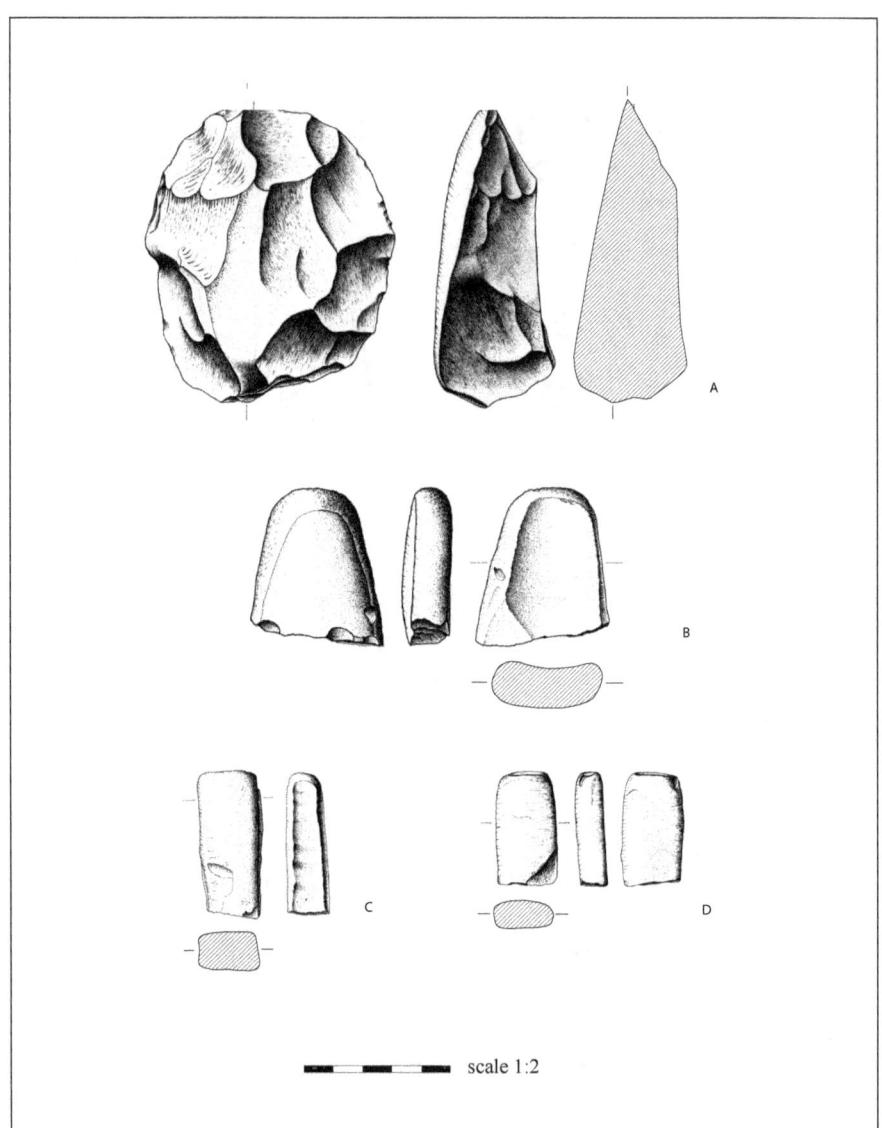

Ground stone tools of Bukit Gombak

Core or percussion tool (A; BG-1501), stone with two retouched negatives (B; BG-0522) and with parallel grooves (C; BG-1017), whetstone (D; BG-0601)

Source: Dayat Hidayat.

his visit of Batusangkar in 1850 and are now stored in the Städtisches Museum in Braunschweig (Haase 2004, pp. 130–32). Heirlooms from Kerinci include four adzes made from different rock materials that have typical rectangular or plano-convex sections (including one from Bukit Koto Payung, east of Semurup (no. DSN/ISK/06-08-C/110)). Among the polished specimens, one from Jerangkang Tinggi, Desa Muak (no. DSN/ISK/06-08-C/111), and one from Bukit Koto Pelih, Desa Lolo Gedang (no. DSN/ISK/06-08-C/109) can be tentatively dated to the tenth to thirteenth centuries due to megalithic remains found near them (Bonatz et al. 2006). The fourth adze which is unpolished and made from non-siliceous grey material obtained in Sungai Penuh provides the best comparison to the ones found on Bukit Gombak (no. DSN/ISK/06-08-C/108).[45]

Other percussion tools on Bukit Gombak are made of magmatic coarse-grained rock of light brown colour. A stone found on the surface has two circular depressions that suggest it was used as a grinding or pulverization slab (see Figure 4.17: A). Similar objects called *kundale* on the Salamon Islands, East Timor, and the Philippines, are used for cracking nuts.[46] A subspherical hammerstone found near the water source shows use traces on both smaller ends (see Figure 4.17: B). A pestle with a rectangular section has use marks concentrated at the smaller end (see Figure 4.17: C). Similar stones are used today for cracking candlenuts (Charras et al. 2006, figure 62). The traces on its other end suggest a secondary use as grinding tool.

Other handheld tools without obvious traces of use include a peach-shape stone (8.5 × 8 × 5.4 cm), egg-shaped stones of different sizes including a relatively large specimen (9.4 × 6.8 × 6.2 cm) found at the water source and a smaller one (4.3 × 3.4 cm) retrieved near the house site at the eastern hill. Their form is suggestive of potter's anvils, whetstones, or percussion instruments. Ethnographic details provide clues for comparison: peach-shaped stones serve as pulverization tools for gold in Bengkulu, Southwest Sumatra (Miksic 1988, p. 10), and stone anvils with a plano-convex section are used at pottery workshops in Galo Gandang in Tanah Datar and in areas with lineage connections to the Minangkabau, for example, in Bungo Tanjung, Kerinci, and Batubara

FIGURE 4.17

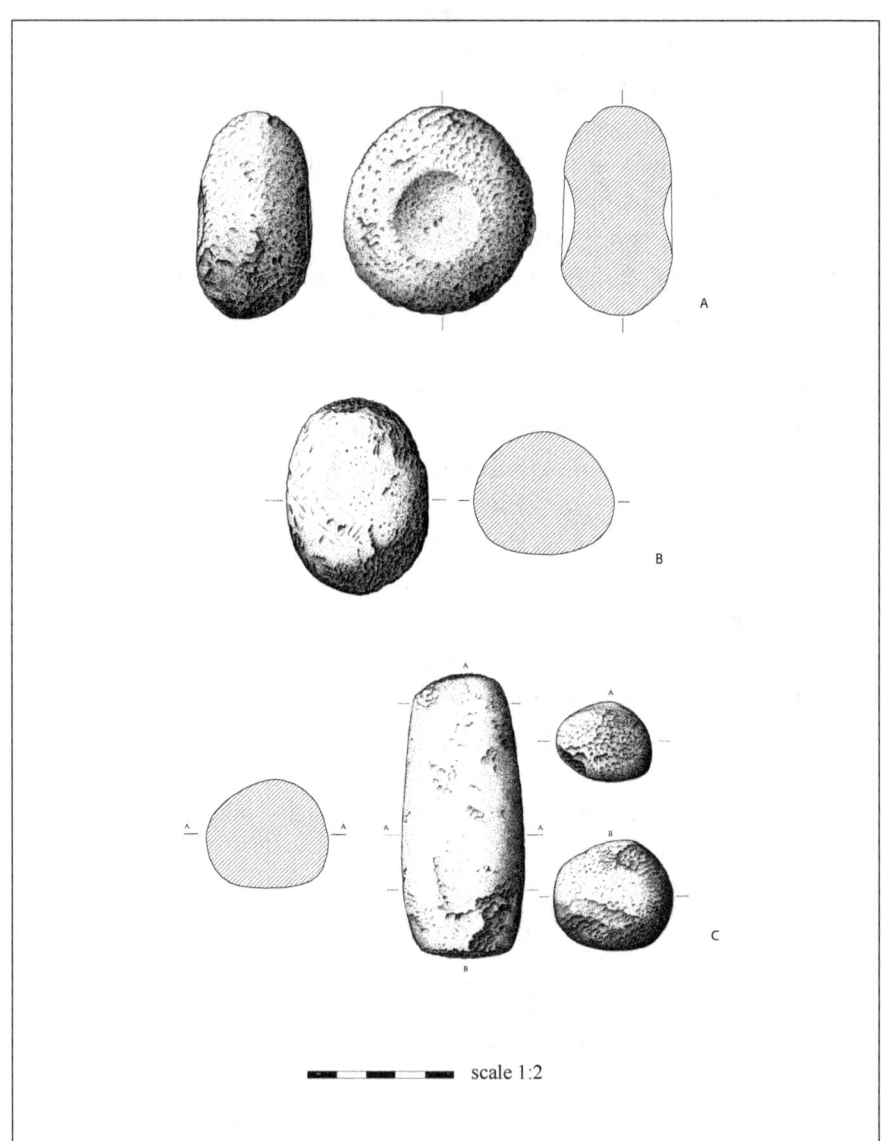

Ground stone tools of Bukit Gombak

Grinding or pulverization slab (A; BG-2013), hammer stone (B; BG-1504), pestle and grinding tool (C; BG-1010)

Source: Dayat Hidayat.

FIGURE 4.18

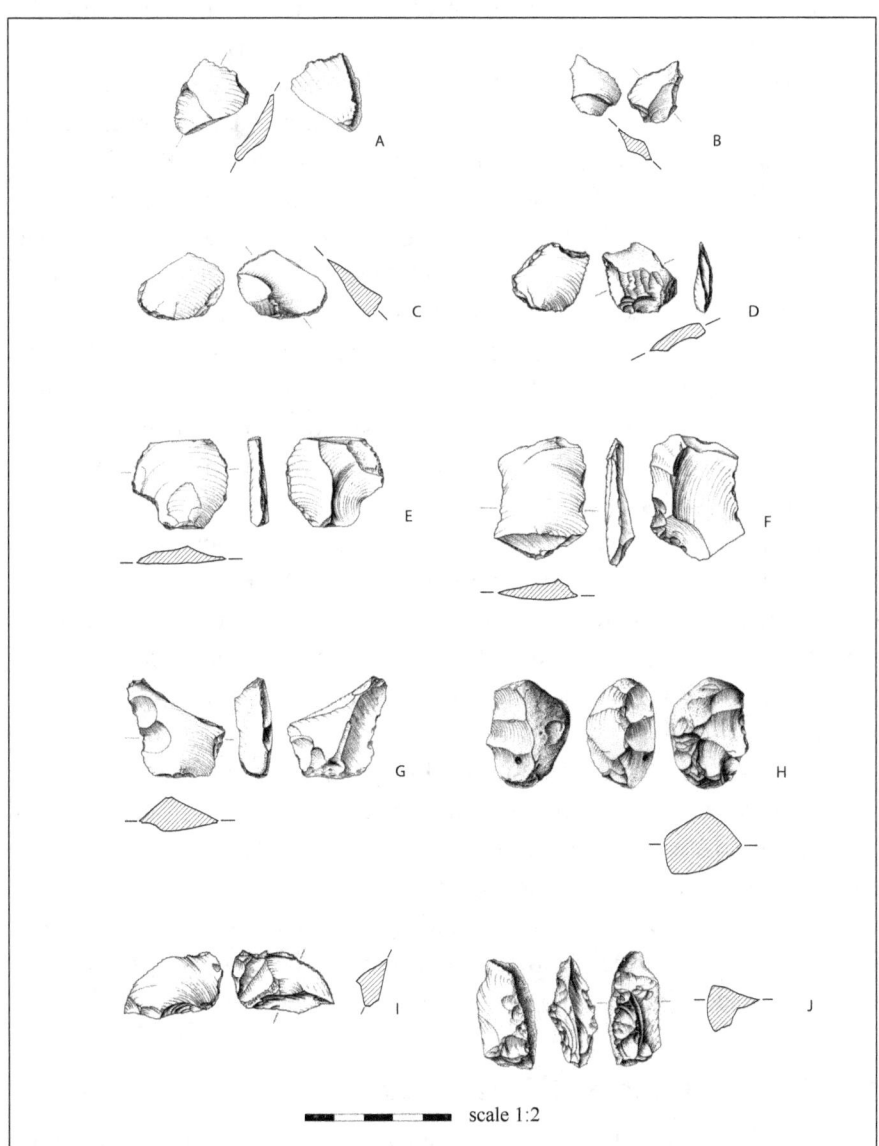

Flaked lithics of Bukit Kincir

Retouches or edge damages (A–B; BG-0691, BG-1376, D; BG-0920, F–G; BG-0900; BG-1374, I–J; BG-0735, BG-0673), core tablet (C; BG-1382), scraper (E; BG-1371), chopping tool (H; BG-0858)

Source: Dayat Hidayat.

(Tiurminar Butar-Butar 1991–92; Tjoa-Bonatz 2012, figure 2.5). Stone anvils are difficult to identify in an archaeological context because the only requirement for a functional anvil is a flat surface, but similarly shaped stones from the tenth to thirteenth centuries have tentatively been assigned to this function although proof is lacking (Tri Marhaeni 2008, p. 45; Bonatz 2006, figure 8). Their size varies between 8 and 15 cm, probably because of differences in the availability of raw material.

Flakes detached all around the edge of a flat core of fine-grained sedimentary rock with a smoothed surface and of beige colour were found at the water source (see Figure 4.16: A). It is difficult to decide whether this was an unused core or a percussion instrument. Due to its large size it has to be held with two hands. Today women use such flat stones at washing sites on rivers to stroke and clean the laundry. A chopping tool from Bukit Kincir is of a similar material and has retouched negatives on both sides (see Figure 4.19: B).

Several sedimentary rocks of brown-greyish colour are smoothed with clear-cut edges: a transversal broken stone fragment with a retouch negative next to a smaller negative (see Figure 4.16: B) and an elongated fragment with parallel grooves and a negative on one side (see Figure 4.16: C). The almost rectangular section of a stone fragment suggests a whetstone (see Figure 4.16: D).

The Bukit Kincir site has similar handstones made from brown-grey magmatic rock, as exemplified by a hammer stone with a plano-convex section and an area of unipolar wear marks at one end (see Figure 4.19: A), and by two pieces with nearly rectangular sections. One can be identified as a *retoucheur* or a grinding stone owing to its facets (see Figure 4.19: C), while another one can tentatively be identified as a whetstone (see Figure 4.19: D). All were recovered in Trench P.

4.3. Glass Vessels and Glass Beads

The excavation at Bukit Gombak yielded a total of 42 glass fragments, including 37 sherds of vessels and five beads (see Table 4.6). In addition, a tiny dark green glass fragment was unearthed at the settlement site of Bukit Kincir. The numbers are small but the mere presence of glass artefacts shows that the highlands participated in the networks that

FIGURE 4.19

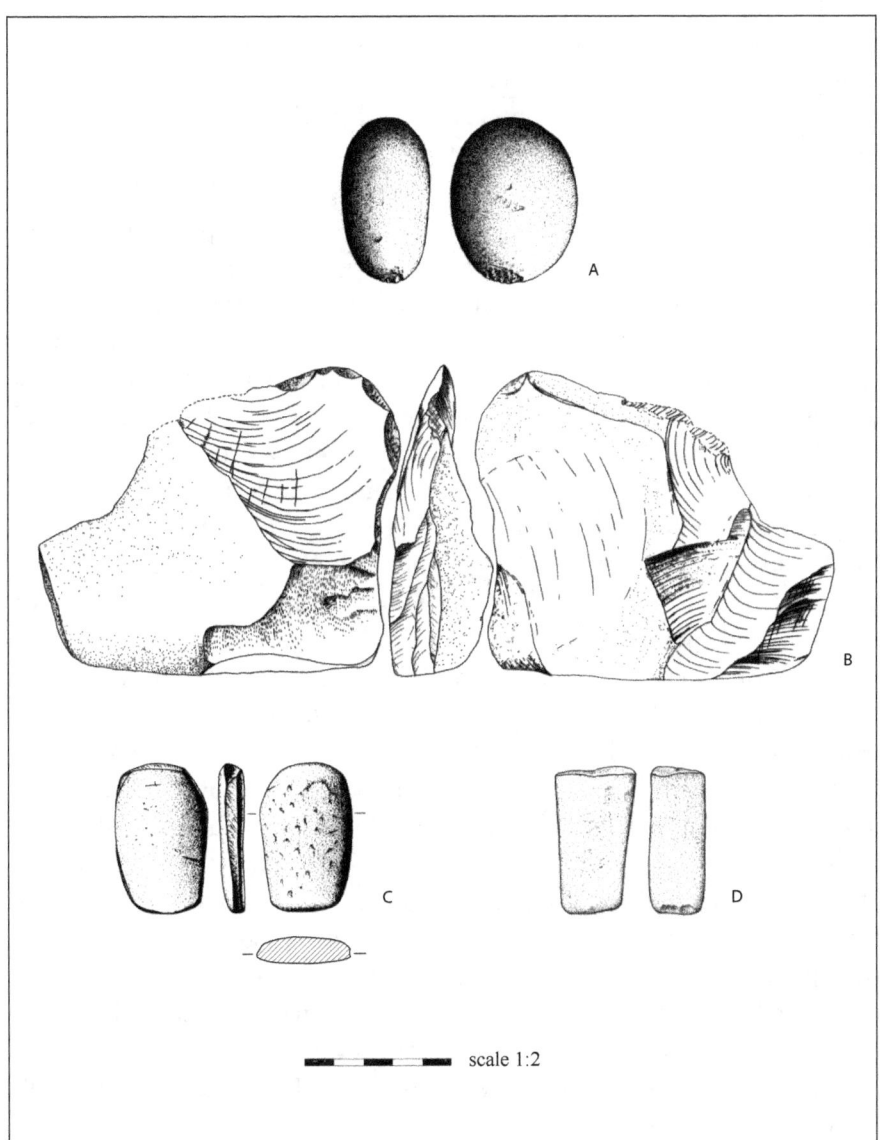

Ground stone tools of Bukit Kincir

Hammer stone (A; BG-0684), chopping tool (B; BG-0749), retoucheur or a grinding stone (C; BG-0913), whetstone (D; BG-0685)

Source: Dayat Hidayat.

traded in glass. No chemical testing was done, which makes identification difficult.

At Bukit Gombak, all fragments of glass sherds came from the foundation pit below street level in Trench N. As a result, the dating of these finds is uncertain (see p. 111). Most of the vessel fragments are translucent with a white tint, but there are also light green, dark and light brown sherds. Some of the translucent glass fragments have floral and geometric patterns. Two of the sherds, which are probably pressed glass from a later period, can be identified as parts of a round foot and a rectangular foot. One green glass sherd shows vertical ribs.

The five glass beads are supposedly drawn. They were all retrieved in the core area of Bukit Gombak (Trenches B–C), which suggests that such ornaments were the property of those who lived on the hill top. Two beads from Trench C are made of translucent blue glass. The first, which is light blue (see Colour Plate 3: I), is a flattened oblate, with a diameter of 0.6 cm that is double its length of 0.3 cm, coloured by dissolved copper oxide (CuO). The second piece, which is darker blue (see Colour Plate 3: H), is slightly larger with a diameter of 0.65 cm and a length of 0.5 cm. Longitudinal striations on the surface and lines of bubbles within the glass clearly indicate that it is a drawn bead coloured with cobalt. Beads made in China were almost always wound, so it is doubtful that they are Chinese. Rather they are "Indo-Pacific glassbeads", which are drawn and made of high alumina mineral-soda-alumina glass. Alison Carter[47] sees correlations with beads found in the Cardamom Mountains in western Cambodia, a fifteenth to seventeenth-century burial place. If this correlation is correct, the beads from Bukit Gombak would be high alumina mineral-soda-alumina glass of subtype 2. This so-called "m-NA-AL 2" glass is found at sites in eastern Africa and western India from the ninth to the nineteenth centuries. They were probably manufactured near the trading port of Chaul, in western India, for the Indian Ocean trade with Africa (Dussubieux et al. 2010, p. 1650).

Three opaque red-orange beads also belong to the Indo-Pacific type of monochrome drawn beads but it is not clear to which of the five subgroups. Two are barrel-shaped and 0.5 cm in diameter and length (see Colour Plate 3: F–G). The third is oblate and smaller, 0.35 cm in diameter, and 0.3 cm in length (see Colour Plate 3: E). Bright orange beads like the first specimen, which displays longitudinal strips from the drawing process, may be quite high in copper and coloured with very small cuprite (Cu_2O) crystals. The others are most likely coloured with metallic copper. The dating and origin of Indo-Pacific drawn beads is still debated. Made in great numbers in India and traded along the Pacific Rim, they were widespread in Southeast Asia over a long period. Southeast Asia's beadmaking industry on Sumatra also developed in the first millennium CE (Perret and Heddy Surachman 2009, p. 383; Dussubieux et al. 2010; Miksic 2013, pp. 340, 344). Sumatra was connected to various trade networks of glass artefacts. This suggests that highland areas participated in different trade networks handling beads and glass vessels.

The Indo-Pacific bead type of high-alumina mineral soda were found in burial contexts or at a house foundation ritual in highland Jambi dating from the eleventh to the thirteenth centuries (Bonatz 2006, pp. 318–21, figures 29.13–6; Tjoa-Bonatz 2013*b*, p. 73). Archaeologists reported that beads were looted from the upper layers of a burial site at Benua Keling Lama, Pasemah (Guillaud 2006, p. 45, ft. 13). Such contexts show that beads were regarded as prestigious items of special value in the highlands. In particular, opaque orange-red beads had a deep cultural meaning for the Minangkabau. Beads of this colour made of coral, rubies, or agate were strung as ceremonial necklaces (*maniak baranggo*) and bracelets (*galang galang*) with alternating beads of precious material (Summerfield and Summerfield 1999, figure 6.77).

4.4. Metal Objects

The 35 metal objects were collected at Bukit Gombak apart from a single find at Bukit Kincir (see Table 4.6).[48] The assemblage consists of 22 objects made of iron, five of brass, five coins from a copper alloy, and a copper weight. The iron implements, which are highly corroded and therefore difficult to study, include weapons and tools used in agrarian contexts and for hunting, in addition to decorative pieces and objects for personal use made from brass. The copper coins originate from the Dutch colonial period. Apart from the coins, none of the metal finds can unequivocally be assigned to a specific time owing to a lack of dated archaeological material. Ethnographic comparisons suggest a relatively recent date.

Iron Implements

Among the 22 iron fragments from Bukit Gombak, several knife blades can be distinguished due to their plano-convex sections and pointed ends. Two fragments with similar dimensions from Trench K (8/8.5 × 1.4/1.5 × 0.2 cm) may represent joints.

A blade for a rice knife (5.6 × 0.8 × 0.3 cm), which locals identified as a *tuai*, is slightly curved upwards at both ends (see Figure 4.20: B). The blade is shafted by a piece of wood to which a bamboo stick can be attached to form a handle that is perpendicular to the blade. I am inclined to think that a metal object found at the twelfth or thirteenth to sixteenth centuries site at Bukit Hasang is a similar blade for a rice knife rather than an ornament as suggested by the excavators (Perret and Heddy Surachman 2009, p. 425, no. 21). Regional comparisons can be drawn with examples from the nineteenth century, for example, at Payakumbuh in Tanah Datar,[49] from Si Rukam and Pasimpai in Limabelas Kota.[50] The shape and size of the decorations on the wooden shafts show regionally distinct features such as trapezoidal, semi-circular, wing- or heart-shaped decorations created by painting or carving. This kind of knife is still used today during the rice harvest to cut the first rice-ears from the stalk, which ripen earlier than the others. The find from Bukit Gombak underlines the significance of rice cultivation and the use of specific tools for the rice harvest.

The function of small iron fragments with round profiles is unknown, but they might have been nails. The same is true of iron sherds, one (4.5 × 2.5 × 0.1 cm) of which is partly rounded with two round perforations. Another one (6.8 × 1.6 × 0.8 cm) is a more solid piece that resembles a chisel with a tapered rectangular profile. The function of a surface find (6.3 × 1.2 × 0.3 cm) is unknown but may be half of the beam of a scale; one end is folded (see Colour Plate 3: C). A tool, 21 cm long with a diameter of 1.3 cm, is made of good quality iron (see Figure 4.20: A). Local residents suggested that it was a wood working tool called *pahat kayu*. The handle is decorated with three engraved bands where

FIGURE 4.20

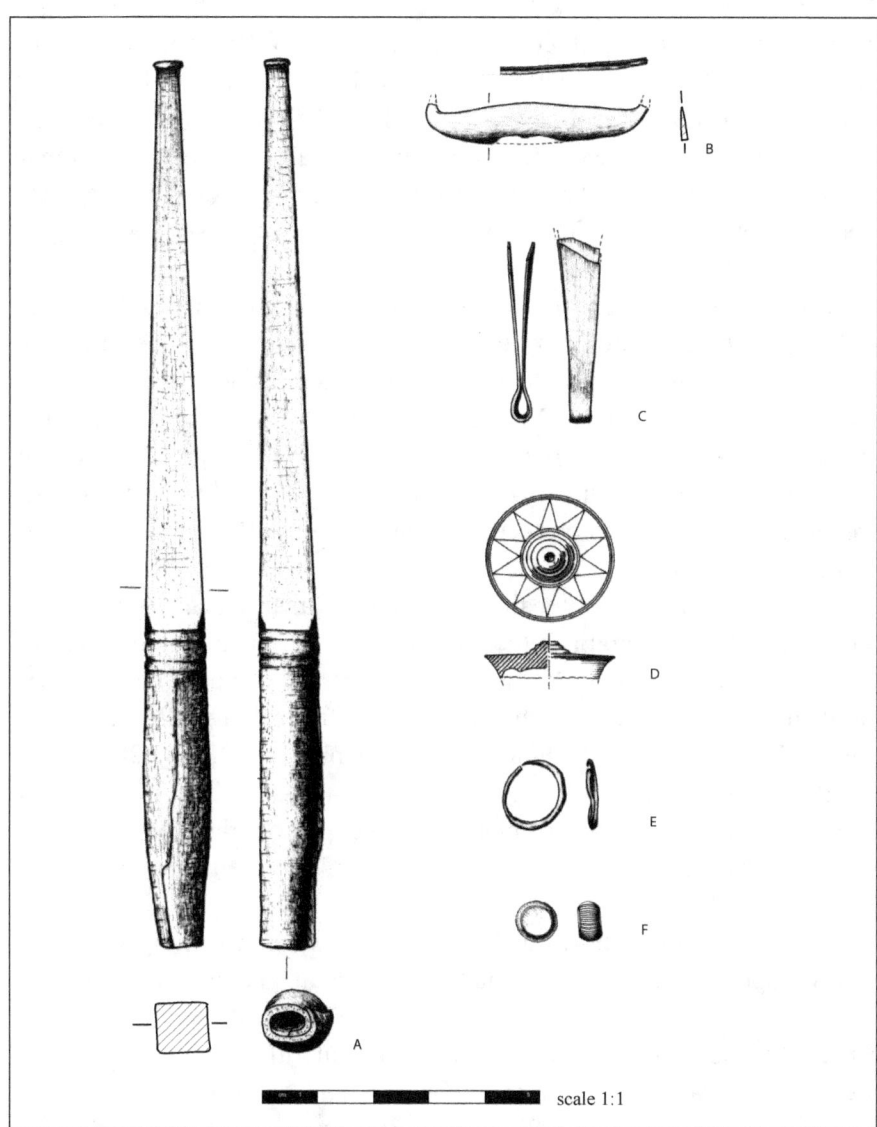

Metal objects of Bukit Gombak

Stick or chisel (A; BG-0051), rice knife (B; BG-0521), pair of tweezers (C; BG-0055), cover of a betel container (D; BG-0602), ring (E; BG-1101), gold weight (F; BG-1103)

Source: Dayat Hidayat.

the tube becomes flatter, and tapers until the end of the round profile. A fragment of a matchlock from a gun with a simple fuse mechanism (6 × 1.2 cm) was unearthed in the core area of Bukit Gombak (see Colour Plate 3: D). The cock of the gun is curved like a floral motif and wavy incisions decorate the lock plate. This decorative repertoire recalls guns which were crafted in the southern area of the Minangkabau region in Sirukam in Payung Sekaki district in Solok Regency and were in common use during the nineteenth century (Hasselt 1881, p. 10, pl. XXVI: 1).

It is not known when iron began to be manufactured in the Sumatran highlands. There is circumstantial evidence of the importance of metals for ritual deposits in an archaeological context during the tenth to the fourteenth centuries (Tjoa-Bonatz 2013*b*, p. 71). In a legal code from the second half of the fourteenth century, "a whittling knife" serves as a fine for an offence, and various kinds of metals of local and foreign provenance are listed as protected private property (Kozok and Waruno Mahdi 2015, p. 77).

The raw material was locally available in Tanah Datar. Iron ore was mined on Mount Merapi, which is known as iron mountain (*gunung bisbissie*), particularly in Panjang-Bauwa district. Copper was mined in the district of Muku near Labuan-Haji, and tin in Sungu-Pagu, today's Sungai Pagu (Marschall 1968, p. 248; Dobbin 1983, pp. 28–29). In addition, foreign iron tools were reused and recast by local ironsmiths. Shipwrecked Portuguese seamen found people on the coast of West Sumatra eager to exchange foodstuffs for iron goods such as knives and nails (Reid 1995, p. 42).

European visitors to Tanah Datar in the sixteenth century described highly sophisticated artefacts made from metal and precious material that were elite status symbols. They were stunned by the weapons carried by the entourage of the Minangkabau ruler, including swords, firearms, standards, "gold-decorated kris", and "a weapon inlaid with silver resembling a halberd" (see p. 76; Barnard 2013, pp. 25–26). Some male accessories, decorated with precious materials and showing refined workmanship, bore royal insignia. The presence of precious metals, iron of local or foreign provenance, gold-copper alloys, steel, copper alloys, and brass point to a developed knowledge of metallurgy.

In addition to these visual identifiers, metal artefacts added sound as an element of royal ceremonies, and instruments were played and guns fired salutes to honour foreign missions (Barnard 2013, pp. 23, 28). European accounts from the sixteenth and seventeenth centuries mention musical instruments made from metal, such as kettle-drums, small bells, and gongs, being played at the Minangkabau royal court (Reid 1995, p. 40; Drakard 1999, p. 88). These early eyewitnesses' sources gave rise to a vague assumption raised since at least the eighteenth century that metal working in the region dates from the sixteenth century. This dating first mentioned by William Marsden (1911, p. 347) was not questioned but repeated by later scholars (e.g., Dobbin 1983, p. 29). The metal finds and evidences of production on the excavated sites are likely to shift local iron casting to the fifteenth or even the fourteenth century.

Metal production in the Minangkabau highland developed into a craft known internationally. European visitors in the nineteenth century knew of Minangkabau's skilled workmanship in the production of iron implements, brass casting, silversmithing, and goldsmithing. At the time, iron smelting was concentrated around the eastern slope of Mount Merapi in northern Tanah Datar in villages such as Limakaum or Salimpaung, where smiths produced hunting implements and weapons such as guns, lances, spears, pikes, swords, harrows, and kris (Marschall 1968, p. 196; Dobbin 1983, p. 29). According to Marsden (1911, p. 347), gun-making was an important industry of the Minangkabau and dated from at least the sixteenth century. Villages became known for certain products. The neighbouring village, Supayang, in the Solok district, specialized in gun barrels, and Tanjung Alam in the Tanjung Baru district produced matchlocks. In the northwest part of the regency, Agam villages near Bukittingi, such as Sungai Puai and Bukik Batabuah, made the locks for guns (Dobbin 1983, p. 29). Iron working became a highly specialized craft in Tanah Datar.

Objects Made of a Copper Alloy

Four objects made of a copper alloy were retrieved on Bukit Gombak, along with a single object of unknown function from Bukit Kincir. The latter is oblong (3.1 × 1.4 cm) with a perforated rounded end and a protrusion (see Colour Plate 3: B).

The following finds from Bukit Gombak represent decorative art and personal items of small size tentatively made of bronze with a high amount of copper added by another alloy. One fragment is a pendent 1.1 cm in diameter belonging to an unknown object, possibly a bell (see Colour Plate 3: A). An undecorated open ear or finger ring just 1.6 cm in diameter has tapered ends (see Figure 4.20: E). Similar simple jewellery was worn by women in the Sakai region in 1910–11 (Ethnological Museum Berlin-Dahlem, inv. no. 35614z). Owing to this comparison and its surface context, it is possible that the ring found on Bukit Gombak is from a later period. Both ends of a pair of tweezers are broken off and the remaining fragment measures 4.7 cm in length and 0.9 cm in width (see Figure 4.20: C). It exhibits a spherical section towards its straight end in order to carry it with a string. As a cosmetic tool it is used to pluck hair or beards, whereas longer iron tweezers were goldsmiths' tools. In an archaeological context, a pair of tweezers was found on a ninth-century Tang shipwreck.[51] More recent examples from the Minangkabau area are similar in shape to the excavated find but have a straight end.[52] Tweezers were carried as private items and worn with other metal tools of personal use on a belt.[53] They were highly esteemed for display and sometimes made of silver in the Minangkabau area (Jasper and Mas Pirngadie 1927, p. 222, figure 325; p. 234, figure 345; Padang Museum inv. no. 4202). Tweezers of iron, brass, or even gold from the late nineteenth century are widespread on Sumatra and the archepelago, and measure up to 10 cm.

A small lid that represents fine artwork in brass casting is 2.9 cm in diameter and 0.6 cm high (see Figure 4.20: D). Its central and depressant knob is built up by three circular levels surrounded by ten incised triangles, creating a star motif. These details and the smoothed surface are the result of highly sophisticated workmanship. The star motif with varying numbers of prongs is widely seen in the crafts of the Minangkabau and beyond. Traces of white colour, possibly chalk, on the underside suggest that it was the lid for a container for betel chewing. In the ethnographic context, portable containers for lime paste are conical, lobed, or drum shaped and made of different materials. Moreover, the material of the container and the cover can differ (Brownrigg 1991, p. 131). A similar though undated box was reported in an archaeological survey from the area of the Kerinci lake with Minangkabau migrants (Hoop 1940, pl. LXXXVII: 3).

Betel chewing is widespread among the Minangkabau, as it is in many parts of Southeast and South Asia, and also featured in royal ceremonies. When the envoy Thomas Dias' met the Minangkabau king in 1684 (see pp. 75–76), the queen offered him "some betel nuts or arecas on a silver salver covered with a yellow cloth" together with a message from the Minangkabau king (Barnard 2013, pp. 23–24). The use of precious material in the container holding the ingredients and the symbolic importance of the yellow cloth, a colour reserved for the royal family, indicates the high status of the giver.

At the end of the nineteenth century, Sirukam in the Solok Regency, the villages Sungai Puar, Kapala Kota, and Tengah Kota in the regency of Agam produced brass objects for export (Martin 1990, pp. 257–58). The lost wax casting method in the Minangkabau region, which oral accounts trace back to a Hindu from Ceylon called Sja Oleh, resembles that used by the Javanese (Marschall 1968, p. 180).

Gold Weights and Coins

The oblate copper weight, locally called *bungkal*, has a trapezoid cross-section and a framed band of vertical lines engraved on its rim (see Figure 4.20: F). It measures 0.9 cm in diameter, 0.5 cm in height, and weighs 2 g. Apart from use-wear traces on the surface, the corrosion product of tenarit is typical for copper. It was probably part of a set of weights used to weigh gold-dust.

Archaeological evidence of early Sumatran weights is still meagre. The trapezoidal cross-section resembles Javanese weights and a bronze weight from the fourteenth-century Singapore (Hoop 1936, figure on p. 465; Borell 2000, pp. 10–11). It is not known if the Javanese provided the prototypes for gold weights based on their weighing system in which a *masa* is 2.4 g and a *kupang* between 0.4 and 0.6 g. The weight from Bukit Gombak nearly matches one *masa* or three *kupang*. In the nineteenth century the standard unit differed in northern and southern Sumatra but was still referred to the *kupang* (Marsden 1911, p. 171).

Ethnographic comparisons can be drawn to five copper weights from the early twentieth century. This kind of weight was widely used in the highland regions in the Mandailing-Batak area of North Sumatra[54] and in Kerinci,[55] which may attest to the wide trading reach of the Minangkabau during that time. The closest comparison is a copper weight of similar shape and decoration weighing 30 g assigned to Kerinci (Rijksmuseum Volkenkunde Leiden, inv. no. 3600c). It belongs to a set along with two heavier copper weights of 42 g and 40 g (Rijksmuseum Volkenkunde Leiden, inv. no. 3600a–b), and a lead weight of 15 g (Rijksmuseum Volkenkunde Leiden, inv. no. 3600-1444d) stored in a finely carved wooden box.[56]

Gold was not only an important export item in the trade of Minangkabau but was also used as a medium of exchange, as a means of payment, and to settle fines or compensation. Sumatra offers a disparate picture of monetary interaction (Wicks 1992, pp. 235–38; Reid 1993, p. 100). Two types of exchanges existed in the highlands of Sumatra: payment with gold dust and exchange of goods, for instance, food stuffs, pepper, and other provisions, as stated in a late fourteenth-century legal code and in another source dated 1560 (Reid 1995, p. 42; Kozok and Waruno Mahdi 2015, pp. 107–8). The use of gold instead of coins in commercial transactions on Sumatra was still being reported in the nineteenth century (Marsden 1911, p. 171). Traders equipped themselves with scales, containers for gold dust, and weights (Pistorius 1871, p. 35).

Base-metal was only used as coinage in the highlands during the eighteenth and early nineteenth centuries. Five copper coins were retrieved on Bukit Gombak and two from the Bukit Kincir burial site (see p. 198).[57] *Half Duit* coins, around 2 cm in diameter, used from 1726 to 1804 carried the VOC-crest and the crowned coat of arms with an upright lion (Trenches C and D), others are highly weathered.

4.5. Finds at the Burial Site

While local pottery had domestic and utilitarian roles, it was also used for ceremonial or other special occasions, as evidenced by the sherd collection at the burial site on Bukit Kincir. The dead for whom a primary burial was performed were not provided with any goods that survive in the archaeological context. However, ceramic sherds, stone artefacts, and metal pieces as well as burnt areas indicate the cemetery was a place of vibrant activity, where ceremonies in connection with the preparation and maintenance of the graves or cremations took place.

Earthenware containers were of three types (see Figure 4.9: A–D). The most common and therefore the most important ritually were plain vessels and neckless jars with an everted rim. They are small and medium sized with a diameter between 14 and 16 cm. Some were footed, lidded, or equipped with a handle. Restricted vessels were more frequently used, but nothing is known about the activities involved. One of the pots shows burnt remains on the interior rim, which suggests either a secondary use as a cooking pot or that cooking or burning activities took place on site. Larger jars, with diameters of 24–33 cm, were only retrieved close to the stone formations in Trenches G and Q. Associated with imported sherds and burnt areas, these large earthenware pots may point to specific actions performed for a larger community close to the geometric stone structures (called Structure 2 on p. 125) or possibly held ashes following a cremation.

Imported wares were only retrieved close to the stone formations (Trenches G–H, L). Within the small group of seven foreign sherds, most belong to green-glazed vessels or one blue-and-white one, but one unique fragment is from a Khmer black-glazed jar (see Colour Plate 1: L).[58] A nearly intact green-glazed plate is one of the most exceptional finds near the stone Structure 2 in Trench H (see Figure 4.9: E). The large and deep dish is 32 cm in diameter and has a vertical mouth lip, with thin striations on the exterior wall. It can be assigned to Longquan wares and is similar to dishes found in the cargo of shipwrecks dated to the last quarter of the fifteenth or the beginning of the sixteenth century.[59] A thick glaze covers the whole vessel, including the base, apart from sandy traces of a tubular support. Minangkabau graves today are marked by stones close to the headstone where dishes are placed for burning incense. They are left at the burial site for repeated rituals over a 100-day period following a burial.

In the context of a burial, Sumatra ceramics served various functions. The custom of placing ceramic dishes, particularly greenware, on graves was also common in other regions, such as Labuanmeringgai, Lampung in South Sumatra in the eighteenth century or West Java (Edwards McKinnon 1994, p. 292). Secondary burials using brown-glazed vessel were conducted near Percut in the Deli-Serdang and Langkat region in North Sumatra from the thirteenth to fourteenth centuries (Edwards McKinnon 1994, p. 291). In the hoard of the "king's grave" at Siguntur, in the regency of Dharmasraya, the deceased was accompanied by an extremely rich assemblage of 25 white-glazed vessels of the eleventh to twelfth centuries (Budi Istiawan 2012, p. 50). A female Sakai grave at the Mandan river in the Riau province held 20 household items made of ceramics, brass, and iron along with a complete betel-set and jewellery.[60] Extremely rich sets of ceramic grave goods, including celadon dishes, are documented in other regions of the archipelago, for example, in the Riau islands of the fourteenth and fifteenth centuries (Miksic 2013, pp. 373–76, 391). These regions are closely connected to the maritime trading routes with Sumatra but seem to have had rather different burial practices.

The stone assemblage at the burial site comprises eight artefacts including six waste flakes from obsidian, a fully preserved triangular adze, and a chert flake. The latter can be associated with the strike-to-light technique. This instrument as well as burnt areas in the same excavation context are firm evidence of burning activities on the burial site. The cutting edges of the adze show no obvious use-ware traces, which would point to grave goods rather than a working tool (see Figure 4.15: F). The waste flakes were probably part of post-deposit infill.

Three metal objects retrieved near the stone structures include a small iron fragment of 2 cm in length with a rectangular section as well as two Dutch copper coins of 2 cm in diameter. Dates of 1810 and 1838 on the verso may suggest the persistent use of the burial place in the early nineteenth century after the settlements sites of Bukit Gombak and Bukit Kincir were already given up.

NOTES

1. The preliminary calculation given in Tjoa-Bonatz (2013*a*, p. 150) has been updated.
2. Samples were taken from Trenches A, B, E, and N from Bukit Gombak and from Trenches R and O from Bukit Kincir.
3. Sample BG-1100-003 from Trench E (lab. no. MD 5128) was selected for Bukit Gombak. Sample BG-0917-070 from Trench R (lab. no. MD 5129) was selected for Bukit Kincir.

4. In Kota Cina 62 per cent were closed vessels, 32 per cent were open vessels, and 5 per cent were *kendi* (Wibisono 1982, tab. 2). At Buki Hasang 61 per cent of the local ware were closed vessels, 4.5 per cent were open vessels, and 4.5 per cent were *kendi* (Perret and Heddy Surachman 2009, p. 160). However, the small number of open vessel may account for the difficult distinction between open vessel and cover which made up 30 per cent of the total at Bukit Hasang.
5. It was possible to estimate the diameter for 533 vessels including 9 from the burial site, 42 from Bukit Kincir, and 482 from Bukit Gombak.
6. At Banten Girang, a site in Northwest Sumatra of the tenth to sixteenth centuries, smaller pots between 7 and 14 cm are distinguished from larger ones with a diameter of more than 30 cm (Wibisono 1994, pp. 170–71, figures 109.1, 109.4). The diameters of cooking pots at Kota Cina are generally larger and range between 25 and 49 cm (Miksic 1979, pp. 190–91). Those on the Pandanan shipwreck of the fifteenth century found in the Philippines have a diameter between 15.6 and 17.1 cm (Tanaka and Dizon 2011).
7. Two sherds of the same ware type were found in close proximity and may therefore belong to a footed jar with a large rim diameter of 35 cm, but a rather small base of only 7.6 cm (see Figure 4.8: B–C).
8. On a photo taken between 1890 and 1912 Minangkabau women carry water jars of this shape, see the photo of Christiaan Benjamin Nieuwenhuis' collection in the Rijksmuseum Volkenkunde Amsterdam, http://hdl.handle.net/10934/RM0001.COLLECT.454703 (accessed 2 April 2014). Today, there are basically two jar types distinguished by their size and body proportions: first, long-necked water jars are either large, carinated bulbous vessels or smaller with rounded shoulders, more elongated with a smooth transition from the body to the foot. The former is 32 cm in height with a maximum body width of 44 cm; the diameter of the rim is 31 cm and that of the foot 17 cm. The latter only reaches 30 cm in height, with a maximum diameter of 28 cm, and a rim diameter of 16 cm (Erman Makmur 1983–84, pp. 13–14, 17–18).
9. This is tentatively assumed due to the same find spot and ware type of two sherds (see Figure 4.8: D).
10. The draughtsman Dayat Hidayat used a different way to illustrate the same grid pattern, compare Figure 4.10: E and Figure 4.2: C.
11. The relief fragment is not spherical. It is thus doubtful whether it belonged to a vessel or was an ornament of unknown function (see Figure 4.10: K). One rarely seen variety with impressed lenticular shapes might not be an intentionally created decoration but sketchy leftovers of the potter's working habits. Similarly, some of the bowls show thin horizontal striations at the interior or exterior rim that are production remains rather than intended to be decorative (e.g., see Figure 4.2: G; Figure 4.4: K).
12. This had been proposed for the earthenware at the contemporaneous site of Singapore (Miksic 2013, p. 275).

13. In Bungo Tanjung, Kerinci, and Batubara, North Sumatra (Tiurminar Butar-Butar 1991–92; Lutfi Yondri 1995; Risnal et al. 1995–96; Eny Christiawaty 2010), see also http://www.blogspot/tanahdatararchaeology (accessed 6 March 2013). In Indonesia, this instrument is only recorded in Flores (Gasser 1969, p. 39) or Pakistan (Rye and Evans 1976, pl. 7).
14. Tjoa-Bonatz (2012, p. 23); see four fragments from a private collection in Sungai Penuh, inv. no. DSN/ISK/06-8-C/131-134, http://pusaka-kerinci.com/ (accessed 9 March 2014).
15. Following the suggestion by Ed Edwards McKinnon and Brian Vincent, which is gratefully acknowledged (personal communication, 9 November 2013).
16. Personal communication, 9 November 2013.
17. The interpretations kindly given by Ed Edwards McKinnon, Brian Vincent, and Joyce White were a great help (personal communication, 15 November 2013).
18. Cf. the Enim district, South Sumatra (Museum der Kulturen Basel, inv. no. IIc 970_2), Tanibar and Matanna, Southeast Sulawesi (Museum der Kulturen Basel, inv. no. II 592/93), Bandung, Java (Museum der Kulturen Basel, inv. no. IIc 13501), on Masbate, Visayas in the Philippines (Gasser 1969, pp. 38, 104).
19. Ed Edwards McKinnon, personal communication, 17 November 2013.
20. Due to stylistic evaluation the dating range of the Lena shoal was slightly broadened to or after 1500 (Miksic 2013, p. 204).
21. Cf. Dupoizat and Naniek Harkantiningsih (2007, pp. 67–69).
22. John Miksic, personal communication, 27 March 2012.
23. Cf. Dupoizat and Naniek Harkantiningsih (2007, p. 55).
24. Tjoa-Bonatz (2013a, figure 6); cf. Brown (2009, pl. 46, no. 16a); Miksic (2013, p. 202, figure 7.17c, first row).
25. The closest comparison is a bowl with a double *vajra* enclosed by double circle discussed in Gotuaco et al. (1997, p. 131).
26. Cf. Chollet (2001, p. 55 below); Goddio and Casal (2002, no. 230); Brown (2009, p. 49, figure 17).
27. Cf. an excavated bowl of the Honghzi-period, see Zhang Bai (2008, p. 161).
28. Cf. Chollet (2001, p. 55 below); Goddio and Casal (2002, nos. 228–30); Dupoizat (2009, pl. 17, no. 5); Miksic (2013, figure 7.17c).
29. Cf. the Lena wreck (Goddio and Casal 2002, nos. 208, 219), Santa Cruz wreck of c. 1510 (Brown 2009, p. 49, no. 16, pl. 63, no. 5), and on Sumatra at Bukit Hasang (Dupoizat 2009, pl. 17, no. 4a).
30. Cf. Nguyên Đình Chiên and Pham Quôc Quân (2008, no. 496); Brown (2009, p. 58, no. 33; the back of the plate is not shown so the comparison may not be fully drawn); Dupoizat (2009, pl. 21.6).
31. Cf. cover from a box from Trowulan with a similar scroll is assigned to the middle of the fifteenth century (Dupoizat 2009, p. 92, figure 28).
32. John Miksic, personal communication, 27 March 2013. Cf. Burmese ware found in North Sumatra (Edwards McKinnon 2017).

33. John Miksic, personal communication, 27 March 2013.
34. Cf. found on the Java Sea wreck, see the latest dating to the twelfth century (Niziolek et al. 2018).
35. John Miksic, personal communication, 27 March 2013.
36. Apart from the artefact in Figure 4.15: C, where the hatched parts indicate breakage, damage caused by use is not distinguished from features of the artefacts in any special way.
37. Hubert Forestier cited in Perret and Heddy Surachman (2009, p. 470).
38. Guillot et al. (1994, pp. 207–9), Perret and Heddy Surachman (2009, pp. 463–72). At Bengkulu the stone assemblage consists of nine artefacts including a slab and four flakes (find nos. 488, 545). Miksic kindly granted access to the unpublished excavation finds which were analysed by J. Barry and PUSLIT ARKENAS in 1988.
39. See Adam Brumm's (2007) ethnoarchaeological study from Flores; an example of fire-making equipment from Sakai, Riau, found around 1910, includes an angular quartz tinder called *sumpit lama* and a steel segment of 6.1 cm in length, 2 cm in width, and 0.8 cm in height (Ethnological Museum Berlin-Dahlem, inv. no. Ic 35563 a, b).
40. Johannes Moser, personal communication, 20 July 2011.
41. It resembles a piece from Banten in West Java, classified as type 2, variety A (Duff 1970, pp. 23, 38, sheet 2). However, none of the artefacts cited by Roger Duff has a precise provenience.
42. The hatched parts in the drawing indicate post-depositional damages.
43. It resembles an adze from Solo in Central Java, classified as type 7, variety A (Duff 1970, pp. 26, 38, sheet 5).
44. This purpose is assigned to a polished adze found around 1879 at Taba Penanjung, Bengkulu. It has a rectangular section and is made of dark brown stone, 6.4 cm long, 3.2 cm wide, and 0.9 cm high (Ethnological Museum Berlin-Dahlem, inv. no. 9817, cf. inv. no. Ic 9731).
45. See all these artefacts from Kerinci, http://pusaka-kerinci.com/ (accessed 6 May 2014).
46. Johannes Moser, personal communication, 4 October 2012.
47. Personal communication, 17 March 2014; Carter et al. (2016).
48. Not included in this list are 32 bullets for a 9 mm handgun, which are listed under "modern" finds in the small find list of Table 4.6. They were collected in the upper levels of Bukit Gombak (18 bullets) and the burial site of Bukit Kincir (five bullets). Local residents explained that the area served as a shooting range until recently.
49. Ethnological Museum Berlin-Dahlem, inv. no. Ic 26510, achieved in 1894.
50. Fischer (1916, p. 97); cf. from Central Sumatra, see Hasselt (1881, pl. XC, 12); Museum Nasional Jakarta, inv. no. 346 from the west coast of Sumatra.
51. Krahl et al. (2011, pp. 234–35, no. 40). Miksic has kindly drawn my interest to this early find.

52. Cf. Rijksmuseum Volkenkunde Leiden, inv. no. 268-309; Hasselt (1881, p. 9, pl. XXIV: 8).
53. Cf. a pair of tweezers from Ladeh in Kerinci (no. LDH/MAR/12-08-A/09), see http://pusaka-kerinci.com/ (accessed 28 Feburary 2014).
54. The weight of 0.40 g from the Mandailing area in Pakantan, North Sumatra is 2.4 cm in diameter, 1.5 cm in height (Ethnological Museum Berlin-Dahlem, inv. no. Ic 37380). It belonged to a set of 26 gold weights achieved in 1910, of which only one remains.
55. Two weights are from Koto Lanang, the district Depati VII in Kerinci. Together with a third plain weight, they total 100 g; the largest is 2.3 cm in diameter and 1.7 cm in height. See a private collection in Sungai Penuh, inv. no. KTL/DAB/10-08-B/10, http://pusaka-kerinci.com/ (accessed 28 February 2014).
56. They entered the collection of the Royal Military Academy in Breda in 1923. This information was kindly provided by Francine Brinkgreve, personal communication, 26 February 2014.
57. In addition, two modern coins dated to 1971 were found in a pit of Trench E.
58. Compare a vessel in Choo (1986, pl. XXVIII A, F).
59. Goddio and Casal (2002, no. 265); Nguyên Đình Chiên and Pham Quôc Quân (2008, p. 194, no. 186); Brown (2009, pl. 16, nos. 9 a/b, 10 a/b, pl. 21, no. 16 a/b). Some of them show additional impressions and the fluted design is applied on the cavetto.
60. These grave goods were acquired in 1910–11 and are now stored in the Ethnological Museum Berlin-Dahlem, inv. no. Ic 35614a-z.

5

CONCLUSION

Mai Lin Tjoa-Bonatz

Despite modern disturbances to the topsoil from agricultural ploughing and the shallow depth of the cultural layers, the archaeological investigation provides solid evidence of continuous settlement activity since prehistory in the fertile highland plain of Tanah Datar in West Sumatra. The newly discovered open site at Tanah Lua, which dates to around BCE 1400–900, indicates a phase of early sendentarization. The absence of domestic architecture as well as the finds of pottery and stone tools indicate that the area, which is on high ground near the water source of Papahat, was temporarily settled by a transient community of foragers.

Not far from this water source stand the twin-mounds of Bukit Gombak and Bukit Kincir, where occupation layers from the fourteenth through the seventeenth centuries have been attested. The residential areas were documented by aerial photography, geomagnetic documentation, and excavations. These areas covered the hilltops and lacked fortifications, but were clearly divided between the residential area uphill and the agricultural land scattered downhill in the plain. This valley was the agricultural core of the region.

On Bukit Gombak and Bukit Kincir, evidence of human activity is demonstrated by occupation debris such as ceramics, glass and metal objects, stone tools, iron slag, charcoal chunks, or anthropogenically-modified soils such as compacted soils, vitrified concretions, burnt clay, or postholes. These remains are most concentrated on the northern slope and central plateau, based on ceramic recovery per square metre and geomagnetic surveys. The hand-made earthenware using the paddle-and-anvil technique was high fired and generally sparsely decorated. It mainly consisted of restricted vessels and less frequent unrestricted vessels that were used for daily consumption. Among the earthenware there is a clear dominance of storing and cooking containers. Metal finds were made of copper alloy or iron and included jewellery, tools, weapons, containers, coins, and a gold weight. In spite of the availability of metal a large variety of stone tools were still used in the settlement, a trait that seems characteristic of this highland region. The stone tools consisted of knapped or naturally crushed grindstones and of flaked lithics that were mainly made of obsidian. These finds reflect both residential and potentially industrial activities. The residential area included small-scale craft production such as metal-working. The small settlement site on the plateau of Bukit Kincir, contemporaneous with Bukit Gombak, was an iron-working site that used various tools made of stone or clay. The settlements on Bukit Gombak and Bukit Kincir provide the first archaeological evidence for iron working in the Minangkabau region since the fourteenth century, a local specialization which gained international recognition. However, the difference in cultural debris and limited amount of tradeware on Bukit Kincir suggest a different population structure from that on Bukit Gombak, and indicate that the inhabitants on Bukit Kincir did not have the same access to imported goods but used comparatively more decorated local earthenware. Archaeometric analyses attest to different clay raw material typical of each of the two sites what indicates on-site production.

Most of the excavation trenches on Bukit Gombak contained postholes of various diameters, evidence of the presence of housing, although most of them did not have any obvious alignment. On the western hilltop on Bukit Gombak, a set of 22 postholes suggests the ground plan of a small dwelling that might date to the fourteenth or fifteenth century.

It consisted of two large longitudinal bays and seven to eight smaller bays perpendicular to the large ones. The ground plan suggests that the ridgepole of the dwelling stretched along the longitudinal north–south axis, so that the long side of the house—and probably the entrance— faced Mount Merapi to the northwest (Tjoa-Bonatz 2013b, pp. 76–77). If so, an ovoid outdoor hearth found along the eastern edge of the excavation trench was at the rear of the house. This plan provides the earliest archaeological evidence relating to a dispute among anthropologists about the orientation of traditional Minangkabau houses. While Lai Chee Kien (1993, p. 60) originally argued that the houses had a north–south alignment, our data supports an alternative hypothesis that houses were oriented with respect to mountains and streams (Vellinga 2004, pp. 268–71, ft. 20). This orientation is still seen in the arrangement of traditional houses and settlements in the Minangkabau region, mapped between 1996 and 1998 (Nakamura 1999). Although pairs of posts were found at the southern and northern sides of the house, it is not known if both pairs were erected at the same time. It is also possible that one of them was removed and later replaced, indicating a chronological sequence of events. If interpreted as architectural feature, a single or double post at the smaller sides of the house seems characteristic of Minangkabau houses within the *koto piliang* tradition and can still be seen today at the Pagaruyung palace. Other notable features include the comparatively small intervals and limited and varying diameters of the posts and the bays. Might the number of house posts have reflected socio-economic status such that a building that was raised on many narrow piles represented a more prestigious house? Does the bigger size of the poles in the centre of the house suggest that they bore a special, symbolic function as the first poles erected, the so-called mother poles? Many questions remain unanswered.

The postholes were identified through their discolouration and the presence of stony, orange-yellow inclusions and charcoal. These layers only went down 15–20 cm and it is not known whether they mark the actual pits for the posts or the location of foundation stones. One circular, flat stone was found in-situ at the western side of the 22 postholes on the western hilltop on Bukit Gombak and may have been a foundation stone. Traditional houses of this region during the nineteenth century and later are commonly stilted on stones to better preserve the wooden structure, but there is evidence that Sumatran houses during the twelfth to fourteenth centuries were sunk directly into the ground (Lai Chee Kien 1993, p. 60; Tjoa-Bonatz 2013b). As this is most likely the case, we may assume that the wooden structure of the house was sufficiently stable without deep grounding.

Bukit Gombak is geostrategically located where two important trading routes using the waterways merged at the southern fringe of the plain of Tanah Datar. This setting along with the attested settlement period strongly suggest that it may have been the seat of Adityavarman's highland kingdom during 1347–75. The site has an excellent view facing Mount Merapi, the place of origin for the Minangkabau people, which would have made it an auspicious choice for Adityavarman. The hypothesis that Bukit Gombak was Adityavarman's royal seat is further supported by the concentration of inscriptions and sculptures, more than any other location in the area.

Adityavarman, formerly a high official at the East Javanese court of Majapahit, might have brought with him artefacts and symbols from Java, among them a stone statue of a Bodhisattva probably dated 700–900 from the Central Javanese period. A water fountain in female form can be associated with similar images in East Java. These artefacts and the inscriptional evidence underline that Adityavarman's statecraft was based on Buddhist beliefs. If interpreted as paraphernalia a gilded dagger depicting Buddhist deities must have been essential to Adityavarman as part of the proper attire to validate his rituals and the local context. A dagger is a sacred symbol of power on both islands, Java and Sumatra, and was of such importance for the continuity of leadership in the region in the seventeenth century that it was probably passed down to the ruling family of Pagaruyung, where it remains a sacred heirloom today. Yet, despite the presence of this limited amount of artwork from or directly associated with Java and a commemorative stone inscribed in Javanese that draws some vocabulary from Javanese political models, no profound Javanese impact on the material culture was found during the excavation. There is thus no evidence of an enduring process of Javanization. The same conclusion can be drawn from the inscriptions that used South Indian script. Tamil speakers were present in

5. Conclusion

the region but did not leave any other cultural remains and it is safe to assume that their numbers were small, that they were fully assimilated, or that they only stayed for a short period of time.

Stone monuments, including inscribed stelae, rocks, and a stone tool, were important for the performance of rituals demonstrating royal status and power. The corpus of inscriptions from Adityavarman includes various kinds of stone types. He re-dedicated two stone statues of Buddhist deities, one at the Jago temple in East Java and one in Dharmasraya, an important polity in the hinterland of Melayu-Srivijaya at the upper Batang Hari River and a halfway point on the way to the highlands. Both were carved in the thirteenth century, long before Adityavarman's time. He showed a particular appreciation for ancient cult images and his epigraphic records repeatedly mention the restoration of older structures, which could imply the refurbishment of religious monuments. Adityavarman's epigraphic corpus in the highland of West Sumatra comprises 22 stone inscriptions carved on rocks or slabs. The most numerous are irregularly shaped stelae and rectangular slabs with a raised upper outline, which was a regional characteristic for burial stones probably dating back to prehistoric times. In one of the inscriptions, the functional context of these monuments is described. Positioned in front of a royal building they addressed a wider audience and were an integral part of royal rituals. Apart from serving as an everyday implement, an inscribed mortar could also have been used for harvest feasts due to its exceptional faceted shape. Some of the stelae were combined as stone seats. The stone seats at Kubarajo represent significant artistic innovation in stone masonry during or shortly after the time of Adityavarman. Probably used during community meetings, these skilfully decorated stones combine Sanskrit writing and non-local patterns with local motifs that were understood as cultural symbols by the community. The decoration includes rich floral and geometric motifs.

Megalithic traditions in the highlands of the Lima Puluh Kota province probably date from as early as the first century BCE. Stone monuments in both Tanah Datar and Lima Puluh Kota were connected to death rituals in a stratified society. Two traditions that used megaliths as cultural symbols likely coexisted and complemented one another during the time of Adityavarman: the tradition in Srivijaya or Java of using inscribed stones as symbols of power, and the local tradition of erecting stones over graves. Both traditions reflect power relations and territorial claims. During the time of Adityavarman, stone inscriptions were political statements used to consolidate royal power, fusing economic, political, and religious achievements. His longest inscription on Bukit Gombak honours the king's construction initiatives and acknowledges the subservience of royal administrators to his state. Through the inscriptions, Adityavarman established a genealogical legitimacy of at least three generations, and the inscription stones define the kingdom's regional boundaries. These stone monuments provided a foundation for the institutional lineage of a ruler whose person represented the symbolic centre of the polity.

Yet, Adityavarman's epigraphic record mentions the importance of acknowledging other clan heads which, together with the remains of stone seats used for council meetings, suggests a federated political system. The existence of a federation is also supported by the distribution of his inscriptions beyond Tanah Datar, namely in the regency of Solok, including emerging sub-centres within the region as evidenced by the spread of luxury goods documented through our survey finds and excavations. These materials demonstrate the capacity for an institutionalized polity that extended beyond personal networks. Adityavarman's syncretic repositioning of local and borrowed models are evidence of state control over the region, a nascent administration, and infrastructural achievements that allowed for the direction and performance of affairs of state.

Apart from these federal but court-centred networks, the economic bases of this increasingly complex polity helped it thrive during its formative period, irrigated rice production, trade, and metal working in particular. Two sides of an inscription mention a water channel for rice irrigation within sight of Bukit Gombak built upon royal order. The archaeological debris on Bukit Gombak yielded a knife used to harvest rice, underlining the significance of this crop as a source of food for the region. The kingdom participated in the international trade networks along the west coast of Sumatra and, through riverine connections, along the east coast as well. With access to both coasts, trade in gold, metals, tropical products, and possibly textiles thrived in the region. By the fourteenth century, the polity had trade contacts with the West via Dharmasraya and in the East with the harbour of Pariaman by way of Lake Singkarak. Both, the latter toponym and the hydronym, occur in Adityavarman's inscriptions. This connection enhanced Tanah Datar's role as an economic intermediary between the maritime waterways of Sumatra. The importance of gold and metal working is indicated by the excavated material from Bukit Gombak, Bukit Kincir, and Ponggongan. A gold weight found at Bukit Gombak underlines the regional extent of the Minangkabau trade throughout the highland regions of Sumatra, although this means of payment only allows comparisons to later periods in the ethnographic context.

Expanding consumer demand for imported goods is most obviously seen in the rising quantities of ceramic tradeware during the late fifteenth and early sixteenth centuries. The number of Chinese white and green glazed sherds from the thirteenth or fourteenth century is small. More abundant are middle Ming period ceramics from China, West Asia, or mainland Southeast Asia. Glass objects, among them red and blue Indo-Pacific beads, provide evidence of the consumption of imported goods and the demand for courtly status markers. These various goods came through different trade routes and were not concentrated on Bukit Gombak alone but were available to wider groups throughout Tanah Datar. Shortly after the middle of the fourteenth century, the Minangkabau entered the historic record and were internationally recognized as a thriving polity.

A burial site located in a depression between the slopes of Bukit Gombak and Bukit Kincir can be directly linked to both habitation areas during the fourteenth and sixteenth centuries. More than 200 erected stones mark graves that were used for full corpse burials, leading to the conclusion that the local population did not adopt the practice of cremation as might have been expected within the realm of a Buddhist ruler like Adityavarman. The stones and the pits are oriented toward Mount Merapi. No bones remained due to the highly acidic soil, and the burials were generally not furnished with grave goods. One stone adze without any use-wear traces was intentionally placed in one grave pit, and local and foreign ceramics, especially green-glazed ware, were used in burial rituals. It cannot be proven when the megalithic gravestone tradition was first introduced to this region, but it probably arrived from northwestern Sumatra, that is, the Sinamar and Mahat valleys in the Lima Puluh Kota region, and through migration. Megalithic grave markers in the form of stones with a slightly raised upper part anticipated the later use of gravestones in cemeteries at Ladang Rojo and *Makam Tuan Kadhi* in Tanah Datar, where survey finds attest to continuous use from the fourteenth to the eighteenth centuries unchanged by Islamic disruption.

The burial site on Bukit Kincir is the earliest archaeological evidence of dating the megalithic tradition in Tanah Datar and coincides with the reign of Adityavarman. The knee-high stones are distinctively smaller, undecorated, and not differentiated in scale in contrast to their antecedents in the stratified society of the adjacent Lima Puluh Kota region or other early megalithic sites in Tanah Datar. At Bukit Kincir the local tradition of using burial stones was clearly subordinated to the tradition of markers signalling power and prestige that was maintained by Adityavarman. The graves are marked by small, uniform stones revealing an egalitarian community. This observation fits well with the assumption of a federated polity. Apart from the erected stones, five structures of aligned stones were excavated on higher ground on Bukit Kincir. Only in this area did the excavators uncover imported ceramics from the fourteenth and fifteenth centuries. These archaeological finds suggest two possible interpretations. First, the differences seen in grave structure and the restricted area where foreign ceramics were found may indicate social strata and distinctions between individuals. Alternatively, layers of fired clay, charcoal, and remains of the strike-a-light technique found close to the stone formations might indicate cremation practices, which would mean that different burial practices were performed over the period that the hill was occupied. Adityavarman's Buddhist traditions, though, such as cremating the dead, did not have any sustained impact on local customs.

The demise of Bukit Gombak can be dated archaeologically to the late seventeenth century. Political crises among competing families led to the abandonment of the site after the Pagaruyung dynasty seized power in 1641. Originally from the Kampar Kiri River, the dynasty moved the centre of power to the present-day village of Pagaruyung.

5. Conclusion

As the Pagaruyung oral traditions, manuscripts, and royal performances spread and additively retold the history of Adityavarman's kingdom, his inscriptions faded into history and even the name of the original site on Bukit Gombak was forgotten. However, it was never built over until just before the excavations started in 2011, and our archaeological investigations have uncovered distant glimpses of the Minangkabau past, otherwise untold in the historic record.

BIBLIOGRAPHY

Adi Haji Taha and Abdul Jalil Osman. "The Excavation of Megalithic Alignment at Kampong Ipoh, Tampin, Negeri Sembilan". *Journal of the Malaysian Branch of the Royal Asiatic Society* 55, no. 1 (1982): 78–81.

Agustijanto. "The Pre-Srivijaya Period on the Eastern Coast of Sumatra: Preliminary Research at the Air Sugihan Site". In *Proceedings of the 13th International Conference of the European Association of Southeast Asian Archaeologists*, edited by Mai Lin Tjoa-Bonatz, Andreas Reinecke, and Dominik Bonatz. Singapore: NUS Press, 2012, pp. 32–42.

Andaya, Barbarya Watson. *To Live as Brothers: Southeast Sumatra in the Seventeenth and Eighteenth Centuries*. Honolulu: University of Hawai'i Press, 1993.

Andaya, Leonard Y. "The Search for the 'Origins' of Melayu". *Journal of Southeast Asian Studies* 32, no. 3 (2001): 315–30.

———. *Leaves of the Same Tree: Trade and Ethnicity in the Straits of Melaka*. Honolulu: University of Hawai'i Press, 2008.

Anonymous. "Berigten oudheiden ter Westkust van Sumatra". *Tijdschrift voor Indische Taal-, Land- en Volkenkunde* 4 (1855): 549–50.

Bacus, Elisabeth A. and Lisa J. Lucero, eds. "Introduction: Issues in the Archaeology of Tropical Polities". *Archaeological Papers of the American Anthropological Association* 9, no. 1 (1999): 1–11.

Balai Pelestarian Peninggalan Purbakala Batusangkar. *Daftar inventaris*. Batusangkar: Balai Pelestarian Peninggalan Purbakala Batusangkar, 1977–78.

Bambang Budi Utomo. *Prasasti-Prasasti Sumatra*. Jakarta: PUSLIT, 2007.

Barnard, Timothy P. "Thomas Dias' Journey to Central Sumatra in 1684". In *Harta Karun: Hidden Treasures on Indonesian and Asian-European History from the VOC Archives in Jakarta, Document 1*. Jakarta: Arsip Nasional Republik, 2013. https://sejarah-nusantara.anri.go.id/hartakarun/item/01/ (accessed 18 November 2016).

Bautze-Picron, Claudine. "Buddhist Images from Padang Lawas Region and the South Asian Connection". In *History of Padang Lawas North Sumatra II: Societies of Padang Lawas (Mid-Ninth-Thirteenth Century CE)*, edited by Daniel Perret. Paris: EFEO, Archipel, Cahiers d'Archipel 43, 2014, pp. 107–16.

Bonatz, Dominik. "Kerinci – Archaeological Research in the Highlands of Jambi on Sumatra". In *Uncovering Southeast Asia's Past: Selected Papers from the 10th International Conference of the European Association of Southeast Asian Archaeologists*, edited by Elisabeth A. Bacus, Ian C. Glover, and Vincent C. Pigott. Singapore: NUS Press, 2006, pp. 310–24.

———. "The Neolithic in the Highlands of Sumatra: Problems of Definition". In *From Distant Tales: Archaeology and Ethnohistory in the Highlands of Sumatra*, edited by Dominik Bonatz, John Miksic, J. David Neidel, and Mai Lin Tjoa-Bonatz. Newcastle upon Tyne: Cambridge Scholars Publishing, 2009, pp. 42–74.

———. "A Highland Perspective on the Archaeology and Settlement History of Sumatra". *Archipel* 84 (2012): 35–81.

———. *4000 Tahun jejak permukiman manusia Sumatera. Perspektif arkeologis di dataran tinggi pulau Sumatera*, edited by Ichwan Azhari. Medan: UNIMED, 2015.

———. "Megalithic Landscapes in the Highlands of Sumatra". In *Megaliths – Societies – Landscapes Early Monumentality and Social Differentiation in Neolithic Europe, Vol 1*, edited by Johannes Müller, Martin Hinz, and Maria Wunderlich. Bonn: Habelt, 2019, pp. 407–45.

Bonatz, Dominik, J. David Neidel, and Mai Lin Tjoa-Bonatz. "The Megalithic Complex of Highland Jambi: An Archaeological Perspective". *Bijdragen tot de Taal-, Land- en Volkenkunde* 162, no. 4 (2006): 490–522.

Bonatz, Dominik, John Miksic, J. David Neidel, and Mai Lin Tjoa-Bonatz, ed. *From Distant Tales: Archaeology and Ethnohistory in the Highlands of Sumatra*. Newcastle upon Tyne: Cambridge Scholars Publishing, 2009.

Borell, Brigitte. "Money in 14th Century Singapore". In *Southeast Asian Archaeology 1998: Proceedings of the 7th International Conference of the European Association of Southeast Asian Archaeologists, Berlin 1998*, edited by Wibke Lobo and Stefanie Reinemann. Kingston upon Hull: Centre for Southeast Asian Studies and Staatliche Museen zu Berlin, 2000, pp. 1–16.

Bosch, F.D.K. "De inscriptie op het Mañjuçrī-beeld van 1265 Çaka". *Bijdragen tot de Taal-, Land- en Volkenkunde van Nederlands-Indië* 77 (1921): 194–201.

———. "De rijkssieradan van Pagar Roejang". *Oudheidkundige Verslag*, Bijlage E (1931): 202–15.

BPPP (Balai Pelestarian Peninggalan Purbakala). *Laporan Hasil Ekskavasi Situs Bukit Braholo*. Batusangkar: Balai Pelestarian Peninggalan Purbakala, 2006.

Brinkgreve, Francine, Pauline Lunsingh Scheurleer, and David Stuart-Fox. *Kemegahan emas di Museum Nasional Indonesia: Golden Splendour in the*

National Museum of Indonesia. Jakarta: National Museum of Indonesia, 2010.

Bronson, Benneth. "Exchange at the Upstream and Downstream Ends: Notes toward a Functional Model of the Coastal State in Southeast Asia". In *Economic Exchange and Social Interaction in Southeast Asia*, edited by Karl L. Hutterer. Ann Arbor: University of Michigan Papers on South and Southeast Asian no. 13. Center for South and Southeast Asian Studies, 1977, pp. 39–54.

Bronson, Benneth, Tegu Asmar et al. *Laporan Penelitian Arkeologi di Sumatra: 20 Mei–Juli 1973*. Jakarta: Lembaga Purbakala dan Peninggalan Nasional, 1973.

Brown, Roxanna M. *The Ming Gap and Shipwreck Ceramics in Southeast Asia: Towards a Chronology of Thai Trade Ware*. Bangkok: River Books, 2009.

Brownrigg, Henry. *Cutters from the Samuel Eilenberg Collection*. Stuttgart, London: Hansjorg Mayer, 1991.

Brumm, Adam. "Fire-Making using a Stone 'Strike-a-Light' in the SOA Basin of Flores, Indonesia". *Indo-Pacific Prehistory Association Bulletin* 26 (2007): 168–70.

Budi Istiawan. *Selintas Prasasti dari Melayu Kuno*. Batusangkar: Balai Pelestarian Peninggalan Purbakala Batusangkar, 2006. 2nd ed., 2011. 3rd ed., 2014. https://kebudayaan.kemdikbud.go.id/bpcbbatusangkar/wp-content/uploads/sites/28/2014/12/Selintas-Prasasti-Melayu-Kuno-Budi-Istiawan.pdf (accessed 28 May 2019).

———. "New Finds of the Classical Period in West Sumatra". In *Connecting Empires and States: Selected Papers from the 13th International Conference of the European Association of Southeast Asian Archaeologists*, Vol. 2, edited by Mai Lin Tjoa-Bonatz, Andreas Reinecke, and Dominik Bonatz. Singapore: NUS Press, 2012, pp. 43–52.

Budi Istiawan and Tegu Hidayat. *Laporan ekskavasi situs Pulau Sawah Tahap VI (Candi Pulau Sawah II Tahap IV)*. Batusangkar: Suaka Peninggalan Sejarah dan Purbakala, Propinsi Sumatera Barat dan Riau, 2001.

Bulbeck, David and Ian Caldwell. *The Land of Iron: The Historical Archaeology of Luwu and the Cenrana Valley*. Hull: Centre for Southeast Asian Studies, University of Hull, 2000.

Butterfields. *Treasures from the Hoi An Hoard: Important Vietnamese Ceramics from a Late 15th/Early 16th Century Cargo* (Two Vols.). San Francisco, Los Angeles: Butterfields Auctioneers Corp., 11–13 October 2000.

Calò, Ambra. *Trails of Bronze Drums in Early Southeast Asia: Exchange Routes and Connected Cultural Spheres*. Singapore: Institute of Southeast Asian Studies, 2013.

Carter, Alison K., Laure Dussubieux, and Nancy Beavan. "Glass Beads from 15th–17th Century CE Jar Burial Sites in Cambodia's Cardamom Mountains". *Archaeometry* 58, no. 3 (2016): 401–2.
Chaniago, Nasrul. "Mengungkap sejarah kerajaan Adityawarman". *Sumbar Post* 123, 20–26 March 2011, p. 4.
Charras, Muriel, Dominique Guillaud, and Usmawadi Amir. "Sistem-sistem teknik, system-sistem Produksi, dan Warisan". In *Menyeleusuri sungai: Merunut waktu: Penelitian arkeologi di Sumatera Selatan*, edited by Dominique Guillaud. Jakarta: Pusat Penelitian dan Pengembangan Arkeologi Nasional, Institut de recherché pour le Développement, École française d'Extrême Orient, 2006, pp. 71–86. http://horizon.documentation.ird.fr/exl-doc/pleins_textes/divers09-05/010039110.pdf (accessed 25 November 2016).
Chollet, Hélène. "La porcelain bleu-et-blanc". In *La memoire engloutie de Brunei une aventure archeologique sous-marine: Cahier de fouille, précis scientique* (Three Vols.), edited by Michel l'Hour. Paris: Édition Textuel, 2001, pp. 29–64.
Choo, Alexandra A. *Report on the Excavation at Fort Canning Hill, Singapore*. Singapore: National Museum Singapore, 1986.
Christie, Jan Wisseman. "Trade and State Formation in the Malay Peninsula and Sumatra, 300 B.C.–A.D. 700". In *The Southeast Asian Port and Polity*, edited by Jeyamalar Kathirithamby-Wells and John Villiers. Singapore: University of Singapore Press, 1990, pp. 39–60.
———. "State Formation in Early Maritime Southeast Asia: A Consideration of the Theories and the Data". *Bijdragen tot de Taal-, Land- en Volkenkunde* 151, no. 2 (1995): 235–88.
———. "The Medieval Tamil-Language Inscriptions in Southeast Asia and China". *Journal of Southeast Asian Studies* 29, no. 2 (1998): 239–68.
———. "Water and Rice in Early Java and Bali". In *A World of Water: Rain, Rivers and Seas in Southeast Asian Histories*, edited by Peter Boomgaard. Leiden: KITLV, 2007, pp. 235–58.
Colombijn, Freek. "The Volatile State in Southeast Asia: Evidence from Sumatra, 1600–1800". *The Journal of Asian Studies* 62, no. 2 (2003): 497–529.
Cort, Louise, Leedom Lefferts, and Charlotte Reith. "'Before' Paddle-and-Anvil: Contributions from Contemporary Mainland Southeast Asia". Symposium on Ceramic Technology and Production, The British Museum, London, 22 November 1997. [typescript].
Couperus, P.Th. "Eenige aantekeningen betreffende de goudproduktie in de Padangsche Bovenlanden". *Tijdschrift voor Indische Taal-, Land- en Volkenkunde* (1856): 122–31. https://babel.hathitrust.org/cgi/pt?id=hvd.hn4jkv;view=1up;seq=11 (accessed 12 December 2016).

Dalboquerque, A. (Afonso de Albuquerque). *The Commentaries of the Great Afonso Dalboquerque*, trans. (Vol. 3). New York: Franklin, 1963 [1518].
Damais, Louis-Charles I. "La date de l'inscription de Hujung Langit ('Bawang')". *Bulletin de l'École française d'Extrême-Orient* 50 (1960): 275–88.
Damanik, Erond L. and Ed. Edwards McKinnon. "Traces of Early Chinese and Southeast Asian Trade at *Benteng Puteri Hijau*, Namu Rambe, Northeast Sumatra". In *Proceedings of the 13th International Conference of the European Association of Southeast Asian Archaeologists*, edited by Mai Lin Tjoa-Bonatz, Andreas Reinecke, and Dominik Bonatz. Singapore: NUS Press, 2012, pp. 53–66.
de Casparis, Johannes G. "Ahmat Majanu's Tombstone at Pengkalan Kempas and its Kawi Inscription". *Journal of the Malaysian Branch of the Royal Asiatic Society* 53, no. 1 (1980): 1–22.
———. "Srivijaya and Melayu". In *Spafa Final Report: Consultative Workshop in Archaeological and Environmental Studies on Srivijaya, Jakarta, Padang, Prapat, and Medan, Indonesia, 16–30 September 1985*. Bangkok: SEAMEO Project in Archaeology and Fine Arts, 1985, pp. 245–55.
———. "Peranan Adityawarman, Putera Melayu di Asia Tenggara". In *Tamadun Melayu* (3), edited by Ismail Hussein, Aziz Deraman, and Abdul Rahman al-Ahmadi. Kuala Lumpur: Dewan Bahasa dan Pustaka, Kementerian Pendidikan Malaysia, 1989, pp. 918–43.
———. "Kerajaan Melayu dan Adityawarman". In *Seminar Sejarah Melayu Kuno, Jambi 7–8 Desember 1992*. Jambi: Pemerintah Daerah, 1992.
Djafar, Hasan. "Prasasti-prasasti masa kerajaan Melayu kuno dan beberapa permasalahannya". In *Seminar Sejarah Melayu Kuno, Jambi 7–8 Desember 1992*. Jambi: PEMDA Tingkat I Propinsi Jambi, Kantor Wilayah DEPDIKBUD Propinsi Jambi, 1992.
Dobbin, Christine. "The Exercise of Authority in Minangkabau in the Late Eighteenth Century". In *Pre-Colonial State Systems in Southeast Asia*, edited by Anthony Reid and Lance Castles. Kuala Lumpur: Royal Asiatic Society, 1975, pp. 77–89.
———. *Islamic Revivalism in a Changing Peasant Economy: Central Sumatra, 1784–1847*. London: Curzon Press, 1983.
Drakard, Jane. *A Malay Frontier: Unity and Duality in a Sumatran Kingdom*. New York: Cornell Southeast Asia Program, 1990.
———. *Kingdom of Words: Language and Power in Sumatra*. Oxford: Oxford University Press, 1999.
———. "Inscribing Sumatra: Perceptions of Place and Space in Achehnese and Minangkabau Royal Letters". *Bulletin de l'École française d'Extrême-Orient* 95–6 (2008–9): 135–89.

Druce, Stephen C. "The Decentralized Austronesian Polity: Of Mandalas, Negaras, Galactics, and the South Sulawesi Kingdoms". *Suvannabhumi* 9, no. 2 (December 2017): 7–34.

Duff, Roger. *Stone Adzes of Southeast Asia*. Christchurch: Canterbury Museum, 1970.

Dunn, Frederick L. *Rain-Forest Collectors and Traders: A Study of Resource Utilization in Ancient and Modern Malaya*. Kulala Lumpur: Malaysian Branch of the Royal Asiatic Society, 1975.

Dupoizat, Maria-France. "Grès et porcelaines des sites de Barus postérieurs à Lobu Tua". In *Histoire de Barus*. Vol. III: *Regards sur une place marchande de l'océan Indien (XIIe-milieu du XVIIe s.)*, edited by Daniel Perret and Heddy Surachman. Paris: EFEO, Archipel, Cahiers d'Archipel 38, 2009, pp. 81–152.

Dupoizat, Maria-France and Naniek Harkantiningsih. "La céramique importée". In *Banten avant l'Islam: Étude archéologique de Banten Girang (Java-Indonésie) 932?–1526*, edited by Claude Guillot, Lukman Nurhakim, and Sonny Wibisono. Paris: Publications de l'E.F.E.O., Monographies no. 173, 1994, pp. 137–68.

———. *Catalogue of the Chinese Style Ceramics of Majapahit: Tentative Inventory*. Paris: EFEO, Archipel, Cahiers d'Archipel 36, 2007.

Dussubieux, Laure, Bernard Gratuze, and Maryse Blet-Lemarquand. "Mineral Soda Alumina Glass: Occurrence and Meaning". *Journal of Archaeological Science* 37 (2010): 1646–55.

Edwards McKinnon, Ed. "Kota Cina: Its Context and Meaning in the Trade of Southeast Asia in the Twelfth to Fourteenth Centuries". PhD dissertation, Cornell University, 1984.

———. "Yue and Longquan Wares in Sumatra". In *New Light on Chinese Yue and Longquan Wares: Archaeological Ceramics Found in Eastern and Southern Asia, A.D. 800–1400*, edited by Chuimei Ho. Hong Kong: The University of Hong Kong, 1994, pp. 284–98.

———. "Historic Period Earthenware from the Island of Sumatra". In *Earthenware in Southeast Asia: Proceedings of the Singapore Symposium on Premodern Southeast Asian Earthenwares*, edited by John N. Miksic. Singapore: NUS Press, 2003, pp. 162–72.

———. "Ceramics, Cloth, Iron and Salt: Coastal Hinterland Interaction in the Karo Region of Northeast Sumatra". In *From Distant Tales: Archaeology and Ethnohistory in the Highlands of Sumatra*, edited by Dominik Bonatz, John Miksic, J. David Neidel, and Mai Lin Tjoa-Bonatz. Newcastle upon Tyne: Cambridge Scholars Publishing, 2009, pp. 120–43.

———. "Burmese Wares in Aceh and North Sumatra". In *Peninsular Siam and its Neighbourhoods: Essays in Memory of Dr. Preecha Noonsuk*, edited by Wannasarn Noonsuk. Nakhon Si Thammarat: Time Printing, 2017, pp. 161–70.

Edwards McKinnon, Ed., Naniek Harkantiningsih Wibisono, Heddy Surachman, Stanov Purnawibowo, Lim Chen Sian, and Benjamin Vining. "The Kota Rentang Excavations". In *Proceedings of the 13th International Conference of the European Association of Southeast Asian Archaeologists*, edited by Mai Lin Tjoa-Bonatz, Andreas Reinecke, and Dominik Bonatz. Singapore: NUS Press, 2012, pp. 67–81.

Eggebrecht, Arne and Eva Eggebrecht. *Versunkene Königreiche Indonesiens*. Hildesheim: von Zabern, 1995.

Eny Christiawaty. "Teknik tatap – laandas di Sentang, Tanjung Tiram, Batubara, Sumatera Utara (teknik pembiatan tembikar tradisi neolitik". *Berkala Arkeologi Sangkhakala* 13, no. 25 (2010): 42–52.

Erman Makmur. *Koleki tembikar*. Padang: Proyek Pengembangan Permuseuman Sumatera Barat, 1983–84.

Fischer, Hendrik W. *Katalog des ethnographischen Reichsmuseums*. Vol. 10: *Mittel-Sumatra*. Leiden: Brill, 1916.

Fontein, Jan. *The Sculpture of Indonesia*. Washington: National Gallery of Art; New York: Abrams, 1990.

Gasser, Stephan A. *Das Töpferhandwerk von Indonesien*. Basel: Pharos, 1969.

Gauri Parimoo Krishnan, ed. *Nalanda, Srivijaya and Beyond: Re-Exploring Buddhist Art in Asia*. Singapore: ACM, 2016.

Goddio, Franck and Gabriel S. Casal. *Lost at Sea: The Strange Route of the Lena Shoal Junk*. London: Periplus, 2002.

Gotuaco, Larry, Rita C. Tan, and Allison I. Diem. *Chinese and Vietnamese Blue and White Wares Found in the Philippines*. Makati: Bookmark, 1997.

Griffiths, Arlo. "Inscriptions of Sumatra: Further Data on the Epigraphy of the Musi and Batang Hari Rivers Basins". *Archipel* 81 (2011): 139–75.

―――. "Short Inscriptions in Old Javanese Found on Sumatra". *Wacana* 14, no. 1 (2012): 1–19.

―――. "Inscriptions of Sumatra. III: The Padang Lawas Corpus Studied Along with Inscriptions from Sorik Merapi (North Sumatra and from Muara Takus (Riau)". In *History of Padang Lawas North Sumatra II Societies of Padang Lawas (Mid-Ninth-Thirteenth Century CE)*, edited by Daniel Perret. Paris: EFEO, Archipel, Cahiers d'Archipel 43, 2014, pp. 211–54.

Guillaud, Dominique, ed. *Menyelusuri sungai: merunut waktu: penelitian arkeologi di Sumatera Selatan*. Jakarta: Pusat Penelitian dan Pengembangan Arkeologi Nasional, Institut de recherché pour le Développement, École française d'Extrême Orient, 2006. http://horizon.documentation.ird.fr/exl-doc/pleins_textes/divers09-05/010039110.pdf (accessed 7 June 2018).

Guillaud, Dominique, Hubert Forestier, and Truman Simanjuntak. "Mounds, Tombs, and Tales: Archaeology and Oral Tradition in the South Sumatra Highlands". In *From Distant Tales: Archaeology and Ethnohistory in the Highlands of*

Sumatra, edited by Dominik Bonatz, John Miksic, J. David Neidel, and Mai Lin Tjoa-Bonatz. Newcastle upon Tyne: Cambridge Scholars Publishing, 2009, pp. 416–33.

Guillot, Claude, ed. *Histoire de Barus: Le Site de Lobu Tua. I.* Étude et Documents. Paris: EFEO, Archipel, Cahiers d'Archipel 30, 1998.

———. *Histoire de Barus Sumatra: Le Site de Lobu Tua II. Étude archéologique et Documents.* Paris: EFEO, Archipel, Cahiers d'Archipel 30, 2003.

Guillot, Claude, Lukman Nurhakim, and Sonny Wibisono, eds. *Banten avant l'Islam: Étude archéologique de Banten Girang (Java-Indonésie) 932?–1526.* Paris: Publications de l'E.F.E.O., Monographies no. 173, 1994.

Guy, John. "Rama, Rajas and Courtesans: Indian Figurative Textiles in Indonesia". In *The Secrets of Southeast Asian Textiles: Myth, Status and the Supernatural, the James H W Thompson Foundation Symposium Papers*, edited by Jane Puranananda. Bangkok: River Books, 2007, pp. 40–57.

Haan, F. van. "Naar Midden Sumatra in 1684". *Verhandelingen van het Koningklijk Bataviaasch Genootschap van Kunsten en Wetenschappen* 39 (1897): 327–66.

Haase, Evelin. *Die ethnographische Sammlung Herzog Johann Albrechts: Souvenirs einer fürstlichen Hochzeitsreise.* Braunschweig: Olms, 2004.

Harrisson, Tom. "The Ming Gap and Kota Batu, Brunei". *The Sarawak Museum Journal* 8, no. 11 June (1958): 273–77.

Hasselt, A.L. van. *Midden-Sumatra: Reizen en Onderzoekingen der Sumatra-Expeditie, uitgerust door het Aardrijkskundig Genootschap 1877–1879* (Four Vols.). Leiden: E.J. Brill, 1881.

Hauser-Schäublin, Brigitta. "The Pre-Colonial Balinese State Reconsidered: A Critical Evaluation of Theories on the Relationship between Irrigation, the State, and Ritual". *Current Anthropology* 44, no. 2 (2003): 153–82.

Herrera, Alexander. "Indigenous Archaeology in Peru?". In *Indigenous Peoples and Archaeology in Latin America*, edited by Cristóbal Gnecco and Patrica Ayala. Walnut Creek, CA: Left Coast Press, 2011, pp. 67–87.

Hess, Elias. *Reisebeschreibungen von deutschen Beamten und Kriegsleuten im Dienst der niederländischen West- und Ost-Indischen Kompagnien 1602–1797.* Den Haag: Nijhoff, 1931 [1602–1797].

Hill, A.H. "Hikayat Raja-Raja Pasai". *Journal of the Malayan Branch of the Royal Asiatic Society* 33, no. 2 (1960): 1–215.

Hunter, Thomas M. "Sanskrit in a Distant Land: The Sanskritized Sections". In *A 14th Century Malay Code of Laws: The Nītisārasamuccaya*, edited by Uli Kozok. Singapore: Institute of Southeast Asian Studies, 2015, pp. 281–379.

Jasper, J.E. and Mas Pirngadië. *De inlandsche kunstnijverheid in Nederlandsch Indië.* Vol. 5: *De bewerking van niet-edele metalen.* The Hague: Mouton, 1927.

Josselin de Jong, Patrick E. *Minangkabau and Negeri Sembilan: Socio-Political Structure in Indonesia.* Leiden: Eduard Ijdo, 1951.

Junker, Laura L. "The Organization of Intra-Regional and Long-Distance Trade in Prehispanic Philippine Complex Societies". *Asian Perspectives* 19, no. 2 (1990): 165–209.

———. *Raiding, Trading, and Feasting: The Political Economy of Philippine Chiefdoms*. Honolulu: University of Hawai'i, 1999.

Kahn, Joel S. *Consituting the Minangkabau: Peasants, Culture, and Modernity in Colonial Indonesia*. Oxford: Berg, 1993.

Kempers, Bernet A.J. *Ancient Indonesian Art*. Amsterdam: C.P.J. van der Peet, 1959.

Kendall, Ann. "Applied Archaeology: Revitalizing Indigenous Agricultural Technology within an Andean Community". *Public Archaeology* 4, nos. 2–3 (2005): 205–21.

Kern, H. "De wij-inscriptie op het Amoghapāça-beeld van Padang Candi (Midden-Sumatra) 1269 Çāka". *Tijdschrift voor Indische Taal-, Land- en Volkenkunde* 49, no. 1 (1907): 165–75.

———. "Het sanskrit-inschrift op den grafsteen van vorst Ādityavarman te Kubur Raja (Mēnangkabau ± 1300 Çāka)". *Verspreide Geschriften* 7 (1917*a* [1913]): 215–21.

———. "Het zoogenaamde rotsinschrift van 'Batu Bēragung' in Mēnangkabau (1269 en 1297 Çāka)". *Verspreide Geschriften* 6 (1917*b* [1872 and 1877]): 249–63.

———. "Nog iets over t' opschrift van Pagarruyung in Mēnangkabau (1278 Çāka)". *Verspreide Geschriften* 6 (1917*c* [1873]): 267–75.

Kieven, Lydia. *Following the Cap-Figure in Majapahit Temple Reliefs: A New Look at the Religious Function of East Javanese Temples, Fourteenth and Fifteenth Centuries*. Leiden, Boston: Brill, 2013.

Klokke, Marijke J. "The Iconography of the so-called Portrait Statues in Late East Javanese Art". In *Ancient Indonesian Sculpture*, edited by Marijke J. Klokke and Pauline Lunsingh Scheurleer. Leiden: KITLV Press, 1994, pp. 178–201.

Koestro, Lucas P., Pierre-Yves Manguin, and Soeroso. "Kota Kapur (Bangka, Indonesia): A Pre-Sriwijayan Site Reascertained". In *Southeast Asian Archaeology 1994: Proceedings of the 5th International Conference of the European Association of Southeast Asian Archaeologists, Paris, 24th–28th October 1994*, edited by Pierre-Yves Manguin. Hull: Centre for Southeast Asian Studies, University of Hull, 1998, pp. 61–81.

Kozok, Uli and Eric van Reijn. "Ādityawarman: Three Inscriptions of the Sumatran 'King of all Supreme Kings' Translated and Annotated from H. Kern and F.D.K. Bosch". *Indonesia and the Malay World* 38, no. 110 (2010): 135–58.

Kozok, Uli and Waruno Mahdi. "Tanjung Tanah Manuscript TK 214". In *A 14th Century Malay Code of Laws: The Nītisārasamuccaya*, edited by Uli Kozok. Singapore: Institute of Southeast Asian Studies, 2015, pp. 50–161.

Krahl, Regina, John Guy, J. Keith Wilson, and Julian Raby, eds. *Shipwrecked: Tang Treasures and Monsoon Winds*. Singapore: Arthur M. Sackler Gallery, Smithsonian Institution, National Heritage Board; Singapore Tourism Board, 2011.

Kroeskamp, Hendrik. *De Westkust en Minangkabau (1665–1668)*. Utrecht: Utrecht Schotanus & Jens, 1931.

Krom, Nicolaas J. "Inventaris der Oudheden in de Padangsche Bovenlanden". *Oudheidkundig Verslag*, Bijlage G (1912): 33–52.

———. *Hindoe-Javaansche Geschiedenis*. s'Gravenhagen: Nijhoff, 1931.

Kulke, Hermann. "'Kadutuan Śrivijaya?' Empire or Kraton of Śrivijaya? A Reassessment of the Epigraphical Data". *Bulletin de l'École française d'Extrême-Orient* 80, no. 1 (1993): 159–80.

———. "Adityavarman's Highland Kingdom". In *From Distant Tales: Archaeology and Ethnohistory in the Highlands of Sumatra*, edited by Dominik Bonatz, John Miksic, J. David Neidel, and Mai Lin Tjoa-Bonatz. Newcastle upon Tyne: Cambridge Scholars Publishing, 2009, pp. 229–52.

Lai Chee Kien. "Deducing from Balimbing: Measuring a Minangkabau House". *Architecture Journal* (1993): 59–69.

Lam, Peter Y.K. *A Ceramic Legacy of Asia's Maritime Trade: Song Dynasty Guangdong Wares and Other 11th to 19th Century Trade Ceramics Found on Tioman Island, Malaysia: [Exhibition] Held in the Muzium Seni Asia, University of Malaya*. Kuala Lumpur: Southeast Asian Ceramic Society, 1985.

Lieberman, Victor. *Strange Parallels: Southeast Asia in Global Context. C 800–1830*. Vol. 1: *Integration on the Mainland*. Cambridge: Cambridge University Press, 2003.

Lombard, Denys. "Pour une histoire des villes du Sud-East asiatique". *Annales, Histoire, Science Sociales* 25, no. 4 (1970): 842–56.

Lukman Nurhakim. "Autres Objets". In *Banten avant l'Islam: Étude archéologique de Banten Girang (Java-Indonésie) 932?–1526*, edited by Claude Guillot, Lukman Nurhakim, and Sonny Wibisono. Paris: Publications de l'EFEO, Monographies no. 173, 1994, pp. 182–84.

Lunsingh Scheurleer, Pauline. "The Well-Known Javanese Statue in the Tropenmuseum, Amsterdam, and its Place in Javanese Sculpture". *Artibus Asiae* 68, no. 2 (2008): 287–332.

Lutfi Yondri. "Pembuatan gerabah tradisional di desa Galogandang, Tanahdatar Sumatera Barat: corak tradisi masa bercocok tanam". *Jurnal Penelitian Balai Arkeologi Bandung* 1 (1995): 69–80.

Machi Suhadi. "Silsilah Adityawarman". *Kalpataru Majalah Arkeologi* 9 (1990): 219–39.

Macleod, N. "De Oost-Indische Compagnie op Sumatra in de 17e eeuw". *De Indische Gids* 28, no. 2 (1906): 1420–49.

Manguin, Pierre-Yves. "The Merchant and the King: Political Myths of Southeast Asian Coastal Polities". *Indonesia* 52 (1991): 41–54.

———. "Les cités-États de l'Asie du Sud-Est côtière: De L'ancienneté et de la permanence des forms urbaines". *Bulletin de l'École française d'Extrême-Orient* 87 (2000): 151–82.

———. "City-States and City-State Cultures in Pre-15th-Century Southeast Asia". In *A Comparative Study of Thirty-City-State Cultures: An Investigation Conducted by the Copenhagen Polis Centre*, edited by Mogens H. Hansen. Copenhagen: Copenhagen Polis Centre, 2002a, pp. 409–16.

———. "The Amorphous Nature of Coastal Polities in Insular Southeast Asia: Restricted Centres, Extended Peripheries". *Moussons* 5 (2002b): 73–99.

———. "The Archaeology of the Early Maritime Polities of Southeast Asia". In *Southeast Asia: From Prehistory to History*, edited by Peter Bellwood and Ian C. Glover. London: Routledge Curzon, 2004, pp. 282–313.

———. "Southeast Sumatra in Protohistoric and Srivijaya Times: Upstream-Downstream Relations and the Settlement of the Peneplain". In *From Distant Tales: Archaeology and Ethnohistory in the Highlands of Sumatra*, edited by Dominik Bonatz, John Miksic, J. David Neidel, and Mai Lin Tjoa-Bonatz. Newcastle upon Tyne: Cambridge Scholars Publishing, 2009, pp. 434–51.

Marschall, Wolfgang. *Metallurgie und frühe Besiedlungsgeschichte Indonesiens*. Köln: E.J. Brill, 1968.

Marsden, William. *The History of Sumatra: Containing an Account of the Government, Laws, Customs, and Manner of the Native Inhabitants, with a Description of the Natural Productions, and a Relation of the Ancient Political State of that Island*. Oxford: Oxford University Press, 1911 [1783].

Marsis Sutopo. *Laporan ekskavasi penyelematan gua Beringin Kecamatan XKota, Kabupaten Solok Suaka Peninggalan Sejarah dan Purbakala Wilayah Provinsi Sumatera Barat dan Riau*, 1991.

———. *Laporan ekskavasi penyelamatan situs Pulausawah*. Batusangkar: Suaka Peninggalan Sejarah dan Purbakala Wilayah Provinsi Sumatera Barat dan Riau, 1996–97.

Marsis Sutopo and Bagyo Prasetyo. "Penelitian tradisi megalitik Gunung Bungsu". *Amoghapasa* 1, no. 1 (July 1994): 19–35.

Martin, P. "Zum Metallguß im Padanger Hochland (Minangkabau)". *Abhandlungen und Berichte des Staatlichen Museums für Völkerkunde Dresden* 44 (1990): 257–67.

Miksic, John N. "Archaeology, Trade and Society in Northeast Sumatra". PhD dissertation, Cornell University, 1979.

———. "Parallels between the Upright Stones of West Sumatra and those in Malacca and Negeri Sembilan". *Journal of the Malaysian Branch of the Royal Asiatic Society* 58 (1985a): 71–80.

———. "Traditional Sumatran Trade". *Bulletin de l'École française d'Extrême-Orient* 74 (1985*b*): 423–67.

———. *Archaeological Research on the 'Forbidden Hill' of Singapore: Excavations at Fort Canning, 1984*. Singapore: National Museum, 1985*c*.

———. "A Valley of Megaliths in West Sumatra: Mahat (Schnitger's Aoer Doeri) Revisited". *Journal of the Malaysian Branch of the Royal Asiatic Society* 59 (1986): 27–32.

———. "From Seri Vijaya to Melaka: 'Batu Tagak' in Historical and Cultural Context". *Journal of the Malayan Branch of the Royal Asiatic Society* 60, no. 2 (1987): 1–42.

———. *Small Finds: Ancient Javanese Gold*. Singapore: Southeast Asian Allery, National Museum, 1988.

———. "Urbanization and Social Change: The Case of Sumatra". *Archipel "Villes d'Insulinde II"* 37 (1989*a*): 3–29.

———. *Old Javanese Gold*, 1st ed. Singapore: Ideation, 1989*b*.

———. "Water, Urbanization, and Disease in Ancient Indonesia". *Archaeological Papers of the American Anthropological* 9, no. 1 (1999): 167–84.

———. "Heterogenetic Cities in Premodern Southeast Asia". *World Archaeology* 32, no. 1 (2000): 106–21.

———. "From Megaliths to Tombstones: Transition from Prehistory to the Early Islamic Period in Highland West Sumatra". *Indonesia and the Malay World* 32 (2004): 191–210.

———. "Chinese Ceramics and the Economics of Early Southeast Asian Urbanisation, 14th to 16th Centuries". *Bulletin of the Indo-Pacific Prehistory Association* 26 (2006): 147–53.

———. "Highland-Lowland Connections in Jambi, South Sumatra, and West Sumatra, 11th to 14th Centuries". In *From Distant Tales: Archaeology and Ethnohistory in the Highlands of Sumatra*, edited by Dominik Bonatz, John Miksic, J. David Neidel, and Mai Lin Tjoa-Bonatz. Newcastle upon Tyne: Cambridge Scholars Publishing, 2009, pp. 75–103.

———. "Before and After Zheng He: Comparing some Southeast Asian Archaeological Sites of the 14th and 15th Centuries". In *Southeast Asia in the Fifteenth Century: The Ming Factor*, edited by Geoff Wade and Sun Laichen. Singapore: NUS Press, 2010, pp. 103–32.

———. *Old Javanese Gold: The Hunter Thompson Collection at the Yale University Art Gallery*, 2nd ed. New Haven, London: Yale University, 2011.

———. *Singapore and the Silk Road of the Sea*. Singapore: NUS Press, 2013.

———. "Kerinci and the Ancient History of Jambi". In *A 14th Century Malay Code of Laws: The Nītisārasamuccaya*, edited by Uli Kozok. Singapore: Institute of Southeast Asian Studies, 2015, pp. 17–49.

———. "Archaeological Evidence for Esoteric Buddhism in Sumatra, 7th to 13th Century". In *Esoteric Buddhism in Mediaeval Maritime Asia: Networks of Masters, Texts, Icons*, edited by Andrea Acri. Singapore: Institute of Southeast Asian Studies, 2016, pp. 253–73.

———. "Buddhism in the Straits of Melaka and the Archaeology of Srivijaya". In *Nalanda, Srivijaya and Beyond: Re-Exploring Buddhist Art in Asia*, edited by Gauri Parimoo Krishnan. Singapore: ACM, 2016, pp. 129–52.

Miksic, John N. and Choon Teck Yap. "Fine-Bodied White Earthenwares of South East Asia: Some X-Ray Fluorescence Tests". *Asian Perspectives* 28, no. 1 (1990): 45–60.

Mill, J.V.G. *Ying-yai Sheng-lan: The Overall Survey of the Ocean's Shores* [1433], by Ma Huan. Cambridge: Cambridge University, 1970.

Moens, J.L. "Het buddhisme op Java en Sumatra in zijn laatste bloeiperdiode". *Tijdschrift voor Indische Taal-, Land- en Volkenkunde* 64 (1924): 521–79.

Nagel Auctions. *Tek Sing Treasures*. Stuttgart: Nagel, 2000.

Nakamura, Selma. "Minangkabau Village Structure and Meanings Upstream and Downstream Orientation". In *International Seminar on Vernacular Settlement: The Role of Local Knowledge in Built Environment*. Jakarta: The Faculty of Engineering University of Indonesia, 1999, pp. 117–32.

Neidel, David. "Settlement Histories of Serampas: Multiple Sources, Conflicting Data, and the Problem of Historical Reconstruction". In *From Distant Tales: Archaeology and Ethnohistory in the Highlands of Sumatra*, edited by Dominik Bonatz, John Miksic, J. David Neidel, and Mai Lin Tjoa-Bonatz. Newcastle upon Tyne: Cambridge Scholars Publishing, 2009, pp. 323–46.

Nguyên Đình Chiên and Pham Quôc Quân. *Gôm Sú Trong Năm Con Tàu Cô O'Vùng Biên Viêtnam* [Ceramics on Five Shipwrecks Off the Coast of Viet Nam]. Hanoi: National Museum of Vietnamese History, 2008.

Ni Komang Ayu Astiti. "Tempayan kubur dan tanah dari situs Padang Sepan, Kec Air Besi, Kab. Bengkulu Utara (Kajian Laboratorium)". *Jurnal Arkeologi Siddhayatra* 9, no. 1 (2004): 1–11.

———. "Pemanfaatan tanah liat bakar pada situs Blandongan dan Candi Jiwa, di kompleks situs Batujaya, Kabupaten Karawang, provinsi jawa barat (studi bahan berdasarkan analisis laboratorium)". *Amerta* 25, no. 1 (2007): 12–23.

Nishimura, Masao. "Long Distance Trade and the Development of Complex Societies in the Prehistory of the Central Philippines – The Cebu Archaeological Project: Basic Concept and First Results". *Philippine Quarterly of Culture and Society* 16, no. 2 (1988): 107–57.

Niziolek, Lisa C., Gary M. Feinman, Jun Kimura, Amanda Respess, and Lu Zhang. "Revisiting the Date of the Java Sea Shiwreck from Indonesia". *Journal of Archaeological Science: Reports* (2018): 781–90.

Pelita. Prasasti kerajaan Minangkabau belum ditemukan, 19 July 1988, p. 7.

Perret, Daniel. "The Sculpture of Padang Lawas: An Updated Inventory". In *History of Padang Lawas North Sumatra II, Societies of Padang Lawas (Mid-Ninth-Thirteenth Century CE)*, edited by Daniel Perret. Paris: EFEO, Archipel, Cahiers d'Archipel 43, 2014, pp. 37–106.

Perret, Daniel and Heddy Surachman, eds. *Histoire de Barus*. Vol. III: *Regards sur une place marchande de l'océan Indien (XIIe–milieu du XVIIe s.)*. Paris: EFEO, Archipel, Cahiers d'Archipel 38, 2009.

———. "South Asia and the Tapanuli Area (North-West Sumatra): Ninth–Fourteenth Centuries CE". In *Early Interactions between South and Southeast Asia: Reflections on Cross-Cultural Exchange*, edited by Pierre-Yves Manguin and Geoff Wade. Singapore: Institute of Southeast Asian Studies, 2011, pp. 161–76.

Perret, Daniel, Heddy Surachman, Ery Soedewo, Repelita Wahyu Utomo, and Mudjiono. "The French-Indonesian Archaeological Project in Kota Cina (North Sumatra): Preliminary Results and Prospects". *Archipel* 86 (2013): 73–111.

Phalgunadi, I Gusti Putu. *The Pararaton: A Study of the Southeast Asian Chronicle*. New Delhi: Sundeep Prakashan, 1996.

Pires, Tomé. *The Suma Oriental of Tomé Pires and The Book of Francisco Rodrigues*, translated by Armando Cortesão. London: Hakluyt Society, 1944 [1512–15].

Pistorius, A.W.P. Verkerk. *Studien over de Inlandsche Huishouding de Padangsche Bovenlanden*. Zalt-Dommel: J.N. Zoon, 1871.

Prapañca, Mpu. *Nāgarakṛtagāma Desawarnana (Nagarakrtagama) by Mpu Prapañca*, translated by Stuart O. Robson. Leiden: KITLV Press, 1995.

Raffles, Lady S. *Memoir of the Life and Public Services of Sir Thomas Stamford Raffles*. Oxford University Press, 1991 [1830].

Rambung, Rosalina and Budi Istiawan. "Survai pendataan gua-gua prasejarah di Balik Bukit". *Amoghapasa* 8, no. 4 (November 1998): 32–39.

Reichle, Natasha. *Violence and Serenity: Late Buddhist Sculpture from Indonesia*. Honolulu: University of Hawai'i, 2007.

Reid, Anthony. "The Structure of Cities in Southeast Asia: Fifteenth to Seventeenth Centuries". *Journal of Southeast Asian Studies* 11, no. 2 (1980): 235–50.

———. *Southeast Asia in the Age of Commerce, 1450–1680*. Vol. 2: *Expansion and Crisis*. New Haven: Yale University Press, 1993.

———. *Witnesses to Sumatra: A Travellers' Anthology*. Oxford: Oxford University Press, 1995.

Rinaldi, Inki. "Tanah Datar menyimpan jejak Adityawarman". *Kompas*, 16 April 2011, p. 22.

———. "Artefak masa neolitikum ditemukan di Tanah Datar". *Kompas*, 27–29 March 2012*a*.

———. "Pembuktian sejarah peradaban di bawah permukaan tanah". *Sains Kompas*, 27 May 2012*b*. http://sains.kompas.com/2012/05/27/03082552 (accessed 30 August 2013).

Risnal, M., Iskandar Zakaria, and Firman Nur. *Tembikar tradisional: desa Bungo Tanjung Kerinci.* Jambi: Departemen Pendidikan dan Kebdudayaan, Bagian Proyek Pembinaan Permuseuman Jambi, 1995–96.

Roth, Gustav. "Mangala-Symbols in Buddhist Sanskrit Manuscripts and Inscriptions". In *Deyadharma: Studies in Memory of Dr. D.C. Sircar*, edited by Gouriswar Bhattacharya. Delhi: Sri Satguru, 1986, pp. 139–250.

Rye, Owen S. and Clifford Evans. *Traditional Pottery Techniques of Pakistan: Field and Laboratory Studies.* Washington: Smithonian, 1976.

Sanday, Peggy R. and Suwati Kartiwa. "Cloth and Custom in West Sumatra: The Codification of Minangkabau Worldview". *Expedition* 26, no. 4 (1984): 13–28.

Sartono, S. "Emas di Sumtera Kala Purba". *Amerta* 8 (1984): 1–16.

Satyawati Suleiman. *The Archaeology and History of West Sumatra.* Jakarta: Pusat Peneltitian Purbakala dan Peninggalan Nasional, Bulletin of the Research Centre of Archaeology of Indonesia 12, 1977.

Schmitt, Anne. "Étude géochimique des pâtes des poteries". In *Histoire de Barus. Vol. III: Regards sur une place marchande de l'océan Indien (XIIe-milieu du XVIIe s.)*, edited by Daniel Perret and Heddy Surachman. Paris: EFEO, Archipel, Cahiers d'Archipel 38, 2009, pp. 301–24.

Schnitger, Frederic M. *The Archaeology of Hindoo Sumatra.* Leiden: E.J. Brill, 1937.

———. *Forgotten Kingdom in Sumatra.* Leiden: E.J. Brill, 1964 [1938].

Scott, James C. *The Art of Not Being Governed: An Anarchist History of Upland Southeast Asia.* Yale: Yale University, 2010.

Setianingsih, Rita M. "Prasasti Ganggo Hilia: Temuan baru dari Sumatera Barat". *Berkala Arkeologi Sangkhala* 16 (November 2005): 64–78.

Sjafiroeddin, David S. "Pre-Islamic Minangkabau". *Berita Kajiau Sumatera* [Sumatra Research Bulletin] 4, no. 1 (1974): 31–57.

Sjarifoedin, Amir. *Minangkabau dari dinasti Iskandar Zulkarnain sampai Tuanku Imam Bonjol.* Jakarta: Gria Media Prima, 2011.

Sumarah Adhyatman. *Kendi: Wadah Air Minum Traditional.* Jakarta: Ceramic Society of Indonesia, 2004.

Summerfield, Anne and John Summerfield, eds. *Walk in Plendor: Ceremonial Dress and the Minangkabau.* Los Angeles: UCLA Fowler Museum of Cultural History, 1999.

Tambiah, Stanley J. "The Galactic Polity: The Structure of Traditional Kingdoms in Southeast Asia". In *Anthropology and the Climate of Opinion.* New York: New York Academy of Sciences, Annals Number 293, 1977, pp. 69–97.

Tanaka, Kazuhiko and Eusebio Z. Dizon. "Shipwrecked Site and Earthenware Vessels in the Philippines: Earthenware Vessels of the Pandanan Shipwreck Site". In *Asia-Pacific Regional Conference on Underwater Heritage Proceedings*, 2011. http://themua.org/collections/items/show/1234 (accessed 28 May 2019).

Taufik Abdullah. "Modernization in the Minangkabau World: West Sumatra in the Early Decades of the Twentieth Century". In *Culture and Politics in Indonesia*, edited by Claire Holt. Ithaca, London: Cornell University, 1972, pp. 179–245.

Tegu Hidayat, Budi Istiawan, and Fitra Arda. *Serpihan-serpihan peradaban dalam khazanah arsip: Laporan pengumpulan data lama Tahun 2010*. Batusangkar: Kementerian Kebudayaan dan Pariwisata, Direktorat Jenderal Sejarah dan Purbakala, Balai Pelestarian Peninggalan Purbakala Batusangkar, 2010.

Teh Gallop, Annabel. "Piagam Serampas: Malay Documents from Highland Jambi". In *From Distant Tales: Archaeology and Ethnohistory in the Highlands of Sumatra*, edited by Dominik Bonatz, John Miksic, J. David Neidel, and Mai Lin Tjoa-Bonatz. Newcastle upon Tyne: Cambridge Scholars Publishing, 2009, pp. 272–322.

Tim Peneliti Tradisi Megalitik Sumatera Barat. *Laporan penelitian tradisi megalitik di Kabupaten Lima Puluh Koto Propinsi Sumatra Barat*. Jakarta: PUSLIT, 1984.

———. *Laporan penelitian kepurbakalaan (ekskavasi) di situs Bawah Parit, Sumatra Barat*. Jakarta: PUSLIT, 1985.

Tiurminar Butar-Butar. *Proses pembuatan tembikar daerah Sum. Utara*. Medan: Departemen Pendidikan dan Kebudayaan Direktorat Jenderal Kebudayaan Museum Negeri Sumatera Utara, 1991–92.

Tjoa-Bonatz, Mai Lin. "The Megaliths and the Pottery: Studying the Early Material Culture of Highland Jambi". In *From Distant Tales: Archaeology and Ethnohistory in the Highlands of Sumatra*, edited by Dominik Bonatz, John Miksic, J. David Neidel, and Mai Lin Tjoa-Bonatz. Newcastle upon Tyne: Cambridge Scholars Publishing, 2009, pp. 196–228.

———. "3400 Years of Earthenware Traditions in Highland Jambi, Indonesia". In *Proceedings of the 13th International Conference of the European Association of Southeast Asian Archaeologists*, edited by Mai Lin Tjoa-Bonatz, Andreas Reinecke, and Dominik Bonatz. Singapore: NUS Press, 2012, pp. 16–31.

———. "Das Entstehen komplexer Siedlungsstrukturen im zentralen Hochland von Sumatra, Indonesien". *Mitteilungen der Berliner Gesellschaft für Anthropologie, Ethnologie und Urgeschichte* 34 (2013*a*): 147–56.

———. "The Earliest Archaeological Sources of Vernacular Architecture on Sumatra". In *Insular Diversity: Architecture – Culture – Identity in Indonesia*, edited by Erich Lehner, Irene Doubrawa, and Ikaputra. Vienna: IVA, 2013*b*, pp. 67–80.

———. "Im Goldland der Minangkabau: Auf der Suche nach dem letzten hindu-buddhistischen Königreich". *Antike Welt* 5, no. 13 (2013*c*): 14–20.

———. "Sea Routes in Sumatran Waters, Indonesia: Surveys of Historic Shipwrecks in the Straits of Bangka, Gaspar and Karimata". In *Advancing Southeast Asian Archaeology 2016: Selected Papers from the Second SEAMEO SPAFA International Conference on Southeast Asian Archaeology, Bangkok, Thailand 2016*, edited by Noel Tan. Bangkok: SEAMEO SPAFA Regional Centre for Archaeology and Fine Arts, 2018, pp. 79–90. http://www.spafajournal.org/index.php/spafapub/issue/view/129/showToc (accessed 7 June 2018).

———. "The Highlands of West Sumatra and their Maritime Trading Connections". In *Imagining Asia(s): Networks, Actors, Sites*, edited by Andrea Acri, Kashshaf Ghani, Murari Kumar Jha, and Sraman Mukherjee. Singapore: Institute of Southeast Asian Studies, 2019, pp. 393–422.

Tjoa-Bonatz, Mai Lin, J. David Neidel, and Agus Widiatmoko. "Early Architectural Images from Muara Jambi on Sumatra, Indonesia". *Asian Perspectives* 48, no. 1 (2009): 32–55.

Tri Marhaeni. *Laporan penelitian kubur tempayan situs Lolo Gedang, Kerinci, Jambi*. Palembang: Balai Arkeologi Palembang, 2008.

Triwurjani, Rr. *Laporan Penelitian: Pengembangan informasi database sistem informasi arkeologi dalam pola sebaran sumberdaya arkeolgi Kawasan Lima Puluh Kota, Sumatera Barat*. Jakarta: Pusat Penelitian dan Pengembagan Arkeologi Nasional Badan Pengembangan Sumber Daya Budaya dan Pariwisata Kemerinterian Kebudayaan dan Pariwisata, 2010.

Uka Tjandrasasmita et al. *Peninggalan Megalitik di Kabupaten Lima Puluh Koto Propinsi Sumatera Barat*. Jakarta: PUSLIT, 1985.

van der Hoop, A.N.J.Th.àTh. *Megalithic Remains in South-Sumatra*. Zutphen: Thieme, 1932.

———. "Ouden gewichten in het Museum". *Tijdschrift vor Indische Taal-, Land- en Volkenkunde* 76, no. 3 (1936): 462–65.

———. "Prehistoric Site near the Lake Kerinchi (Sumatra)". In *Proceedings of the Third Congress of Prehistorians of the Far East*, edited by Frederick N. Chasen and Michael W.F. Tweedie. Singapore: Government Press, 1940, pp. 200–4.

van der Meulen, W.J. "Suvarṇîpa and the Chrysê Chersonêsos". *Indonesia* 18 (October 1974): 1–40.

Vellinga, Marcel. *Constituting Unity and Difference: Vernacular Architecture in a Minangkabau Village*. Leiden: KITLV, 2004.

Vernika Hapri Witasari. "Lambang raja pada kerajaan kuna di kawasan Indonesia abad XI–XV masehi: Sebuah rekonstruksi makna". Thesis, Universitas Indonesia, Fakultas Ilmu Pengetahuan Budaya, Jakarta, 2011.

Verstappen, H. Theodoor. *A Geomorphological Reconnaissance of Sumatra and Adjacent Islands (Indonesia)*. Groningen: Royal Dutch Geographical Society, Verhandelingen 1, 1973.

Wade, Geoff. "Southeast Asia in the Ming Shi-lu: An Open Access Resource". Singapore, 2005. http://www.epress.nus.edu.sg/msl/introduction (accessed 18 September 2018).

Wade, Geoff and Sun Laichen, eds. *Southeast Asia in the Fifteenth Century: The Ming Factor*. Singapore: Institute of Southeast Asian Studies, 2010.

Waruno Mahdi. "Script and Language of the Tanjung Tanah Manuscript". In *A 14th Century Malay Code of Laws: The Nītisārasamuccaya*, edited by Uli Kozok. Singapore: Institute of Southeast Asian Studies, 2015, pp. 162–220.
Westenenk, Louis C. "De Minangkabausche Nagari". *Mededeelingen Encyclopaedisch Bureau* Afl. VIU, Batavia: Bureau voor Bestuurszaken der Buitenbezittingen, 1915, pp. 89–193.
Westerlaken, Rodney. "Banjar Laba Nangga: A Prehistoric Site in North Bali and its Interpretation as Cultural Heritage". MA thesis, Leiden University, 2011.
Wheatley, Paul. *Nagara and Commandery: Origins of the Southeast Asian Urban Traditions*. Chicago: University of Chicago, 1983.
White, Joyce C. "Incorporating Heterarchy into Theory on Socio-Political Development: The Case from Southeast Asia". *Archaeological Papers of the American Anthropological Association* 6 (1989): 101–23.
Wibisono, Sonny. "Tembikar Kota Cina, Sumatera Utara". *Amerta* 6 (1982): 13–26.
———. "Poterie". In *Banten avant l'Islam: Étude archéologique de Banten Girang (Java-Indonésie) 932?–1526*, edited by Claude Guillot, Lukman Nurhakim, and Sonny Wibisono. Paris: Publications de l'EFEO, Monographies no. 173, 1994, pp. 169–81.
Wicks, Robert S. *Money, Markets, and Trade in Early Southeast Asia: The Development of Indigenous Monetary Systems to A.D. 1400*. Ithaca: Cornell University, 1992.
Wiyoso Yudhoseputro, ed. *Album keramik traditional: Aceh, Sumatera Barat, Sulawesi Selatan, Nusa Tenggara Barat*. Jakarta: Departemen Pendidikan dan Kebudayaan, 1995–96.
Wolters, O.W. *Early Indonesian Commerce: A Study of the Origins of Śrivijaya*. Ithaca: Cornell University Press, 1967.
———. *The Fall of Srivijaya in Malay History*. Ithaca: Cornell University Press, 1970.
———. *History, Culture and Region in Southeast Asian Perspectives*. Singapore: Institute of Southeast Asian Studies, 1982.
Yuwono Sudibyo. *Menhir di kawasan Lima Puluh Kotasebuah pengamatan*. Padang: PPSP Sumatera Barat, 1984.
———. "Lasung batu Sumatra Barat antara cerita rakyat dan peninggalan sejarah". *Kebudayaan* 12 (1996–97): 32–40.
Zhang Bai, ed. *Zhongguo chu tu ci qi quan ji* [Complete Collection of Ceramic Art Unearthed in China]. Vol. 10: *Guangdong, Guangxi, Hainan, Sichuan, Chongqing, Hong Kong, Macau & Taiwan*, edited by Huang Daoqin, Land Riyong, and Li Mingbin. Beijing, Leiden: Brill, 2008.

Online-Sources
http://www.blogspot/tanahdatararchaeology (accessed 6 March 2013).
http://hdl.handle.net/10934/RM0001.COLLECT.454703 (accessed 2 April 2014).
http://pusaka-kerinci.com/ (accessed 9 March 2014).

Maps
Topographisch Bureau te Batavia "Sumatra", 1887–92.
Valentyn, F. "Nieuwe kaart van het Eyland Sumatra". In *Oud en nieuw Oost-Indiën*. Dordrecht: Joannes van Braam; Amsterdam: Gerard onder de Linden, 1724–46.

INDEX

Note: Page numbers followed by "n" refer to endnotes.

A
Adityavarman
  archaeological context of, 42–46
  Batu Bapahat, 51–53
  Bukit Gombak, 46–51
  Buddhist traditions, 210
  connection to Java, 35–42, 206
  in Dharmasraya, 37–42
  gold processing, 72–74
  Gudam, 60–61
  inscriptions of, 1, 3–4, 7, 10, 47, 48, 61–66, 79–85
  irrigation channel, 52
  Minangkabau and, 30–35
  Ombilin, 69–70
  Pagaruyung, 74–79
  Paninggahan, 69–70
  Pariangan, 68–69
  Ponggongan, 57–60
  Rambatan, 66–68
  river-based trading system, 14
  royal centre, 96–120
  Saruaso, 53–57
  settlement process, 118
Air Sugihan, 8
Akarendravarman, 52, 60, 86n22
Albrecht, Johann, 180
Alexander the Great, 32, 33
Alfonso d'Albuquerque, 33
Amoghapasa Lokeswara, 37–39
Ananggavarman, 55
archaeometric analyses, 138–40

B
Banten, 154, 171, 173, 199n6
Barisan Mountains, 5, 13
Batang Hari River, 30, 37, 39, 42, 207
Batu Bapahat, 46, 91, 51–53
Batu Batikam, 79–81
Batu Giriang-Girian, 89n56
Bawah Parit, 2, 4
Bhairawa statue, 40–41
Bijayandrawarman, 87n30
Bodhisattva statue, 49, 54, 206
BPCB, 1, 4, 16
Bukit Batu Larung, 6
Bukit Gombak, 3, 46–51, 91, 208–9
  ^{14}C-dating and TL-dating, 94
  earthenware, 136–46, 140–52, 153–58, 149, 150
  excavations, 15, 16, 20–28, 176, 186, 204
  glass sherds, 188

stone artefacts, 17, 20, 43, 47–50, 173–74, 178, 180–81, 182, 184
imported ceramics, 160–61, 166–69
topography, 46, 97–98, 203, 206
magnetometer, 17–18
metal objects, 191, 190–95, 209
settlement site, 96–98
Southeast Asian ceramics, 166–70
storage jars, 172
water spring, 112–13
Bukit Kincir
metal objects, 193–95
earthenware, 136–52, 154–58
excavations, 24, 176
imported ceramics, 160–62, 168
topography, 46, 97, 203
stone artefacts, 173, 175, 177, 179, 181, 185–86, 187
Bukit Kincir, burial site, 26, 28, 94, 209, 210
dating, 125–26
erected stones, 120
Bukit Kincir, settlement site, 94
excavations, 128–31
topography, 127–28, 131–33
burial site, 82–85,120–27
imported ceramics, 197–98
material culture studies, 196–98
vessel, 157

C
^{14}C-dating, 65, 106, 108, 130, 131
ceramics
archaeometric analyses, 138–40
clay objects tools, 153–58
earthenware, 135–38
fabric, 138–40
imports from China, 159–70

imports from Southeast Asia and Persia, 166–70
pottery making process, 152–53
charcoal sample, 117, 118, 126, 130, 131
chronogram, 43, 88n42, 88n47
coins, 189, 195–96, 198
copper alloy, 193–95

D
dagger, 34, 35, 206
Datuk Ketemanggungan, 32, 79
Datuk Perpatih Nan Sabatang, 79
Datuk Tantejo Gerhano, 82
dendritic model, 11–13
Dharmasraya, 37–42
Dias, Thomas, 54, 75, 195
Dvarapala, 87n23

E
earthenware, 135–38
archaeometric analyses, 138–40
chemical analyses of, 136
tools, 153–58
fabric, 138–40
pottery making process, 152–53
vessel types, 140–52, 197
ethnoarchaeological comparison, 152–53

F
fire-making equipment, 179
flaked lithic, 173–79
floral decoration, 65, 73, 165

G
Galo Gandang, 152, 183
geophysical surveys, 17–20
glass, 186–89
gold, 72–74, 195–96, 209
Grantha script, 43, 53
gravestones, 84, 90n77, 126–27

grinding stone, 71, 186, 187
ground stone tools, 179–87
   adzes, 180–83
Gudam, 60–61
Gujerati ceremonial cloths, 65
guns, 100, 108, 193, 201n48
Gunung Bungsu, 4, 83

H
Hayam Wuruk, 30–31
Hikayat Raja Pasai, 31
Hujung Langit, 35

I
iconography, 6, 35, 41, 84–85
iron implements, 190–93
   slag, 100, 130, 132, 134, 154
   smelting, 179, 193

J
Jambi highlands, 6–7
Java, 35–42

K
Kapalo Bukit Gombak, 50
Karangagung, 8
Kawi script, 43
kendi, 147, 151, 172, 199n4
kincir, 132
King Matralot, 36
Kota Cina, 8
Kota Kapur, 8
Kota Rentang, 8
Koto Gadang, 89n56
koto piliang, 32, 205
Kuburajo, 61–66
kundale, 183
kupang, 195

L
Ladang Rojo, 84, 210
Lake Singkarak, 69–70, 209

Lakshmana, 54
Lima Puluh Kota regency, 2–4, 64, 207
lost wax casting method, 195
Lubuk Layang, 87n30
Luhak Kandikia, 25–26

M
Mahakala, 41
Mahat valley, 1–4
Makam Tuanku Indomo, 84, 90n77
malayapura, 38, 39
mandala polity, 9
Manjusri statue, 36
maritime trade, 8–9, 76, 119
masa, 195
material culture studies
   ceramics. *See* ceramics
   finds at burial site, 196–98
   glass beads, 186–89
   glass vessels, 186–89
   metal objects, 189–96
   stone artefacts, 172–86
Median Graben, 5
Megaliths, 1–7, 210
Melayu-Srivijaya, 6, 9, 42, 207
menggu, 147
Minangkabau
   and Adityavarman, 30–35
   artefacts, 33–35
   artwork, 64
   betel chewing, 195
   chronicles and myths of origin, 30–33
   excavating, 20–28
   kingdom, 5, 10
   socio-political organization, 85
   Tamil-speaking community, 53
Mount Merapi, 192, 193, 205
Muara Jambi, 9, 12

N
Nagarakrtagama, 37

O
obsidian, 132, 172, 177, 179, 198
Ombilin, 69–70
Optically Stimulated Luminescence (OSL), 126

P
Padang Lawas, 8, 87n23
Padang Roco, 37, 39–40
padma, 47
Pagaruyung V, 87n31, 74–76
panggisa, 151
Paninggahan, 69–70
Pararaton, 36
Pariangan, 68–69
Persia, 166–70
Pondok, 6, 114
Ponggongan, 57–60, 155
postholes, 100, 104, 177, 204–5
prehistoric settlement site, 91–96, 173
pre-Srivijaya polities, 6
PUSLIT ARKENAS, 2, 15, 201n38

R
Raja Adat, 66
Raja Alam, 88n49
Raja Ibadat, 66
Rambatan, 66–68

S
Sang Sapurba, 32
Saruaso, 53–57, 85
sedentarization, 6, 95, 203
selayan, 117

Semangko Graben, 5
Sikatimuno, 32–34
Si Mandang Giri, 32, 34
Simawang, burial sites, 82–83
Sinamar valley, 1, 210
Singosari period, 36
Sri Marmadewa, 36
strike-a-light tool, 179
sumpit lama, 201n39
Sungai Langsat. *See* Padang Roco
surāvāsa, 54
Suri Maharajo Dirajo, 32
swidden agriculture, 95–96
syncretism, 41

T
tambo, 32
Tamil-speaking community, 53
Tanah Datar, 1–4, 7, 15–16, 28, 39–46, 73–74, 76–79, 82, 180, 203, 207, 210
Tanah Lua, 91–96, 141–43, 150, 153, 158, 173, 175, 178, 181, 203
Tanjung Tanah manuscript, 37, 88n39
Tantrism, 47
tapayan, 147
tarenang, 146–47
tembaga suasa, 76
thermoluminescence dating, 100
Tuhan Parpatih, 60–61

W
water management, 53
waterways, 12, 46, 71, 206, 209
wavelength-dispersive x-ray fluorescence (WD-XRF), 139
wet-rice irrigation, 51–53

COLOUR PLATE 1

scale 1:2

Imported monochrome ceramics of Bukit Gombak (A–E, H–N) and Ladang Rojo (F–G)

Chinese greenware (A–B; BG-BG-0600-015, BG-0600-001, D–G; BG-0063-034/-038, BG-1006-082, BG-2007-039, BG-2007-038), Longquan dish with fish-relief of the thirteenth to fourteenth centuries (A), base (B), Sawankhalok dish, second half of the fifteenth century (C; BG-1000-183), Longquan dish of the late fifteenth century (D), dish of the Yuan and Ming dynasties (E), base with floral motif (F), Longquan(?) bowl of the thirteenth to fourteenth centuries (G), whiteware of the thirteenth to fourteenth centuries: rim sherd with parallel ribs (H; BG-0501-155), bowl with fluted sides (I; BG-0063-074/-075); Chinese brown-glazed jars of Fujian brittle ware: with gold-brown glaze (J; BG-0063-072/-077), looped jar (K; BG-1000-021), Khmer jar (L; BG-0260-001), *kendi* of fine-paste ware (M; BG-1503-002), Persian stoneware (N; BG-0260-001)

COLOUR PLATE 2

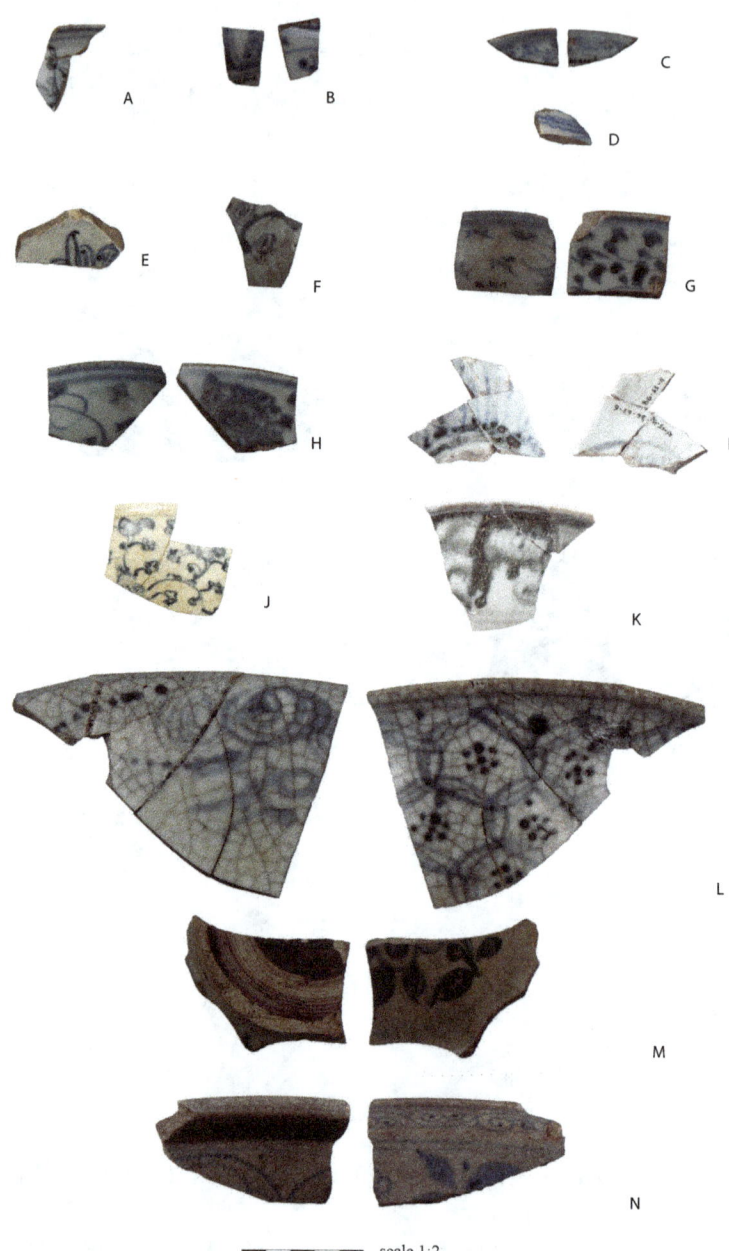

scale 1:2

Imported blue-and-white dishes of Bukit Gombak

Middle Ming period bowls, c. 1490–1510 (A–D; BG-0501-186/BG-0001-090, BG-084-009, BG-0600-009, BG-0300-006, G; BG-0084-007, I; BG-0063-006–011/BG-0050-067, L; BG-0514-039), bowl of the late fourteenth or early fifteenth century (E; BG-0302-015), Jingdezhen-bowl of the second half of the fourteenth or early fifteenth century (F; BG-0001-001, J; BG-0050-068), Jingdezhen-bowl of the fourteenth or fifteenth century (K; BG-003-019), Vietnamese dishes (M–N; BG-1022-001, BG-1006-160)

COLOUR PLATE 3

Metal fragments of Bukit Gombak (A, C–D) and of Bukit Kincir (B)

Pendant of copper alloy (A; BG-1002), tag of copper alloy (B; BG-0915), iron fragment (C; BG-2011), matchlock of a gun (D; BG-1040), drawn beads of Bukit Gombak: red colour (E–G; BG-1007, BG-0530, BG-1003), dark blue (H; BG-1042), and light blue (I; BG-0126)

COLOUR PLATE 4

Sample Number	Sample before Refiring	Sample after Refiring in Air		
		1.100°C	1.150°C	1.200°C
Bukit Gombak				
BG-1100-003				
BG-0005-001				
BG-0514-047				
BG-0412-001				
Bukit Kincir				
BG-0919-070				
BG-0919				
BG-0701				

scale 1:1

Archaeometric analyses of seven pottery samples from Bukit Gombak and Bukit Kincir: clay raw material, thermal behaviour after refiring

Source: Malgorzata Daszkiewicz, Gerwulf Schneider.

www.ingramcontent.com/pod-product-compliance
Lightning Source LLC
Chambersburg PA
CBHW072137290426
44111CB00012B/1894